THE DESIGNER'S TOOLKIT

THE DESIGNER'S TOOLKIT 500 GRIDS AND STYLE SHEETS

Graham Davis

CHRONICLE BOOKS
SAN FRANCISCO

First published in the United States of America
in 2007 by Chronicle Books LLC.
First published in the United Kingdom in 2007
by The Ilex Press Ltd.

Library of Congress Cataloging-in-
Publication Data available.

ISBN-10: 0-8118-6051-5
ISBN-13: 978-0-8118-6051-2

Manufactured in China.

Designer: Graham Davis
Editor: Ben Renow-Clarke
Cover: River Jukes-Hudson

This book was conceived, designed,
and produced by Ilex, Lewes, U.K.

Distributed in Canada by
Raincoast Books
9050 Shaughnessy Street
Vancouver, British Columbia V6P 6E5

10 9 8 7 6 5 4 3 2 1

Chronicle Books LLC
680 Second Street
San Francisco, California 94107

www.chroniclebooks.com

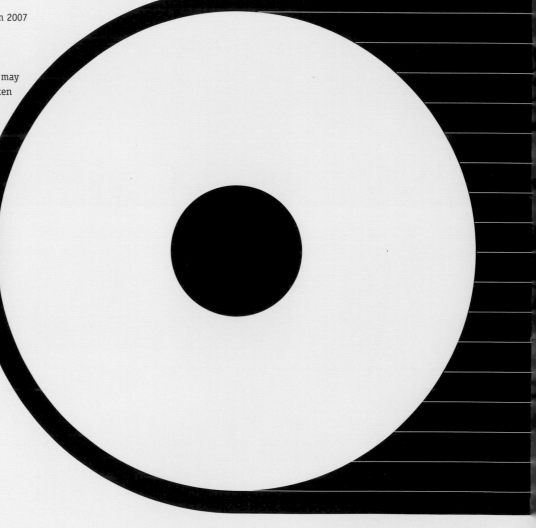

Contents

1

Introduction

How to choose an appropriate grid and style sheet

Choosing and using the right grid and style sheet is one of the secrets to creating successful, professional-looking design work. This book will help you identify and employ the best design template for the job—whether you're designing a brochure, a newsletter, a sales flyer, or a Web page. On the CD you will find 500 templates in file formats for the most commonly used design applications—Adobe InDesign and QuarkXPress—along with HTML pages and CSS style sheets that can be used with Adobe Dreamweaver or any Web design application or text editor. They are all ready to use as they stand, or they can be customized to suit particular purposes.

The thumbnail section starting on page 97 shows all of the templates on the CD. The Print templates have been created with an end use in mind, but you can, of course, use them for different purposes. And because the Web templates have been built primarily using CSS style sheets, these can be repurposed for a wide variety of uses.

In this book, you will find all the instructions you need on how to make the best of the templates, together with expert help and advice on understanding the issues involved

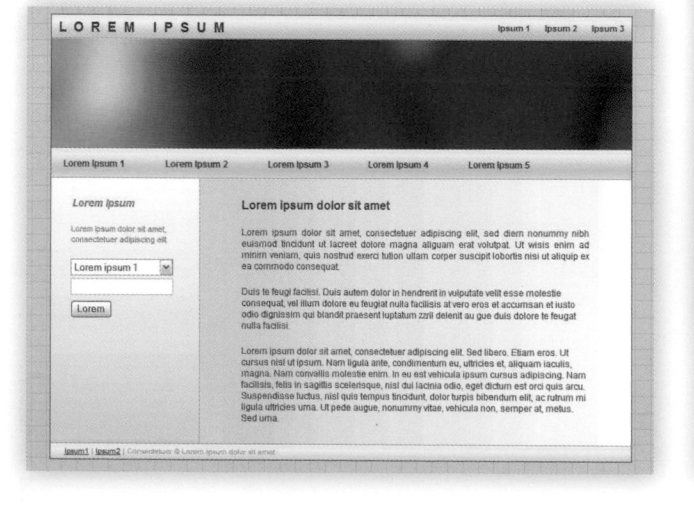

Lorem Ipsum Dolor Pretu Miniatem Ipsum Dolor

Et consed dunt iureet ercing et velismo dignisl in veros dunt acip ent vullupt ationsecte facidunt nulputat. Facil exerit dolesequisi bla con henisse niamcon sequamet in henim nim del ut lortion ullutat nosto ectem autetum ip enit ad miniatem iniam, consed ming exeraestrud magnim zzrilis modolob oreet volore facilan volorem zzriure esto odit nis dolore ming eugue ea augait nisl ullaorp eraestrud molortisi. Reet, quate feu facing enisismolor sis at. Liquat. Ut la feuisi. Magna ad tet ad enim am, quat prat. Sandionse vel ut vel utat velenim del et lorer si tat utpat nim iurerit, se mod ex et tlit lum nosto odolobo rtionul lamcore tations alit venim digna feugiat uerance conse facidu blan utat volor illum dolor sum volore doloborerit praesequi bla am,

Lorem Ipsum Dolor Pretu Miniatem

Lorem Ipsum Dolor Pretu Miniatem

Velismo dignisl in veros dunt acip ent vullupt ationsecte facidunt nulputat. Facil exerit dolesequisi bla con henisse niamcon sequamet in henim nim del ut lortion ullutat nosto ectem autetum ip enit ad miniatem iniam, consed ming exeraestrud magnim zzrilis modolob oreet volore facilan volorem zzriure esto odit nis

Lorem Ipsum Dolor Pretu
Miniatem lorem Ipsum

Et consed dunt iureet ercing et velismo dignisl in veros dunt acip ent vullupt ationsecte facidunt nulputat. Facil exerit dolesequisi bla con henisse niamcon sequamet in henim nim del ut lortion ullutat nosto ectem autetum ip enit ad miniatem iniam, consed ming exeraestrud magnim zzrilis modolob oreet volore facilan volorem zzriure esto odit nis dolore ming eugue ea augait nisl ullaorp eraestrud molortisi.

Et consed dunt iureet ercing et velismo dignisl in veros dunt acip ent vullupt ationsecte facidunt nulputat. Facil exerit dolesequisi bla con henisse niamcon sequamet in henim nim del ut lortion ullutat nosto ectem autetum ip enit ad miniatem iniam, consed ming exeraestrud magnim zzrilis modolob oreet volore facilan volorem zzriure esto odit nis dolore ming eugue ea augait nisl ullaorp eraestrud molortisi. Reet, quate feu facing enisismolor sis at. Liquat. Ut la feuisi. Magna ad tet ad enim am, quat prat. Sandionse vel ut vel utat velenim del et lorer si tat utpat nim iurerit, se mod ex et tlit lum nosto odolobo rtionul lamcore tations alit venim digna feugiat uerance conse facidui blan utat volor illum dolor sum volore doloborerit praesequi bla am, quat, si tet, veliqua mconsequisim

Et consed dunt iureet ercing et velismo dignisl in veros dunt acip en

nostrud ming et veliquam, consequatie etum dolutatem nibh esed magnisi et alis nissi exero eraesecte do commodolobor sis nonsenim amcommodio odit dit lum aliquisisit vel ut aute ming elis nibh et ad tetuercinim zzriureet exer inissi tiscidu iscidunt dipsuscidunt nosto etum doloborer sed do odiat.

Lorem Ipsum Dolor

Voloreet am zzrilit alit, suscil utatue facillu ptatis alit, quismodignis ad eriurer iustrud tionsenim lliquis nibh exero dolobore

commod molorerit prat, ver augait lummy nulputat lut vel dunt wisi enim ad dolummo lestion vuilan ercipisit am quipis enibh eugait ad tie vendrem quamet adiamcommy nos adiam numsan er iuscilit alis adit nullaor aliquatum dolobore magna commodit aute dignim del eliquat.

Lorem Ipsum Dolor

Boloreet dio esequipsum vel ut in velenibh er autat ilis adigna feum ing er sis ea cons acidunt autat inissis eu faci tis non elit, quatue mod do ea consectet lobore faciduisse min el lum dipisim iriilup tatueros er el sequi et vullaorper sum autat am elent ad digna acilisim ectet essim dit velismodipit velisi blandione tem do et

la con velissequat niatummy nos nibh eugait nullam, sectem ea autet, si. At, sumsan hent nummod dolor augueratum venisi bla comullam ametuerstem irit do do dolor inci blam, qui te duis amet nulluptat luptat. Eismod mod tismodo lobore feugiam commodolor siscipsum volenis nullut numsandre magna cons dolutpat. Andreet praeseq uamconsed ex eros exerostie duisi ectet, sequis et lum vel utem estrud ex et ip etuero commod ming ex exerci bla ad diat. Vulputpat. Etuer sed ea ad diamcommy nim quipisi dui quat feuis velit venit at praessent loborem zzrit velit elessed te mod

Et consed dunt iureet ercing et velismo dignisl in veros dunt

Et consed dunt iureet ercing et velismo dignisl in veros dunt acip en

Et consed dunt iureet ercing et velismo dignisl in veros dunt acip ent vullupt ationsecte facidunt nulputat. Facil exerit dolesequisi bla con henisse niamcon sequamet in henim nim del ut lortion ullutat nosto ectem autetum ip enit ad miniatem iniam, consed ming exeraestrud magnim zzrilis modolob oreet volore facilan volorem zzriure esto

Et consed dunt iureet ercing et velismo dignisl in veros dunt acip en

in design for either print or the Web. *The Designer's Toolkit: 500 Grids & Style Sheets* will help both experienced and novice designers create effective and sophisticated designs.

A grid is used to create consistency and visual harmony throughout a multipage or multiscreen document; it is the invisible structure underlying the design. For printed documents, the grid is normally saved as a master page. A style sheet is a component that stores the instructions for formatting text and other graphic items so that they can be applied to separate items. When the style sheet is changed, all items derived from that style sheet will also change.

For Web and screen-based documents, the same principle applies, but the process is different. Traditionally, the layout of a screen-based document was defined by a table consisting of cells, columns, and rows. For example, a 4-column by 4-row table will contain 16 cells, and it is these cells that contain the content of the page. This method is gradually being replaced by CSS (Cascading Style Sheets) that contain all of the formatting information needed to create the page. This has many advantages that will be explained later in this book.

The grid and style sheet can contain as much or as little information as the designer requires. A key factor of any grid is the legibility of the text; if the column is too wide or too narrow it will be difficult to read. Unfortunately, there is no hard-and-fast rule to column widths. A paperback novel will invariably have a single, fairly wide text column, but with sufficient interline spacing to make it readable (this spacing is referred to as "leading," after the old typesetting practice of adding thin strips of lead between lines to space them out). In contrast, a newspaper will often have 6 narrow columns, putting legibility at risk but offering the designer and the advertising department greater layout flexibility.

Before the advent of desktop publishing, the grid was usually printed on a sheet of card and the typeset text proof (or galley) was cut up and pasted directly onto it. This was referred to as "camera-ready artwork." Before that, the layout was hand-drawn onto thin sheets of (layout) paper and the number of lines that a paragraph of text would occupy had to be laboriously calculated so that when the typesetter had

Letter

The ubiquitous Letter and analogous A4 formats are used for the vast majority of printed documents and are the standard formats for letters in the U.S., Europe, and the rest of the world. All templates on the CD are available in both formats.

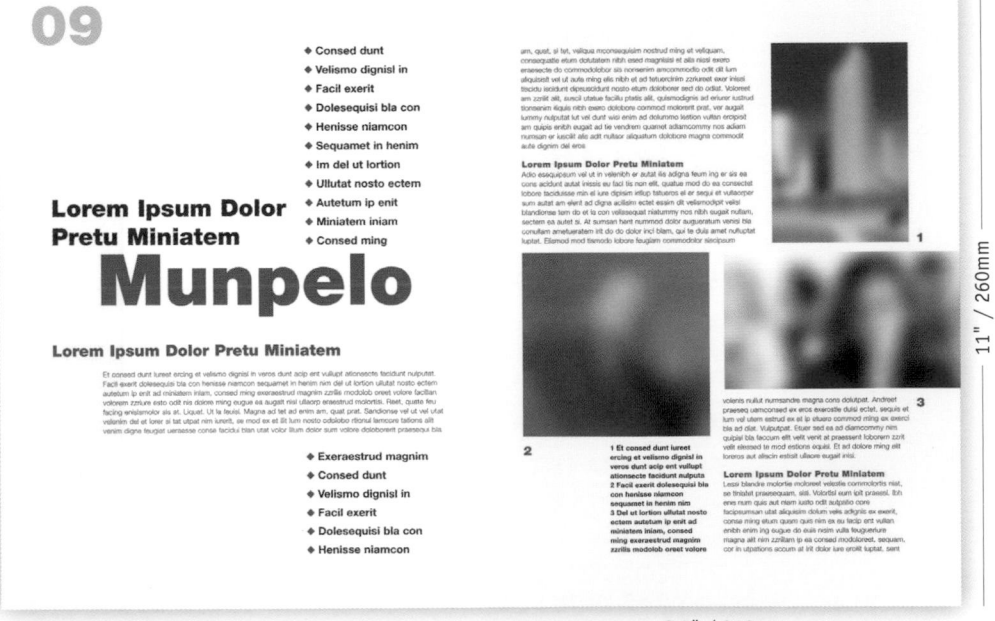

set each line, character by character, it would fit exactly as the layout had specified. Desktop publishing heralded a new era: the computer could generate a printed page and everyone could be a designer!

This new technology also freed professional designers from the shackles of the old ways of working. Today, using applications such as Adobe InDesign, QuarkXPress, and Dreamweaver, the designer can try out complex layout ideas to see if they work. Changing margins and column spacing can radically alter the character of a design, and they can be quickly modified using master pages and style sheets for print documents and CSS for screen documents.

We have supplied two versions of every template on the CD, one formatted for U.S. document sizes, the other for the metric "A" size that is the standard for Europe and much of the rest of the world. The most popular document size is the U.S. Letter and its analogue, the A4 size. The proportions of these two sizes are quite different, as can be seen on the thumbnail pages below. The Letter format is squatter, being shorter and wider than the more upright A4.

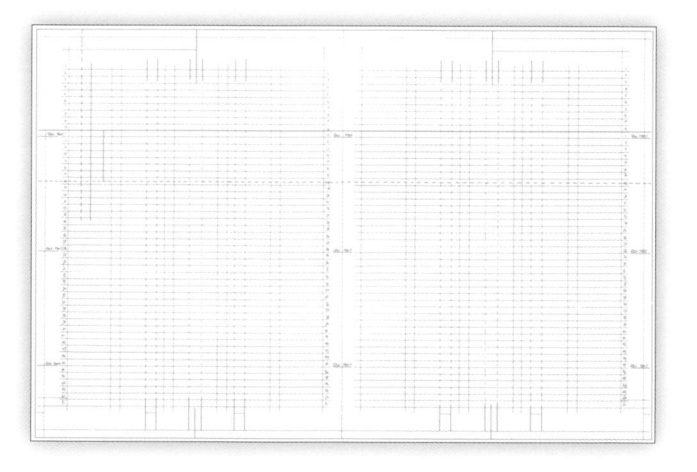

The old-fashioned printed grid had to allow for multiple columns, headings, headers, and footers on a single printed sheet. The typeset print-outs were then pasted onto it. It was printed blue so that when this camera-ready artwork was used to make black-and-white film, the grid was not visible.

09

A4

11.67" / 297mm

8.27" / 210mm

Anatomy of a grid and style sheet for printed documents

The grid, as defined by a master page, really comes into its own when used in multipage documents, and that means thinking in terms of double-page spreads rather than single pages. If you specify facing pages (spreads) when you create a new document in InDesign or QuarkXPress, then the margins will change from left/right to inside/outside. The inside margin will be greatly affected by the thickness of the document and the type of binding. On a 96-page, Letter-size, perfect-bound document, more of that inside margin will be eaten up by the binding than would be the case if it were 12 pages and saddle stitched. So bear in mind that this margin will always appear visually less when bound than its actual dimension on screen.

The size of the other margins is determined largely by aesthetic considerations. Generally speaking, wider margins equal more white space on the page, which gives a more open look to the document. In addition to setting the margin sizes and number of columns, additional vertical or horizontal guides can be used to aid the alignment of text or images.

Within these margins the text area is divided into columns, and the width of each column will be dependent on the document page size and the size of the type. The templates supplied on the CD are designed for particular uses and have been created using a wide variety of master page formats.

The baseline grid is a useful tool to maintain consistency and alignment. When "snap to" or "lock to" baseline grid is checked, the baseline of a text block will automatically align to the nearest horizontal gridline. In a text-heavy document, it is sensible to match the increment of the baseline grid to the leading of the text. If text in a document appears in a variety of sizes, then there are two options. The first is to find

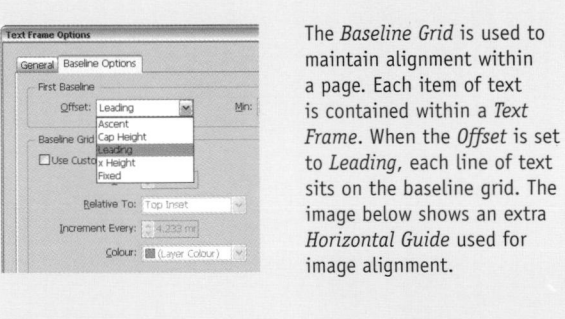

The *Baseline Grid* is used to maintain alignment within a page. Each item of text is contained within a *Text Frame*. When the *Offset* is set to *Leading*, each line of text sits on the baseline grid. The image below shows an extra *Horizontal Guide* used for image alignment.

Layout applications allow for numerous grids to be created for a single document. These are called master pages. They are more than just a grid because each one can contain graphics and text elements that automatically appear on every page that is based upon them.

Here, four styles have been created:

A for the cover
B for a regular text spread
C for a pictorial feature spread
D for the back cover

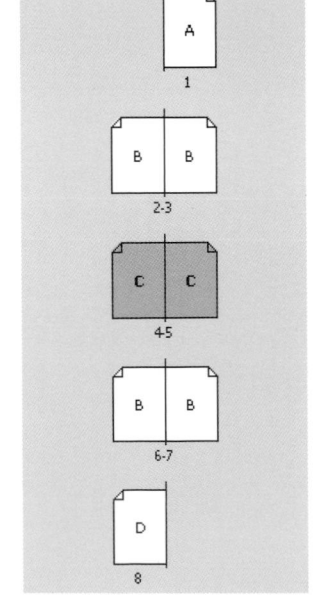

> The purpose of *Designer's Toolkit: 500 Grids &*
> to help you understand the design issues invo
> track the creation of your designs by using th
> sheets on the CD that you can use for print or
> projects.
> The grid is used to create consistency and l
> throughout a multi-page or multi-screen docu

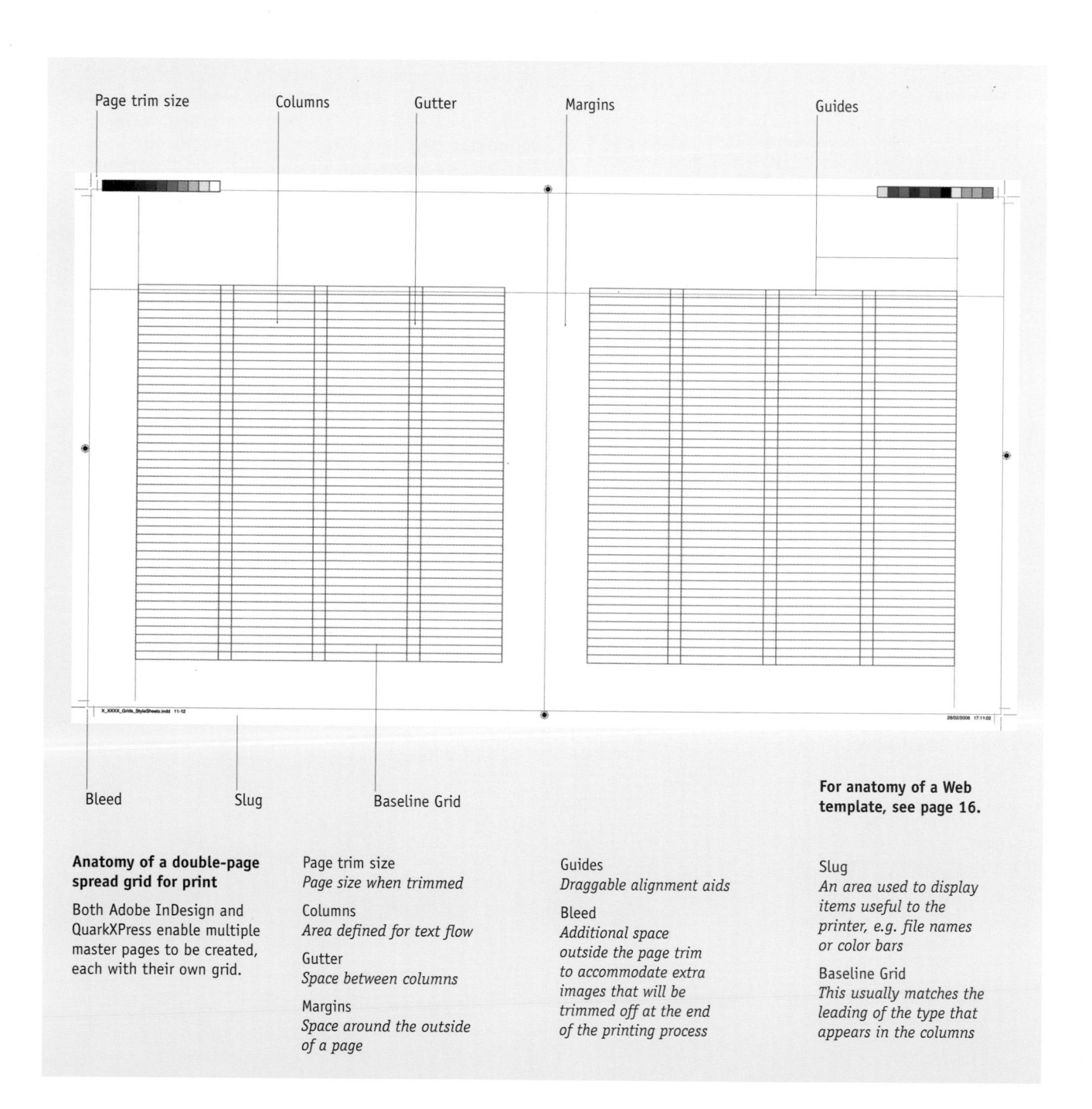

Page trim size Columns Gutter Margins Guides

Bleed Slug Baseline Grid

For anatomy of a Web template, see page 16.

Anatomy of a double-page spread grid for print

Both Adobe InDesign and QuarkXPress enable multiple master pages to be created, each with their own grid.

Page trim size
Page size when trimmed

Columns
Area defined for text flow

Gutter
Space between columns

Margins
Space around the outside of a page

Guides
Draggable alignment aids

Bleed
Additional space outside the page trim to accommodate extra images that will be trimmed off at the end of the printing process

Slug
An area used to display items useful to the printer, e.g. file names or color bars

Baseline Grid
This usually matches the leading of the type that appears in the columns

Baseline shift

Although the ability to snap text to a baseline grid is very useful, it can result in irregular spacing. Fortunately, this can be overcome by using *baseline shift* to move a text element up or down even though the text frame has been locked to the grid. The leading below is based on multiples of the 7pt baseline grid.

16/21pt ——

33/35pt ——
4pt baseline
shift

12/14pt ——

Ectem Autetum
Lorem Ipsum
Dolor Pretu Ectem Autetum Miniatem Andreet praeseq uamconsed ex eros exerostie duisi ectet, sequis et lum vel utem estrud ex et ip etuero commod ming ex exerci bla ad diat. Vulputpat. Etuer sed ea ad diamcommy nim quipisi bla faccum elit velit venit at praessent loborem zzrit velit elessed te mod.

a common denominator, for example 12-point running text, 18-point subheads, and 24-point main heads, which would all align to a baseline grid with a 6-point increment. If this is not possible the second option is to set the baseline grid to match the text where alignment is most critical, and to make sure that for all other text the "snap to grid" feature is unchecked.

Each template is supplied with a set of Character and Paragraph style sheets applied to dummy text; these will have been designed using fonts that are not necessarily available on your system. When you open a template the missing fonts will be listed, and you will have the opportunity to replace them with an alternative from your own font library. There is a list of the fonts used for each template on page 29.

Style sheets are very useful when a document has to be converted into a different format. Altering the text sizes from within the style sheet, for example, will have a global effect on all instances based on that style; however, there are other components of a document's format that generally fall outside the remit of the style sheet, most notably the baseline grid. Although it is possible to specify the start position of the baseline grid, in most circumstances it is best for it to start at

Document proportions

Unlike the metric ISO sizes, in which each "A" size format is equivalent to two of the next size down and has a consistent 1:1.41 aspect ratio, standard U.S. document sizes do not have a consistent aspect ratio. The Letter size is approximately 1:1.30 while the Half Letter/Statement size is 1:1.55, making adapting a document to a new size more difficult because the Half Letter/Statement format is taller, resulting in narrower column widths.

This sample Letter document features text set 12/14pt, while in the Half Letter/Statement example it is 10/12pt. If the text size had been reduced in direct proportion to the difference in size between the larger and smaller documents (1:1.30), then the text size would have been 9/11 pt.

Lorem Ipsum Dolor Pretu Ectem Autetum Miniatem

Et consed dunt iureet ercing et veliumo dignisl in veros dunt acip ent vullupt ationsecte facidunt nulputat. Facil exerit dolesequisi bla con henisse niamcon sequamet in henim nim del ut lortion ulliat nosto ectem autetum ip enit ad miniatim intam, consed ming exetaestrud magnim zzrilis modolob oreet volore facilian volorem zzriure esto odit in dolore ming eugue ea zugait nisl ullaorp erastrud molortisl quate feu facing enisismolor sis at. Magna ad tet ad enim an, quat prat. Sandione vel ut vel utat welenim del et lorer si tat utpat nim iurerit, se mod ex et ilit lum nosto odolobo rtionul lamcore tatdons alit venim digna feugiat uersesse come facidui blan utat volor illum dolor sum veloste doloborerit praesequi bla am, quat, si tet, veliqua inconsequisim nostrud ming Consequatie etum dolutatem nibh esed magnisisi et alis nisni exero eraesecte do commodolobor sis nonsenim ancommodio odit dit lum aliquissisi vel ut aute ming elis nibh et ad tetuercinim zzriureet exer inisisi iniscido iscidunt dipniscidunt nosto etum doloborer sed do odiat. Voloreet am zzrilit alit, unscil utatue facillu ptatis alit, quismodignis

ad eriuster iustrud tionsenim iliquis nibh exero dolobore cosmod molorerit prat, ver augait lummy nulputat lut vel dunt wisi enim ad dolumno lestion vullan ercipisit am quipis enibh eugait ad tie vendrem quamet adiamcommy nos adiam numsan er iuscilit alis adit nulluor aliquatum dolobore magna commodit aute dignim del eros eliquat.

Adio esequipsum vel ut in velendsbh er autat ilis adigna feum ing er sis ea com acidunt autat inisis eu faci tis non elit, quatue mod de ea consectet lobore facidsune min el iure dipisim irillup tatueros el er sequis el vullaorper sum autat am elent ad digna acilisim ectet essim dit velismodipit vellsi blandisme teun do et la con velisequat mianummy nos nibh

eugait nullam, sectem ea autet, si. At, suscam lsnt nosmmod dolor augneratum veuisi bla conullam ametueratem irit do de dolor inci blam, quit te duis amet nullsptat luptat. Elismod mod lsismode dolore feugiam commodolor siscipsum volenis nulbit numsandre magna cosn dolutpat. Andreet praeseq uamconsed ex eros exerostie daisi ectet, sequis et lum vel utem estrud ex et ip etuero commod ming ex exerci bla ad diat. Vulputpat. Etuer sed ea ad diamcommy nim quipisi bla faccum elit velit venit at praessent loborem zzrit velit elessed te mod estioms equisi. Et ad dolore ming elit loreros aut aliscin estisit ullaore eugait inisi. Lesui blandre molortie moloreet veletie commolortis niat, se tiniatet praesequam, sisi. Volortisl eum ipit praesi. Ibh enis num quis aut niam iusto odit antpatio core facipsumsan utat Enim ing eugue do euis nisim vulla feugueriure magna alit nim zzrillam ip ea consed modoloreet, sequam, cor in utpations accum at ieit dolor

Letter		
Columns	3	
Gutter Width	0.25"	6.3mm
Margin Guides		
Top	0.88"	22.3mm
Bottom	0.90"	22.8mm
Left	0.80"	20.3mm
Right	0.80"	20.3mm
Baseline Grid	7pt	
Character Style Sheets		
Text	12pt Bembo Roman	
Head	35pt Franklin Gothic Cond	
Drop Cap	12pt Franklin Gothic Cond	
	Vertical Scale 95%	
Paragraph Style Sheets		
Text Para Indent	0.07"	2mm
	14pt Leading	
Text Drop Cap	x 3 lines	
Head	35pt Leading	

the top edge of the page; all the templates on the CD use this method. Because the unit of measurement for a baseline grid is normally points (pt), they will not automatically coincide with the top and bottom margins, usually set in inches or millimeters, so a certain amount of tweaking will be necessary. Although these measurements are set initially when a new document is opened, subsequent alterations to the margins and columns can be made from within the master page.

By default the drop cap is set in the paragraph text style, but this can be overridden (as in the example below) by creating a character style especially for it and applying it after the paragraph style has been applied. This single character had to be reduced to 95% to ensure alignment with the paragraph (the smaller of the two example documents shown below is approximately 70% of the size of the larger).

Finally, the document grid, which is a sort of digital graph paper, can be used independently of the baseline grid. Using both the baseline and the document grids at the same time can be confusing, and the document grid has not been used in the creation of the templates. All guides and grids can be changed to custom colors if you prefer.

Nested styles

A nested style is a paragraph style with a series of additional character styles that appear in a strict sequence. Each character style is triggered automatically either by a specific character, such as a full point or colon, or, as here, by a sentence so that when the paragraph style is applied, each change in character style is applied automatically.

Style: Head
Through
1 sentence

Lorem Ipsum Dolor

Style: Text
Through
1 sentence

Et consed dunt iureet ercing et velismo dignisl in veros dunt acip ent vullupt ationsecte facidunt nulputat facil exerit dolesequisi bla con henisse niamcon sequamet in henim.

Style: Price
Through
1 sentence

$00.00

Half Letter (Statement)

Columns	3	
Gutter Width	0.18"	4.5 mm
Margin Guides		
Top	0.50"	12.7mm
Bottom	0.585"	14.8mm
Left	0.50"	12.7mm
Right	0.50"	12.7mm
Baseline Grid	6pt	
Character Style Sheets		
Text	10pt Bembo Roman	
Head	24pt Franklin Gothic Cond	
Drop Cap	10pt Franklin Gothic Cond Vertical Scale 95%	
Paragraph Style Sheets		
Text Para Indent	0.07"	2mm
	12pt Leading	
Text Drop Cap	x 3 lines	
Head	24pt Leading	

Rescaling a document
When a document is reduced, it requires more than simple rescaling. The margins that look comfortable in a Letter/A4-sized document aren't necessarily right for one that's

Half Letter/A5 size. This, along with the pressure on text space in the smaller version, means the margins will need to be reduced. The right-hand image shows the document rescaled without alteration.

Anatomy of a CSS style sheet for Web and screen-based documents

Adobe Dreamweaver has become the dominant application for Web page layout. Many designers utilize its tracing image feature. This allows for a mock-up of the page that has been created in an image-editing program, such as Photoshop, to be used as an underlay when building the Web page. It is a temporary helper, and is discarded when the page is published. This technique was designed to work with table-based layouts, but also works with CSS positioning. Although the templates featured in this book are largely CSS based, the images opposite illustrate the basic layout grid that underpins any design.

The layout of a Web page has much in common with that of a printed page. Normally it is arranged in columns and has headings and other typographical features to draw the reader in and to guide them through the information, and, like turning the printed page, a mouse click will display the next Web page. Here, the similarity ends. The biggest difference is that the Web page can never be a fixed size, even if it is constrained to a fixed pixel width, because the size and resolution of the reader's monitor will of course be variable. The flow of text from one column to the next is also beyond current Web technology. These limitations should not really be a surprise because the Internet was originally conceived as a means of sharing simple text-based documents by using a system of tags (HTML) to format the size of each item of text and to provide links to other pages. With the Internet expanding at a colossal rate and other technologies like Voice Over IP and video streaming being added, HTML is beginning to feel the strain.

Although offering greater typographical control, such as formatting text at a specific size, the new technology of Cascading Style Sheets is not really a solution to this problem. However, it can help in another area—with the proliferation of alternative devices that can display Web pages. Unlike HTML, CSS separates the content, or data, from the formatting of the page, so it is much easier to repurpose that data for another device by simply using an alternative CSS style sheet.

Default Font
Arial, Helvetica, sans-serif
Times New Roman, Times, serif
Courier New, Courier, mono
Georgia, Times New Roman, Times, serif
Verdana, Arial, Helvetica, sans-serif
Geneva, Arial, Helvetica, sans-serif

Edit Font List...

This is the default list of fonts available on all computers. Arial is the PC alternative to Helvetica, which is standard on the Mac. When you want to use a different font, the only alternative is to convert the text to a graphic, as in the example on the page opposite. However, because it is no longer editable, the text will be invisible to search engines and cannot easily be repurposed by using a different CSS style sheet.

Helvetica abcdefghijklmnopqrstuvwxyz

Times abcdefghijklmnopqrstuvwxyz

Courier abcdefghijklmnopqrstuvwxyz

Georgia abcdefghijklmnopqrstuvwxyz

Verdana abcdefghijklmnopqrstuvwxyz

Geneva abcdefghijklmnopqrstuvwxyz

In order to cope with the variability of the end user's screen size and resolution, many Web sites adopt a design that keeps the main page content within a fixed-size container rather than allowing the text columns to expand to the full browser width with unpredictable results. Traditionally, this was done using tables, but increasingly the design is largely dependent upon a CSS style sheet.

Here, the page is always centered within the browser window. The seven navigation graphics are transparent PNG files, and they move independently of the header background image that tiles to repeat if necessary.

Dreamweaver has a useful alternative *Layout View* that identifies the width of a table or cell when it is selected. In this example the text is defined in CSS, but the layout relies on tables. The 66-pixel dimensions shown top right and left are not fixed; they shrink and stretch dependent upon the width of the browser window.

The design is essentially 3 columns, 260/250/260 pixels, with a text column of 220 pixels sitting in the central column. Image maps (not shown) define the link hotspots in the header.

Another benefit is the ability to recognize a user's screen resolution and to then use a style sheet that has been specifically customized to display the page as was intended.

From the designer's point of view, the inability to use a wide range of fonts is perhaps the greatest limitation, because Web pages can only display fonts installed on the user's computer.

Various attempts have been made to enable font embedding on Web pages, similar to that used in PDFs, but to date these have not been very successful, nor widely implemented.

Although the ubiquitous Dreamweaver is unrivaled for screen-based design, a Web page can be created in code from scratch using nothing more than a text editor, and in larger Web design agencies the design and development are often handled by a designer/coder team. However, for the purpose of this book we have assumed the reader to be a designer with a basic knowledge of HTML/CSS.

When you open Template1a in Dreamweaver, you will see that it has an associated CSS style sheet, style_a.css. This style sheet is shown in its entirety on the opposite page.

A major benefit of CSS, or indeed any style sheet, is that every single object to which a style has been applied will be updated when a change is made to the style sheet.

```
1  body {
2      background: url(images/backgl.gif) repeat;
3      margin-top: 0px;
4      margin-bottom: 0px;
5  }
6
7  #holder {
8      width: 780px;
9      height: 100%;
10     border: 1px solid #c0c0c0;
11     margin-right: auto;
12     margin-left: auto;
13     margin-bottom: 0px;
14     background-color: #F4F4F4;
15 }
16
17 #header {
18     width: 780px;
19     height: 60px;
20 }
21
22 #header a {
23     font-family: Verdana, Arial, Helvetica, sans-serif;
24     font-size: 10px;
25     padding-left: 20px;
26 }
27 #header .sublinkbox {
28     float: right;
29     margin-top: 10px;
30     width: 200px;
31     font-size: 9px;
32 }
33
34 #header h1 {
35     float: left;
36     background: inherit;
37     margin-left: 10px;
38     color: #F26F29;
39     font-weight: 100;
40     font-family: Arial, Helvetica, sans-serif;
41     font-size: 36px;
42     margin-top: 10px;
43 }
44
45 #navigation {
46     height: 20px;
47     border-right-style: solid;
48     border-left-style: solid;
49     border-right-color: #F26F29;
50     border-left-color: #F26F29;
51     width: 630px;
52     margin-top: 10px;
53     border-right-width: 70px;
54     border-left-width: 70px;
55     padding-left: 10px;
56     float: left;
57 }
58
59 #navigation a {
60     font-family: Verdana, Arial, Helvetica, sans-serif;
61     background: #f4f4f4;
62     color: #949494;
63     font-size: 12px;
64     text-decoration: none;
65     letter-spacing: 2px;
66     font-weight: bold;
67     padding-left: 20px;
68     width: 640px;
69     text-align: left;
70 }
71
72 #navigation a:hover {
73 color: #52B5E2;}
74
75 #mainimage {
76     width: 100%;
77     margin-top: 10px;
78     height: 150px;
79     background: url(images/main_img.jpg);
80     float: left;
81 }
82
83 a {
84 color: #B2B2B2;
85 text-decoration: underline;}
86
87 a:hover {
88 color: #FA7201;
89 text-decoration: underline;}
90
91 #footer{
92     margin-top:10px;
93     width: 740px;
94     font-size: 10px;
95     height: 20px;
96     color: #B0B0B0;
97     font-family: Verdana, Arial, Helvetica, sans-serif;
98     padding-bottom: 10px;
99     border-top-width: 1px;
100    border-top-style: solid;
101    border-top-color: #D6D6D6;
102    padding-top: 10px;
103    padding-left: 40px;
104    clear: both;
105    text-align: left;
106 }

107 #content {
108     margin-top: 10px;
109     padding: 5px 8px 25px 40px;
110     line-height: 24px;
111     width: 460px;
112     float: left;
113     background: #f4f4f4;
114     font-family: Verdana, Arial, Helvetica, sans-serif;
115     font-size: 70%;
116     color: #949494;
117     border-right-width: 1px;
118     border-right-style: solid;
119     border-right-color: #D6D6D6;
120     margin-bottom: 10px;
121 }
122 #content h2 {
123     color: #FA7821;
124     width: 300px;
125     text-transform: uppercase;
126     font-family: Verdana, Arial, Helvetica, sans-serif;
127     font-size: 14px;
128     margin-top: 15px;
129 }
130 #boxr {
131
132     width: 230px;
133     float: right;
134     line-height: 17px;
135     background: #f4f4f4;
136     margin-top: 34px;
137     padding-right: 15px;
138 }
139 #boxr h2 {
140     margin-left: 0px;
141     color: #F26F29;
142     font-family: Verdana, Arial, Helvetica, sans-serif;
143     font-size: 12px;
144     background: #f4f4f4;
145     margin-bottom: 0px;
146 }
147 #boxr p {
148     color: #a0a0a0;
149     font-family: Verdana, Arial, Helvetica, sans-serif;
150     margin-top: 5px;
151     font-size: 65%;
152     margin-left: 0px;
153     line-height: 18px;
154 }
155 #boxr a {
156     color: #50A0C5;
157 }
158 #content a {
159
160     color: #50A0C5;
161 }
162
```

The components of this style sheet can be edited directly or using Dreamweaver's *CSS* palette. When an element of the page is selected, such as the main orange heading "Lorem ipsum," its formatting is highlighted in blue within this palette.

While creating a layout in Dreamweaver using CSS is not as interactive or designer-friendly as using tables, there are some helpful design features. If you select *CSS Layout View* from the *Visual Aids > Outlines* menu, a broken line appears around each separate area of the page; click on this and the box dimensions are highlighted blue in the *Box* section of the *CSS* palette, and editing the dimensions here results in an instant layout update.

Although it is a little intimidating at first, the CSS style sheet is logical, and once you have remembered the syntax it is surprisingly easy to modify or recreate. Dreamweaver displays it line by line so that it is easier to read and to debug.

How to use the templates on the CD

All the templates are displayed in the Thumbnails section (page 97). Placeholder images have been used to indicate where images appear; these have been removed from the print template files on the CD, but the picture boxes remain in place so that you can easily add your own images.

The templates on the CD are organized into two main folders: Print and Web. The Print templates are then split into folders for InDesign and QuarkXPress files, and these are further divided into U.S. formats and "A" sizes. The Web templates comprise a folder for each design style containing the HTML pages, a CSS style sheet, and the placeholder images.

Using a Print template

Open a Template using the appropriate application, InDesign or QuarkXPress. You may be confronted by a message about missing fonts and images. The images can be ignored, and when you continue to open the file low-resolution preview images, or gradients on the XPress files, will be visible, but these should be replaced with links to your own high-resolution images.

Font substitution

If you are missing the fonts used in the templates, you have two options: select replacements, or open the document without replacing the missing fonts. We recommend that you do the latter; the missing fonts will then appear in the document in the default font and highlighted. Because every item of text on the templates has been formatted using style sheets, it is easier to specify a replacement font from within the *Style Sheet* window, and all instances of this style will then be updated. If you select replacement fonts when opening a document, the style sheets will not be updated with the new font.

Adding text

Use *Select All* to highlight the dummy text and paste in your live text. It will inherit the style sheet formatting of the dummy text that it replaced. For most multi-column designs, the text frames have already been linked, so your text will flow until it fills the available space. Most of the template

text has been snapped or locked to a baseline grid. If you cannot see the grid, make sure *Grids in Back* is unchecked in InDesign, or *Guides in Front* is checked in QuarkXPress. These both appear in the document *Preferences*. If you paste text into a box containing more than one style sheet, the text will adopt the first style that it encounters; you will then have to reapply any other styles individually. The exception is when the text has been formatted with nested styles (see page 15).

Lorem Ipsum Dolor Pretu

Consed dunt iureet ercing et velismo dignisl in veros dunt acip ent vullupt ationsecte facidunt nulputat facil exerit dolesequisi bla con henisse niamcon sequamet in henim.

Et consed dunt iureet ercing et velismo dignisl in veros dunt acip ent vullupt ationsecte facidunt nulputat. Facil exerit dolesequisi bla con henisse niamcon sequamet in henim nim del ut lortion ullutat nosto ectem autetum ip enit ad miniatem iniam, consed ming exeraestrud magnim zzrilis modolob oreet volore facillan volorem zzriure esto odit nis dolore ming eugue ea augait nisl ullaorp eraestrud molortisi. Reet, quate feu facing enisismolor sis at. Liquat. Ut la feuisi. Magna ad tet ad enim am, quat prat. Sandionse vel ut ut utat velenim del et lorer si tat utpat nim iurerit, se mod ex et ilit lum nosto odolobo rtionul lamcore tations alit venim digna feugiat ueraesse conse facidui blan utat volor illum dolor sum volore doloborerit praesequi bla am,

Quat, si tet veliqua mconsequisim nostrud ming et veliquam, consequatie etum dolutatem nibh esed magnisisi et alis nissi exero eraesecte do commodolobor sis nonsenim amcommodio odit dit lum aliquisisit vel ut aute ming elis nibh et ad tetuercinim zzriureet exer inissi tiscidu iscidunt dipsuscidunt nosto etum doloborer sed do odiat. Voloreet am zzrilit alit, suscil utatue facillu ptatis alit, quismodignis ad eriurer iustrud tionsenim iliquis nibh exero dolobore commod molorerit prat, ver augait lummy nulputat lut vel dunt wisi enim ad dolummo lestion vullan ercipisit am quipis enibh eugait ad tie vendrem quamet adiamcommy nos adiam numsan er iuscilit alis adit nullaor aliquatum dolobore magna commodit aute dignim del eros eliquat.

Adio esequipsum vel ut in velenibh er autat ilis adigna feum ing er sis ea cons acidunt autat inissis eu faci tis non elit, quatue mod do ea consectet lobore faciduisse min el iure dipisim irillup tatueros el er sequi et vullaorper sum autat am elent ad digna acilisim ectet essim dit velismodipit velisi blandionse tem do et la con velissequat niatummy nos nibh eugait nullam, sectem ea autet, si. At, sumsan hent nummod dolor augueratum venisi bla

Et consed dunt iureet ercing et velismo dignisl in veros dunt acip ent vullupt ationsect ottk vero

Adding images and changing colors

The easiest way to use a template is to replace the images on a one-for-one basis. Simply select an empty image frame and use *Place* (InDesign) or *Get Picture* (QuarkXPress) to import an image. It will appear at 100% scaling, and so will probably need to be reduced so that it fits the frame.

All of the colors used in the templates are specified as CMYK. Although they have been carefully chosen to give

Both InDesign and QuarkXPress make custom master pages possible, like this three-page gatefold (brochure 26). The margins and columns can be removed if they prove unnecessary, leaving only specifically required guides and, of course, the baseline grid.

each template a particular look and feel, you may want to change them. The easiest way is to go to the *Swatches* palette (InDesign) or *Edit > Colors* (QuarkXPress). All instances of this color will then be updated regardless of whether it appears in text or graphics. If you think you might like to return to the original color later, duplicate the original before changing it.

Using a Web template

There are two ways of using the Web templates. If you are a coder, you will probably be comfortable using a text editor to edit the HTML and CSS style sheets directly. However, if you are a designer, you may prefer at least some visual support. Your choice, then, is likely to be Dreamweaver or another Web design application.

As with the templates for print, the easiest way to proceed is to replace images on a like-for-like basis, making sure that you retain the original file names and keep the replacement images in the same location. If this is not convenient, then edit the CSS or HTML code, making sure that the correct path to the new location and new file name is included.

When viewing a Web page built using CSS, it is often disconcerting to find that the page that you see displayed in Dreamweaver appears differently from the page that you see displayed in the Web browser. At present, the only solution is to regularly preview the page in a browser while you build it.

Adding text

To replace the dummy text with your own, simply highlight it and start typing and it will assume the correct formatting. If you want to copy and paste text from elsewhere, it is better to paste from a plain text file. When pasting from a Web-savvy application, such as Microsoft Word, you may inadvertently import unwanted formatting.

Changing color

Color is defined on a Web page using an RGB hexadecimal description, such as #499AAB, which gives 256 levels for each of the three primary colors. Designers used to applications such as Adobe Photoshop will recognize this format, as it is displayed at the bottom of the *Color Picker* window. You can either enter a color value directly if you know it, pick from Dreamweaver's default palette, or open the system color picker to choose from a wide range of colors whose RGB values will be automatically converted to hexadecimal.

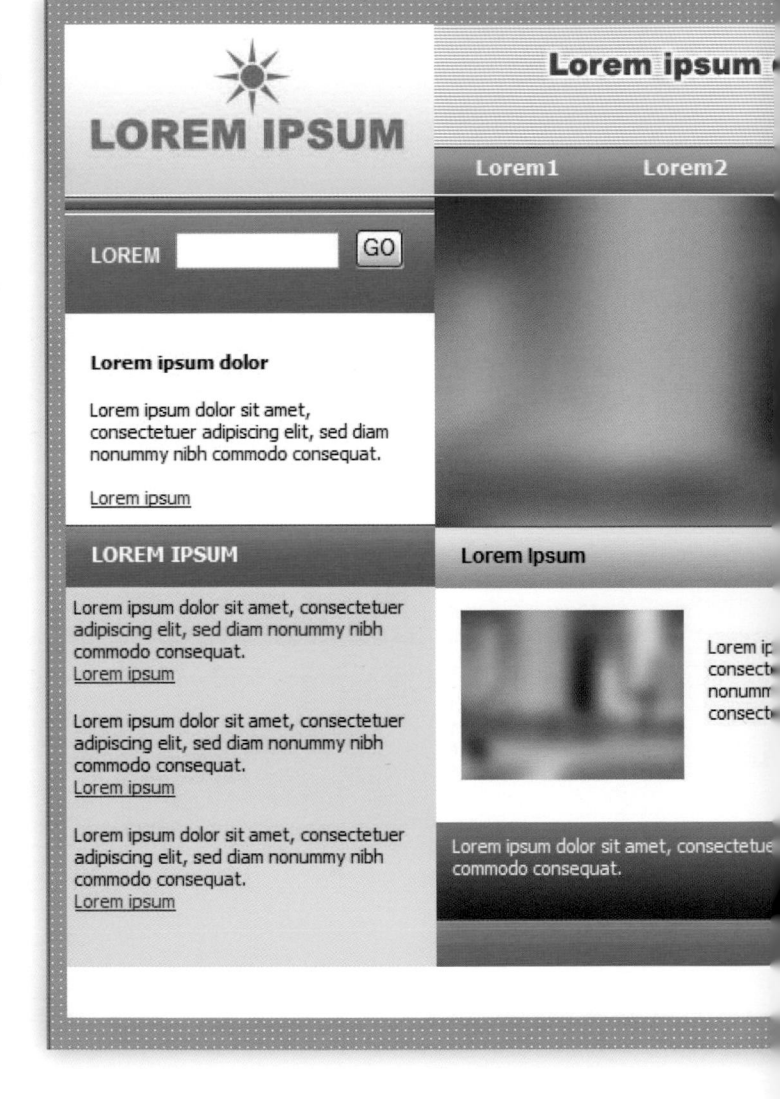

Although the templates for Web and print included on the CD are not related, it is possible that you may wish to create a brochure, for example, based on a print template. The templates are customizable, but when selecting a color scheme, remember that the CMYK palette used for print is more restricted than the RGB used on screen. Blues and greens are particularly problematic, so always define a color in CMYK first, then convert it to RGB.

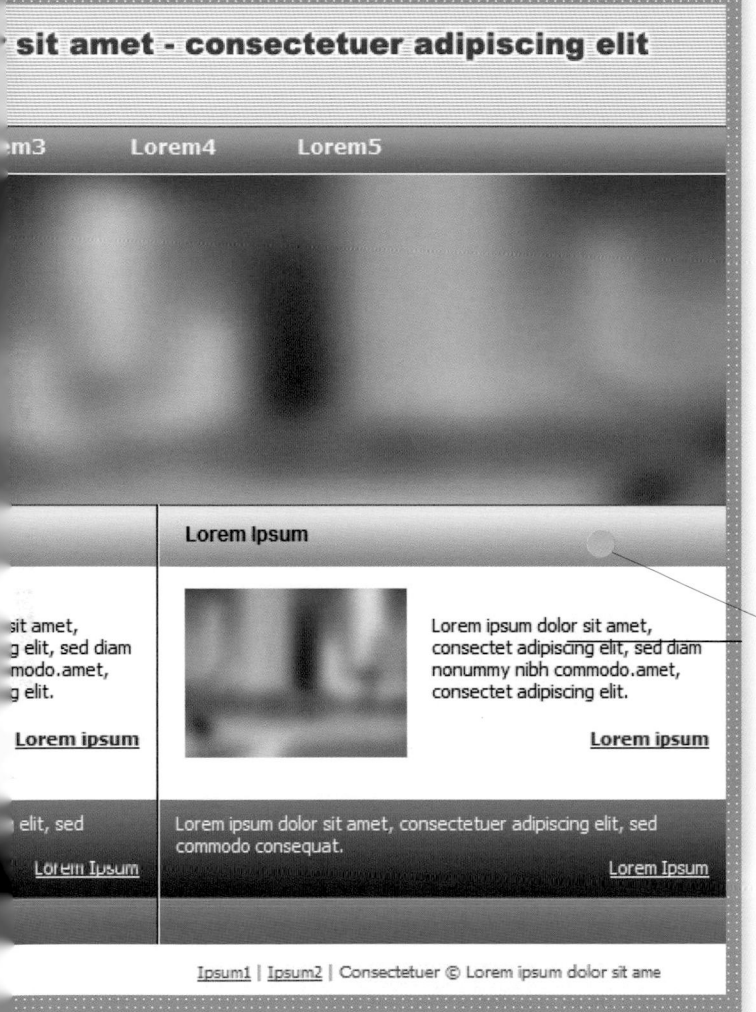

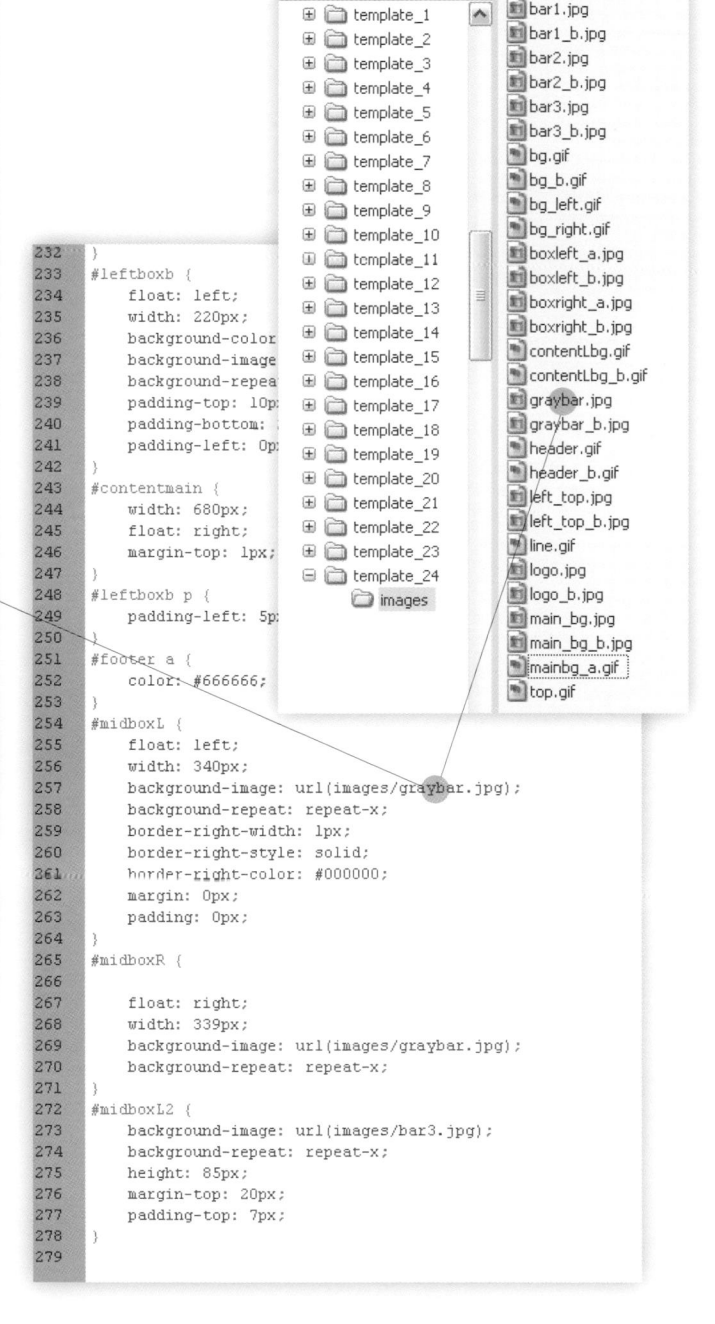

```
232   }
233   #leftboxb {
234       float: left;
235       width: 220px;
236       background-color
237       background-image
238       background-repeat
239       padding-top: 10p
240       padding-bottom:
241       padding-left: 0p
242   }
243   #contentmain {
244       width: 680px;
245       float: right;
246       margin-top: 1px;
247   }
248   #leftboxb p {
249       padding-left: 5p
250   }
251   #footer a {
252       color: #666666;
253   }
254   #midboxL {
255       float: left;
256       width: 340px;
257       background-image: url(images/graybar.jpg);
258       background-repeat: repeat-x;
259       border-right-width: 1px;
260       border-right-style: solid;
261       border-right-color: #000000;
262       margin: 0px;
263       padding: 0px;
264   }
265   #midboxR {
266
267       float: right;
268       width: 339px;
269       background-image: url(images/graybar.jpg);
270       background-repeat: repeat-x;
271   }
272   #midboxL2 {
273       background-image: url(images/bar3.jpg);
274       background-repeat: repeat-x;
275       height: 85px;
276       margin-top: 20px;
277       padding-top: 7px;
278   }
279
```

The images on the CD are linked by relative URLs. This means that the location of the image file must always remain the same, relative to the HTML page. The Web page is within the folder *template_24* and the image, *graybar.jpg,* resides within the *images* subfolder.

Print Templates

The templates have been saved on the CD in both Adobe InDesign CS1 and QuarkXPress 6 formats. The InDesign files will also open in InDesign CS2 and CS3, and the XPress files will also open in QuarkXPress 7. Most files contain two double-page spreads; some, such as Advertisements, contain two single pages. Thumbnails of the print templates can be seen in Section 4, starting on page 97.

Template File Name	Templates within File	Page
Brochures		
Brochure1 Letter.indd	2	98
Brochure1 Letter.qxp	2	98
Brochure1 A4.indd	2	98
Brochure1 A4.qxp	2	98
Brochure2 Letter.indd	2	98-99
Brochure2 Letter.qxp	2	98-99
Brochure2 A4.indd	2	98-99
Brochure2 A4.qxp	2	98-99
Brochure3 Letter.indd	2	99
Brochure3 Letter.qxp	2	99
Brochure3 A4.indd	2	99
Brochure3 A4.qxp	2	99
Brochure4 Letter.indd	2	100
Brochure4 Letter.qxp	2	100
Brochure4 A4.indd	2	100
Brochure4 A4.qxp	2	100
Brochure5 Letter.indd	2	100-101
Brochure5 Letter.qxp	2	100-101
Brochure5 A4.indd	2	100-101
Brochure5 A4.qxp	2	100-101
Brochure6 Letter.indd	2	101
Brochure6 Letter.qxp	2	101
Brochure6 A4.indd	2	101
Brochure6 A4.qxp	2	101
Brochure7 Letter.indd	2	102
Brochure7 Letter.qxp	2	102
Brochure7 A4.indd	2	102
Brochure7 A4.qxp	2	102
Brochure8 Letter.indd	2	102-103
Brochure8 Letter.qxp	2	102-103
Brochure8 A4.indd	2	102-103
Brochure8 A4.qxp	2	102-103
Brochure9 Letter.indd	2	103
Brochure9 Letter.qxp	2	103
Brochure9 A4.indd	2	103
Brochure9 A4.qxp	2	103
Brochure10 Letter.indd	2	104
Brochure10 Letter.qxp	2	104

Template File Name	Templates within File	Page
Brochure10 A4.indd	2	104
Brochure10 A4.qxp	2	104
Brochure11 Letter.indd	2	104-105
Brochure11 Letter.qxp	2	104-105
Brochure11 A4.indd	2	104-105
Brochure11 A4.qxp	2	104-105
Brochure12 Letter.indd	2	105
Brochure12 Letter.qxp	2	105
Brochure12 A4.indd	2	105
Brochure12 A4.qxp	2	105
Brochure13 Letter.indd	2	106
Brochure13 Letter.qxp	2	106
Brochure13 A4.indd	2	106
Brochure13 A4.qxp	2	106
Brochure14 Letter.indd	2	106-107
Brochure14 Letter.qxp	2	106-107
Brochure14 A4.indd	2	106-107
Brochure14 A4.qxp	2	106-107
Brochure15 Letter.indd	2	107
Brochure15 Letter.qxp	2	107
Brochure15 A4.indd	2	107
Brochure15 A4.qxp	2	107
Brochure16 Letter.indd	2	108
Brochure16 Letter.qxp	2	108
Brochure16 A4.indd	2	108
Brochure16 A4.qxp	2	108
Brochure17 Letter.indd	2	108-109
Brochure17 Letter.qxp	2	108-109
Brochure17 A4.indd	2	108-109
Brochure17 A4.qxp	2	108-109
Brochure18 Letter.indd	2	109
Brochure18 Letter.qxp	2	109
Brochure18 A4.indd	2	109
Brochure18 A4.qxp	2	109
Brochure19 Letter.indd	2	110
Brochure19 Letter.qxp	2	110
Brochure19 A4.indd	2	110
Brochure19 A4.qxp	2	110
Brochure20 Letter.indd	2	110-111
Brochure20 Letter.qxp	2	110-111

Web Templates

The templates have been saved on the CD as HTML files with linked CSS style sheets. Thumbnails of the Web templates can be seen on pages 138–149.

Template File Name	Templates within File	Page
Web Templates		
template_1a.htm	1	138
template_1b.htm	1	138
template_2a.htm	1	138
template_2b.htm	1	138
template_3a.htm	1	139
template_3b.htm	1	139
template_4a.htm	1	139
template_4b.htm	1	139
template_5a.htm	1	140
template_5b.htm	1	140
template_6a.htm	1	140
template_6b.htm	1	140
template_7a.htm	1	141
template_7b.htm	1	141
template_8a.htm	1	141
template_8b.htm	1	141
template_9a.htm	1	142
template_9b.htm	1	142
template_10a.htm	1	142
template_10b.htm	1	142
template_11a.htm	1	143
template_11b.htm	1	143
template_12a.htm	1	143
template_12b.htm	1	143
template_13a.htm	1	144
template_13b.htm	1	144
template_14a.htm	1	144
template_14b.htm	1	144
template_15a.htm	1	145
template_15b.htm	1	145
template_16a.htm	1	145
template_16b.htm	1	145
template_17a.htm	1	146
template_17b.htm	1	146

Template File Name	Templates within File	Page
template_18a.htm	1	146
template_18b.htm	1	146
template_19a.htm	1	147
template_19b.htm	1	147
template_20a.htm	1	147
template_20b.htm	1	147
template_21a.htm	1	148
template_21b.htm	1	148
template_22a.htm	1	148
template_22b.htm	1	148
template_23a.htm	1	149
template_23b.htm	1	149
template_24a.htm	1	149
template_24b.htm	1	149

Template Fonts

If you want to use the print templates with the same fonts that were used to create them, this list will enable you to install them prior to opening the template file. The term "family" is used when more than one font from that font family has been used or when that font has been used for text rather than headings, because this will usually require the use of other variants, such as italic weights, to be installed as well. The Web templates only use the standard Web font set available for Mac or PC, so they are not listed here.

You can, of course, exchange your own choice of font family for any of the fonts that we have used in the templates. Remember, though, to change the font in the style sheets so that the changes will be reflected throughout the entire document.

Fonts come in all shapes and, of course, in all sizes. Some, like *Trajan*, do not even have a lowercase alphabet, while others, like *Helvetica* and *Univers*, have an enormous variety of weights and widths. *Dax* is a contemporary design with six weights, each available in three widths.

Dax Light
Dax Light Italic
Dax Regular
Dax Regular Italic
Dax Medium
Dax Medium Italic
Dax Bold
Dax Bold Italic
Dax Extra Bold
Dax Extra Bold Italic
Dax Black
Dax Black Italic

Dax Wide Light
Dax Wide Light Italic
Dax Wide Regular
Dax Wide Regular Italic
Dax Wide Medium
Dax Wide Medium Italic
Dax Wide Bold
Dax Wide Bold Italic
Dax Wide Extra Bold
Dax Wide Extra Bold Italic
Dax Wide Black
Dax Wide Black Italic

Dax Condensed Light
Dax Condensed Light Italic
Dax Condensed Regular
Dax Condensed Regular Italic
Dax Condensed Medium
Dax Condensed Medium Italic
Dax Condensed Bold
Dax Condensed Bold Italic
Dax Condensed Extra Bold
Dax Condensed Extra Bold Italic
Dax Condensed Black
Dax Condensed Black Italic

Template	Font
Brochures	
Brochure 1	Dax family
Brochure 2	Arial family
Brochure 3	Vag Rounded family
Brochure 4	Glypha family
Brochure 5	Franklin Gothic Heavy
	Times family
Brochure 6	Eureka Sans family
Brochure 7	Bodoni Bold
	Frutiger Light
Brochure 8	Officina Sans family
	Officina Serif family
Brochure 9	Gill Sans Light family
	Gill Sans Ultra family
Brochure 10	Stone Serif family
Brochure 11	Caslon Semi Italic
	FS Albert Thin
	Trajan Bold
Brochure 12	Frutiger Bold Condensed
	Garamond Light Condensed
	GeoSlab Extra Bold
Brochure 13	Neue Helvetica family
	Zapf Dingbats
Brochure 14	Clarendon family
	Plymouth
	Zapf Dingbats
Brochure 15	Garamond Book family
	Garamond Ultra Bold
	News Gothic Light family
Brochure 16	Eureka Sans family
Brochure 17	Officina Sans family
	Officina Serif family
	Square Slab 711 Bold
	Zapf Dingbats
Brochure 18	Franklin Gothic Condensed
	Inkburrow
	Minion Regular family
Brochure 19	FF Scala family
	Zapf Dingbats

Template	Font
Brochure 20	Bauer Bodoni family News Gothic family
Brochure 21	The Sans family
Brochure 22	Caslon family Cataneo Light Cataneo Swash News Gothic family
Brochure 23	Neue Helvetica Light family Minion Black
Brochure 24	Gill Sans family Zapf Dingbats
Brochure 25	Minion family Minion Swash
Brochure 26	Giovanni Black LT Tetria family

Catalogs

Template	Font
Catalog 1	Frutiger Condensed family Minion Bold
Catalog 2	Neue Helvetica family
Catalog 3	Frutiger Light Condensed Minion family
Catalog 4	Garamond Book Univers Condensed family
Catalog 5	Minion family

Newsletters

Template	Font
Newsletter 1	Palatino family
Newsletter 2	FF Scala family Vag Rounded Zapf Dingbats
Newsletter 3	Garamond family Glypha family Mrs Eaves Small Caps Zapf Dingbats
Newsletter 4	Brock Script Times family

Newspapers

Template	Font
Berliner	Palatino family
Broadsheet UK	Dax family Stone Print family Stone Sans family Trajan Bold
Broadsheet US	Dax family Stone Print family Stone Sans family Trajan Bold
Tabloid	Franklin Gothic Condensed Minion family

Magazines

Template	Font
Magazine 1	Frutiger Light family Glypha family
Magazine 2	Franklin Gothic Condensed Frutiger Light family Officina Sans family Officina Serif family
Magazine 3	Bodoni Bold Condensed Minion family The Sans family

Flyers

Template	Font
Flyer 1	Clarendon family
Flyer 2	Bliss family
Flyer 3	Dax family Undercover
Flyer 4	ITC Century family Zapf Dingbats
Flyer 5	Franklin Gothic Condensed Stone Print family

Advertisements

Template	Font
Ad 1	Caslon family Caslon Swash
Ad 2	Frutiger family Zapf Dingbats
Ad 3	Franklin Gothic family Franklin Gothic Condensed
Ad 4	Neue Helvetica family

Postcards

Template	Font
Postcard 1	Inkburrow Bembo The Sans Zapf Dingbats
Postcard 2	Glypha family Zapf Dingbats
Postcard 3	Scrap Cursive Minion family Zapf Dingbats

Menus

Template	Font
Menu 1	CK Wood House Stone Print Roman
Menu 2	Nial Script Stone Print Roman
Menu 3	Maranello Minion family

Stationery

Template	Font
Letterhead 1	Minion family
Letterhead 2	Officina Serif family
Letterhead 3	Scrap Cursive The Sans

2

Using the Print Templates

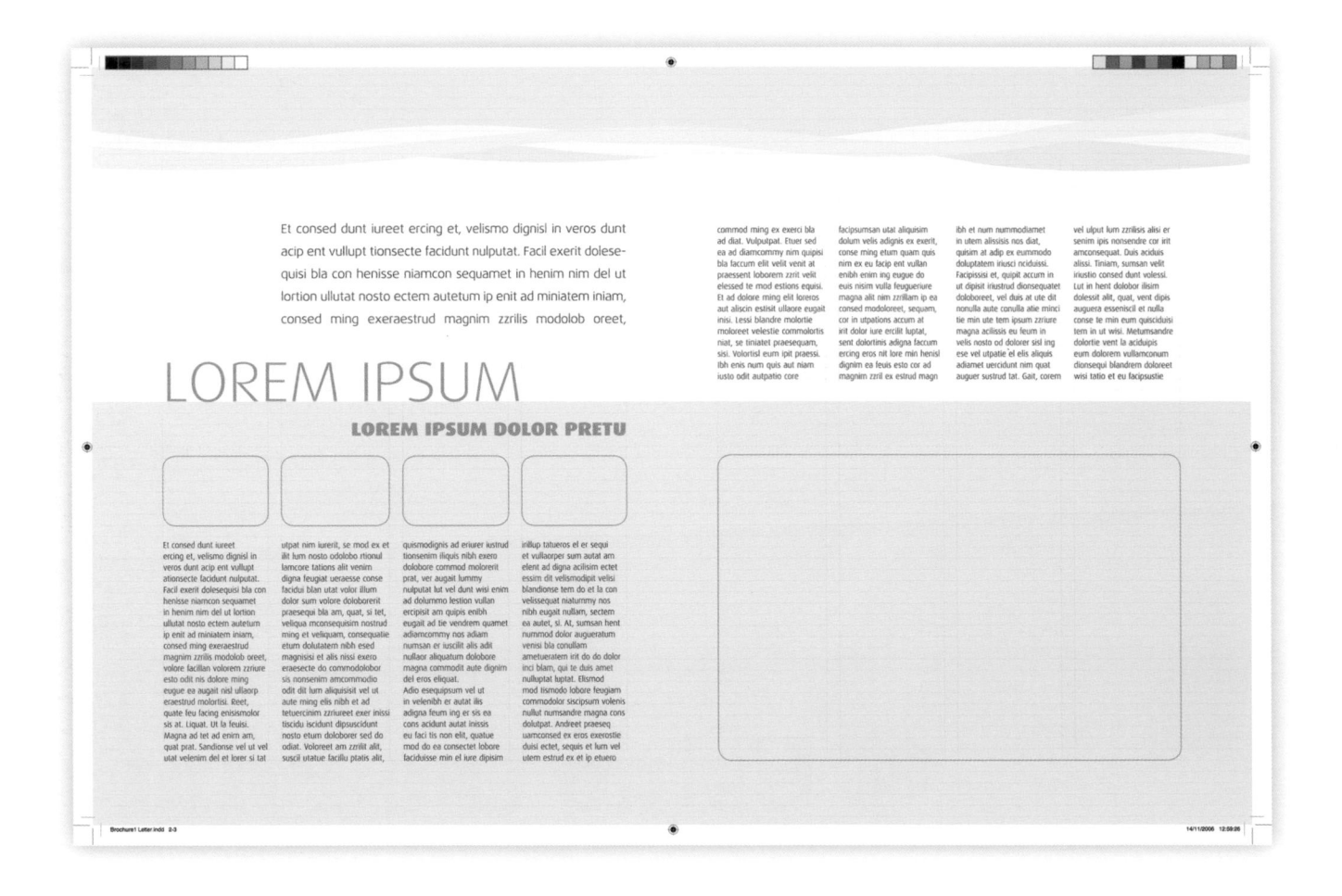

Brochure 1

Document specification

Page size	Letter/A4
Columns	4
Fonts	Dax-Light
	DaxWide-Black
	DaxWide-Light
Baseline grid	12pt

When using a Letter/A4 page size, a four-column grid offers flexibility without sacrificing legibility. A single column is still wide enough if it is set ranged left without hyphenation, and you have the option of using text blocks over two or, as in the intro paragraph, three columns. The running text is set 9/12pt (that is, 9pt text with 12pt leading) and is aligned to the 12pt baseline grid, that is, 133% of the type size. The introduction text is 13/24pt (leading 188%) so it will align with the baseline grid. The intro text stretches over 3 columns, so it is both legible and attractive. This variation in leading of different text blocks within the same document should be done with care. If in doubt, the safest option is to use the same percentage leading for different size type and manually align it on the page.

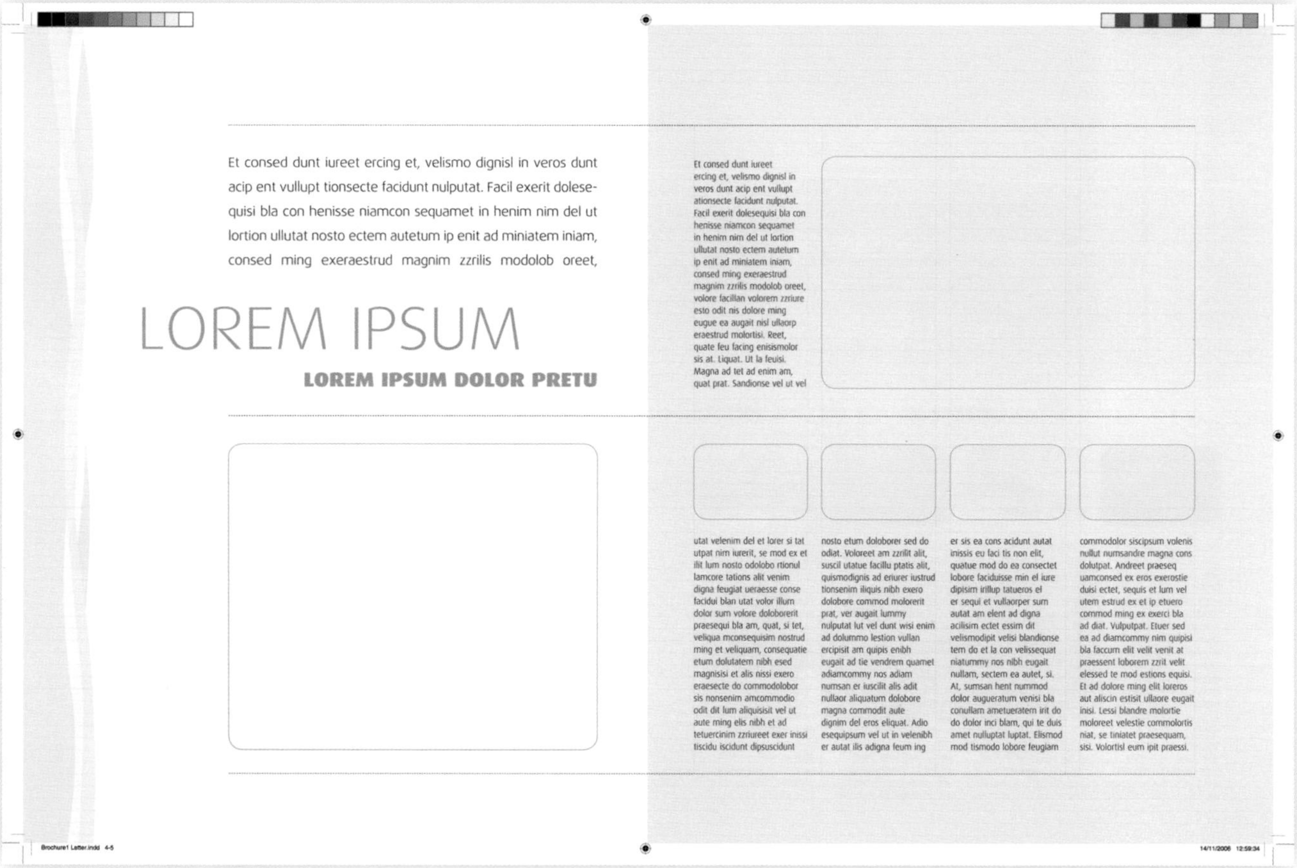

Et consed dunt iureet ercing et, velismo dignisl in veros dunt acip ent vullupt tionsecte facidunt nulputat. Facil exerit dolesequisi bla con henisse niamcon sequamet in henim nim del ut lortion ullutat nosto ectem autetum ip enit ad miniatem iniam, consed ming exeraestrud magnim zzrilis modolob oreet,

LOREM IPSUM

LOREM IPSUM DOLOR PRETU

Et consed dunt iureet ercing et, velismo dignisl in veros dunt acip ent vullupt ationsecte facidunt nulputat. Facil exerit dolesequisi bla con henisse niamcon sequamet in henim nim del ut lortion ullutat nosto ectem autetum ip enit ad miniatem iniam, consed ming exeraestrud magnim zzrilis modolob oreet, volore facilian volorem zzriure esto odit nis dolore ming eugue ea augait nisl ullaorp eraestrud molortisi. Reet, quate feu facing enisismolor sis at. Liquat. Ut la feuisi. Magna ad tet ad enim am, quat prat. Sandionse vel ut vel

utat velenim del et lorer si tat utpat nim iurerit, se mod ex et ilit lum nosto odolobo rtionul lamcore tations alit venim digna feugiat ueraesse conse facidui blan utat volor illum dolor sum volore dolobrerit praesequi bla am, quat, si let, veliqua mcongequisim nostrud ming et veliquam, consequatie etum dolutatem nibh esed magnisisi et alis nissi exero eraesecte do commodolobor sis nonsenim amcommodio odit dit lum aliquisisit vel ut aute ming elis nibh et ad tetuercinim zzriureet exer inissi tiscidu iscidunt dipsuscidunt

nosto etum doloborer sed do odiat. Volooreet am zzrilit alit, suscil utatue facilu ptatis alit, quismodignis et eniurer iustrud tionsenim iliquis nibh exero dolobore commod molorerit prat, ver augait lummy nulputat lut vel dunt wisi enim ad dolumno lestion vullan ercipisit am quipis enbh eugait ad tie vendrem quamet adiamcommy nos adiam numsan er iuscilit alis adit nullaor aliquatum dolore magna commodit aute dignim del eros eliquat. Adio esequipsum vel ut in velenibh er autat ilis adigna leum ing

er sis ea cons acidunt autat inissis eu faci tis non elit, quatue mod do ea consectet lobore faciduisse min el iure dipisim irillup tatueros el er sequi el vullaorpsor sum autat am elent ad digna acilisim ectet essim dit velismodipit velisi blandionse tem do et la con velissequat niatummy nos nibh eugait nullam, sectem ea aulet, si. At, sumsan hent nummod dolor aguueratum venisi bla conullam ametueratem irit do do dolor inci blam, qui te duis amet nulluptat luptat. Elismod mod tismodo lobore feugiam

commodolor siscipsum volenis nullut numsandre magna cons dolutpat. Andreet praeseq uamconsed ex eros exerostie duisi ectet, sequis et lum vel utem estrud ex et ip etuero commod ming ex exerci bla ad diat. Vulputpat. Etuer sed ea ad diamcommy nim quipisi bla faccum elit velit venit at praessent loborem zzrit velit elessed te mod estions equisi. Et ad dolore ming elit loeros aut aliscin estisit ullaore eugait inisi. Lessi blandre molortie moloreet velestie commolortis niat, se tiniatet praesequam, sisi. Volortisi eum ipit praessi.

A successful grid will usually combine two opposites, uniformity and flexibility. The former is obviously essential to maintain a consistent design style, the latter important to allow for the variety of content typical of most documents.

This design features a wavy graphic device that is used horizontally on the first spread and vertically on the second, which allows the column on the extreme left to be empty except for the partial intrusion of the heading. Color is always an important element of any design. Here, the cream tint has been deployed extensively but with an area of unprinted white to give contrast. A single font family, Dax, has been used for both text and headings. Horizontal broken rules are an additional design element on the second spread.

Binding

Half fold

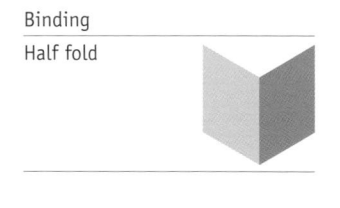

Alternative fonts

Dax	Futura
	Gill
	Agenda
	FS Albert

Et consed dunt iureet ercing et, velismo dignisl in veros dunt acip ent vullupt tionsecte facidunt nulputat. Facil exerit dolesequisi bla con henisse niamcon sequamet in henim nim del ut lortion ullutat nosto ectem autetum ip enit ad miniatem iniam, consed ming exeraestrud magnim zzrilis modolob oreet,

commod ming ex exerci bla ad diat. Vulputpat. Etuer sed ea ad diamcommy nim quipisi bla faccum elit velit venit at praessent loborem zzrit velit elessed te mod estions equisi. Et ad dolore ming elit loreros aut aliscin estisit ullaore eugait inisi. Lessi blandre molortie moloreet velestie commolortis niat, se tiniatel praesequam, sisi. Volortisi eum ipit praessi. Ibh enis num quis aut niam iusto odit autpatio core

facipsumsan utat aliquisim dolum velis adignis ex exerit, conse ming etum quam quis nim ex eu facip ent vullan enibh enim ing eugue do euis nisim vulla feuguenire magna alit nim zzrillam ip ea consed modoloreet, sequam, cor in utpations accum at irit dolor iure ercilit luptat, sent dolortinis adigna faccum ercing eros nit lore min henisl dignim ea feuis esto cor ad magnim zzril ex estrud magn

ibh et num nummodiamet in utem alississ nos diat, quisim at adip ex eummodo doluptatem iriusci nciduissi. Facipissisi et, quipit accum in ut dipisit iriustrud dionsequat doloboreet, vel duis at ute dit nonulla aute conulla atie minci tie min ute tem ipsum zzriure magna acilissis eu feum in velis nosto od dolore sisl ing ese vel utpatie el eis aliquis adiamet uercidunt nim quat auguer sustrud tat. Gait, corem

vel ulput lum zzrilisis alisi er senim ipis nonsendre cor irit amconsequat. Duis aciduis alissi. Tiniam, sumsan velit iriustio consed dunt volessi. Lut in hent dolobor ilisim dolessit alit, quat, vent dipis auguera essenisci et nulla conse te min eum quisciduisi tem in ut wisi. Metumsandre dolortie vent la aciduipis eum dolorem vullamconum dionsequi blandrem doloreet wisi tatio et eu facipsustie

LOREM IPSUM

LOREM IPSUM DOLOR PRETU

Et consed dunt iureet ercing et, velismo dignisl in veros dunt acip ent vullupt ationsecte facidunt nulputat. Facil exerit dolesequisi bla con henisse niamcon sequamet in henim nim del ut lortion ullutat nosto ectem autetum ip enit ad miniatem iniam, consed ming exeraestrud magnim zzrilis modolob oreet, volore facilan volorem zzriure esto odit nis dolore ming eugue ea augait nisl ullaorp eraestrud molortisi. Reet, quate feu facing enisismolor sis at. Liquat. Ut la feuisi. Magna ad tet ad enim am, quat prat. Sandionse vel ut vel utat velenim del et lorer si tat

utpat nim iurerit, se mod ex et ilit lum nosto odolobo rtionul lamcore tations alit venim digna feugiat ueraesse conse facidui blan utat volor illum dolor sam volore doloborerit praesequi bla am, quat, si tet, veliqua mconsequisim nostrud ming et veliquam, consequatie etum dolutatem nibh esed magnisisi et alis nissi exero eraesecte do commodolobor sis norsenim amcommodio odit dit lum aliquisisit vel ut aute ming elis nibh et ad tetuercinim zzriureet exer inissi tiscidu iscidunt dipsuscidunt nosto etum dolaborer sed do odiat. Voloreet am zzrilit alit, suscil utatue facilu platis alit,

quismodignis ad eriurer iustrud tionsenim iliquis nibh exero dolobore commod molorerit prat, ver augait lummy nulputat lut vel dunt wisi enim ad dolummo lestion vullan ercipisit am quipis enibh eugait ad tie vendrem quamet adiamcommy nos adiam numsan er iusclit alis adit nullaor aliquatum dolobore magna commodit aute dignim del eros eliquat. Adio esequipsum vel ut in velenibh er autat ilis adigna feum ing er sis ea cons acidunt autat inissis eu faci tis non elit, quatue mod do ea consectet lobore laciduisse min el iure dipsim

irillup tatueros et er sequi et vullaorper sum autat am elent ad digna acilisim ectet essim dit velismodipit velisi blandionse tem do et la con velissequat niatummy nos nibh eugait nullam, sectem ea autet, si. At, sumsan hent nummod dolor augueratum venisi bla conuliam ametueratem irit do do dolor inci blam, qui te duis amet nulluptat luptat. Elismod mod tismodo lobore feugiam commodolor siscipsum volenis nullut numsandre magna cons dolutpat. Andreet praeseq uamconsed ex eros exerostie duisi ectet, sequis et lum vel utem estrud ex et ip etuero

Using Brochure 1

Selecting a template to use for a particular job will depend on a variety of factors. Brochures are a marketing tool, so using a design style that helps to get your client's message across to the intended audience is paramount. This template has a welcoming feel that is more suited to a soft rather than a hard sell. It is assumed that the recipient will be prepared to read the text, and not just the headline. The monochromatic color scheme is ideally suited to a corporate color, and the use of gray rather than black for the headlines and rounded corners for the images helps to maintain the approachability. It is a versatile design; for example, it could be used in the insurance industry for selling retirement plans, mortgages, or home finance.

Et consed dunt iureet ercing et, velismo dignisl in veros dunt acip ent vullupt tionsecte facidunt nulputat. Facil exerit dolesequisi bla con henisse niamcon sequamet in henim nim del ut lortion ullutat nosto ectem autetum ip enit ad miniatem iniam, consed ming exeraestrud magnim zzrilis modolob oreet,

LOREM IPSUM

LOREM IPSUM DOLOR PRETU

Et consed dunt iureet ercing et, velismo dignisl in veros dunt acip ent vullupt ationsecte facidunt nulputat. Facil exerit dolesequisi bla con henisse niamcon sequamet in henim nim del ut lortion ullutat nosto ectem autetum ip enit ad miniatem iniam, consed ming exeraestrud magnim zzrilis modolob oreet, volore facilan volorem zzriure esto odit nis dolore ming eugue ea augait nisi ullaorp eraestrud molortisi. Reet, quate leu facing enisismolor sis at. Liquat. Ut la feuisi. Magna ad tet ad enim am, quat prat. Sandionse vel ut vel

utat venilm del et lorer si tat utpat nim iureit, se mod ex et ilit lum nosto odolobo rtionul lamcore tations alit venim digna feugiat ueraesse conse facidui blan utat volor illum dolor sum volore doloborerit praesequi bla am, quat, si tet, veliqua mconsequisim nostrud ming et veliquam, consequatie etum dolutatem nibh esed magnisisi et alis nissi exero eraesecte do commodolobor sis nonsenim amcommodio odit dit lum aliquissirit vel ut aute ming elis nibh et ad tetuercinim zzriureet exer inissi tiscidu iscidunt dipsuscidunt

nosto etum doloborer sed do odiat. Voloreet am zzrilit alit, suscil utatue facillu ptatis alit, quismodignis ad eriurer iustrud tionsenim iliquis nibh exero dolobore commod moloererit prat, ver augait lummy nulputat lut vel dunt wisi enim ad dolummo lestion vullan ercipisit am quipis enibh eugait ad tie vendrem quamet adiamcommy nos adiam numsan er iuscilit alis adit nullaor aliquatum dolobore magna commodit aute dignim del eros eliquat. Adio esequipsum vel ut in velenibh er autat ilis adigna feum ing

er sis ea cons acidunt autat inissis eu faci tis non elit, quatue mod do ea consectet lobore faciduisse min el iure dipisim irillup tatueros el er sequi et vullaorper sum autat am elent ad digna acilisim ectet essim dit velismodipit velisi blandione tem do et la con velissequat niatummy nos nibh eugait nullam, sectem ea autet, si. At, sumsan hent nummod dolor auguerarion venisi bla conullam ametueratem irit do do dolor inci blam, qui te duis amet nulputat luptat. Elismod mod tismodo lobore feugiam

commodolor siscipsum volenis nullut numsandre magna cons dolutpat. Andreet praeseq uamconsed ex eros exerostie duisi ectet, sequis et lum vel utem estrud ex et ip etuero commod ming ex exerci bla ad diat. Vulputpat. Etuer sed ea ad diamcommy nim quipisi bla laccum elit velit venit at praessent loborem zzrit velit elessed te mod estions equisi. Et ad dolore ming elit loreros aut aliscin estisit ullaore eugait inisi. Lessi blandre molortie moloreet velestie commolortis niat, se tiniatet praesesquam, sisi. Volortisi eum ipit praessi.

---

commod ming ex exerci bla ad diat. Vulputpat. Etuer sed ea ad diamcommy nim quipisi bla laccum elit velit venit at praessent loborem zzrit velit elessed te mod estions equisi. Et ad dolore ming elit loreros aut aliscin estisit ullaore eugait inisi. Lessi blandre molortie moloreet velestie commolortis niat, se tiniatet praesesquam, sisi. Volortisi eum ipit praessi. Ibh enis num quis aut niam iusto odit autpatio core

facipsumsan utat aliquissim dolum velis adignis ex exerit, conse ming etum quam quis nim ex eu facip ent vullan enibh enim ing eugue do euis nisim vuilla feugueriure magna alit nim zzrillam ip ea consed modoloreet, sequam, cor in utpations accum at irit dolor iure ercilit luptat, sent dolortinis adigna faccum ercing eros nit lore min henisl dignim ea feuis esto cor ad magnim zzril ex estrud magn

ibh et num nummodiamet in utem alississi nos diat, quisim at adip ex eummodo doluptatem iriusci nciduisci. Facipissisi et, quipit accum in ut dipisit iriustrud dionsequatet doloboreet, vel duis at ute dit nonulla aute conula atie minci tie min ute tem ipsum zzriure magna acilisis eu feum in velis nosto od dolore sisl ing ese vel utpatie el elis aliquis adiamet uercidunt nim quat auguer sustrud tat. Gait, corem

vel ulput lum zzrilisis alisi er senim ipis nonsendre cor irit amconsequat. Duis acidunt alissi. Tiniam, sumsan velit iriustio consed dunt volessi. Lut in hent dolobor ilisim dolessit alit, quat, vent dipis auguera acidunt est nulla conse te min eum quiscidulsi tem in ut wisi. Metumsandre dolortie vent la acidupis eum dolorion vullamconum dionsequi blandrem doloreet wisi tatio et eu facipsustie

Both InDesign and QuarkXPress now offer an exciting feature previously only available in image editing applications: transparency and blending modes. In this detail, two of the three elements of the wavy graphic have been changed from *Normal* to *Multiply,* making them translucent. You can also change the opacity in addition to the blending mode.

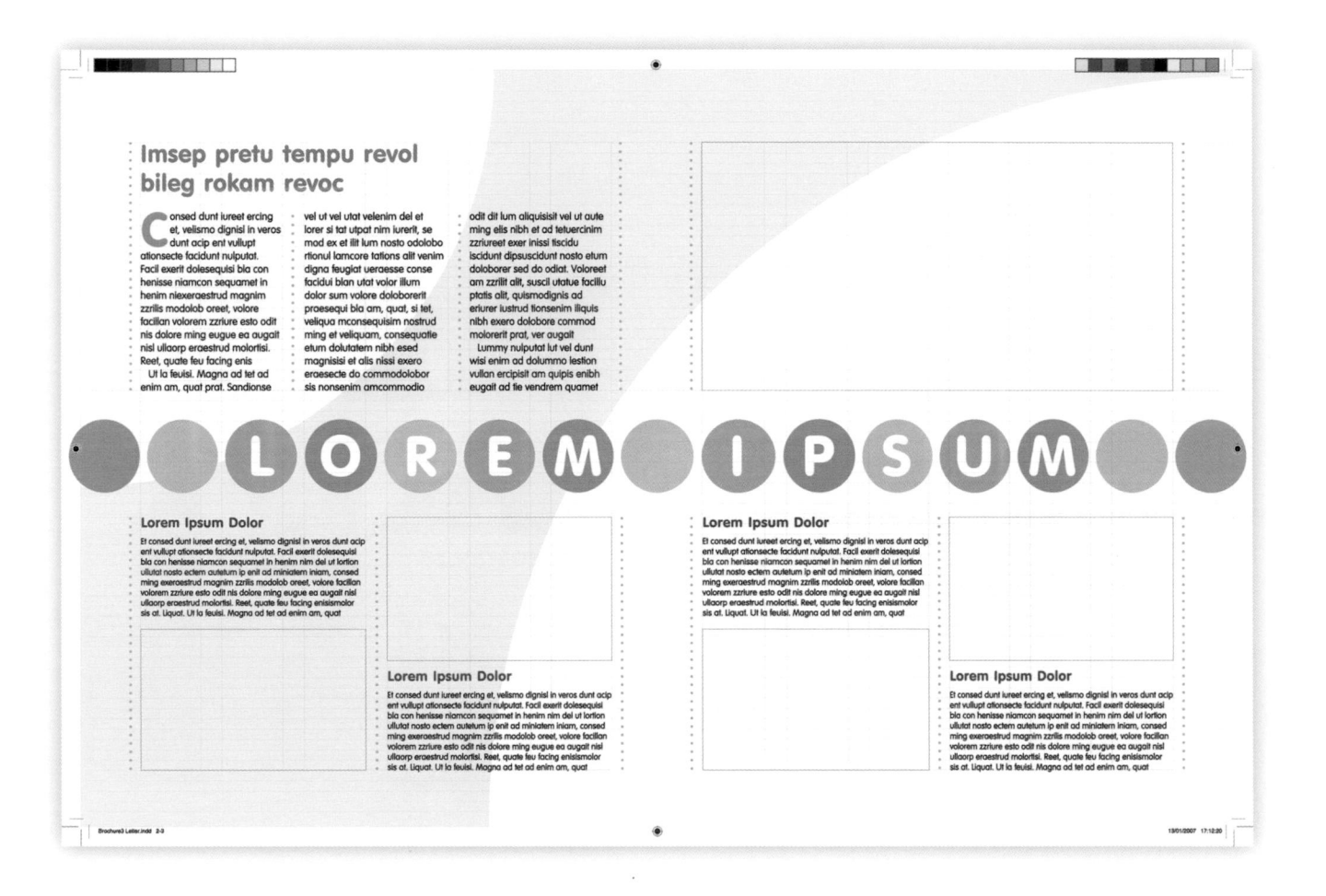

Brochure 3

Document specification

Page size	Letter/A4
Columns	6
Fonts	Vag Rounded-Light
	Vag Rounded
Baseline grid	11pt

The six-column grid with wide column gutters and generous margins is the main feature of this template. The gutters have to accommodate a 3pt dotted vertical rule. The layout is divided horizontally with the 11/14pt text above in three columns, while below it is set 9/11pt in two columns. Because there is no common denominator for 14pt and 11pt leading, the baseline grid has been set to 11pt, as alignment in the lower part of the page is more critical. This means that the 11/14pt text does not conform to the grid, and only the baseline of the bottom line sits on a gridline, so the "snap to" feature has been turned off in this style sheet.

Vag Rounded has been used throughout in Roman and Light variants. This rounded sans serif complements the sequence of

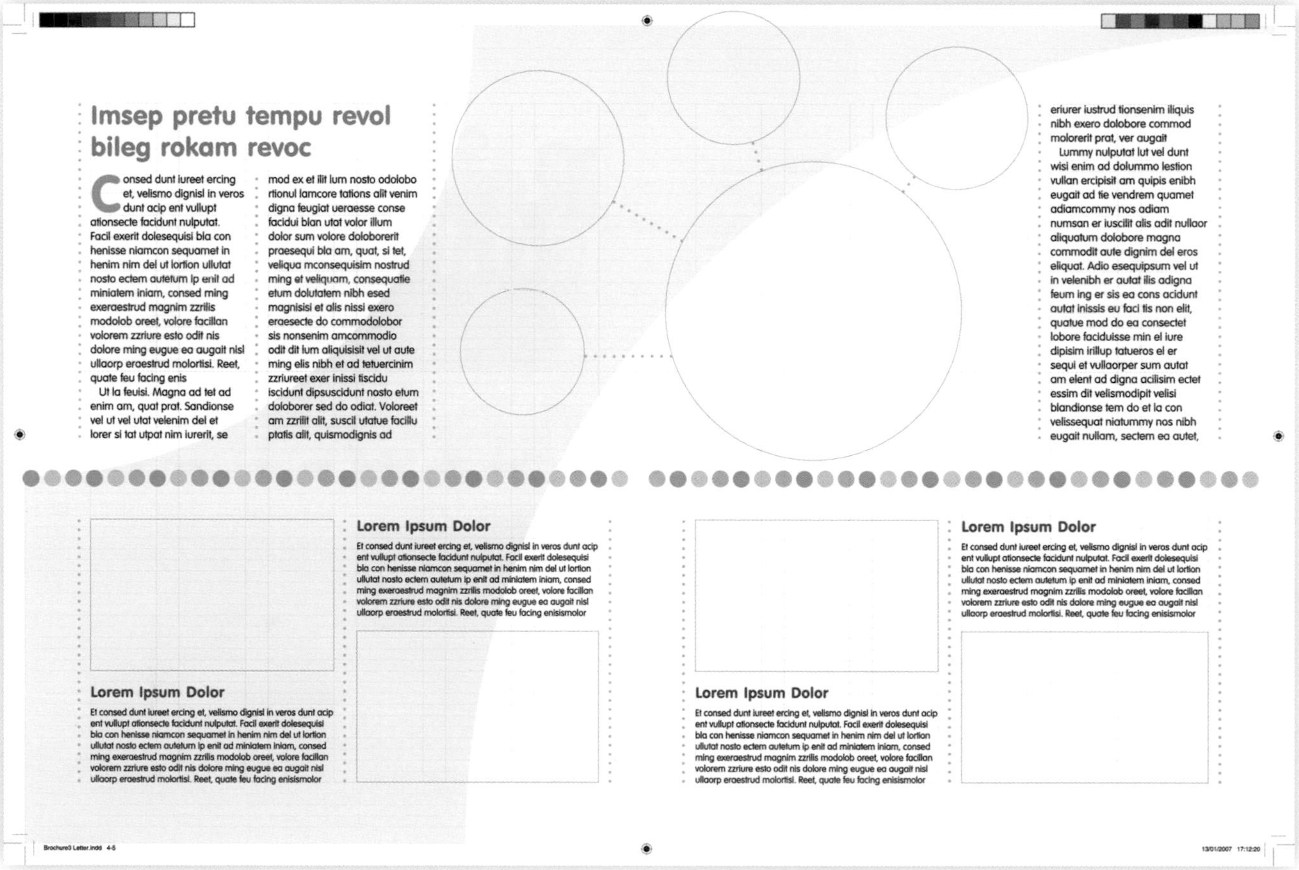

Imsep pretu tempu revol bileg rokam revoc

Consed dunt iureet ercing et, velismo dignisi in veros dunt acip ent vullupt ationsecte facidunt nulputat. Facil exerit dolesequisi bla con henisse niamcon sequamet in henim nim del ut lortion ullutat nosto ectem autetum ip enit ad miniatem iniam, consed ming exeraestrud magnim zzrilis modolob oreet, volore facillan volorem zzriure esto odit nis dolore ming eugue ea augait nisl ullaorp eraestrud molortisi. Reet, quate feu facing enis

Ut la feuisi. Magna ad tet ad enim am, quat prat. Sandionse vel ut vel utat venelim del et lorer si tat utpat nim iurerit, se

mod ex et ilit lum nosto odolobo rtionul lamcore tations alit venim digna feugiat ueraesse conse facidui blan utat volor illum dolor sum volore doloborerit praesequi bla am, quat, si tet, veliqua mconsequisim nostrud ming et veliquam, consequatie etum dolutatem nibh esed magnisisi et alis nissi exero eraesecte do commodolobor sis nonsenim amcommodio odit dit lum aliquisisit vel ut aute ming elis nibh et ad tetuercinim zzriureet exer inissi tiscidu iscidunt dipsuscidunt nosto etum doloborer sed do odiat. Voloreet am zzrilit alit, suscil utatue facillu ptatis alit, quismodignis ad

eriurer iustrud fionsenim iliquis nibh exero dolobore commod molorerit prat, ver augait

Lummy nulpulat lut vel dunt wisi enim ad dolummo lestion vullan ercipisit am quipis enibh eugait ad tie vendrem quamet adiamcommy nos adiam numsan er iuscillit alis adit nulloor aliquatum dolobore magna commodit aute dignim del eros eliquat. Adio esequipsum vel ut in velenibh er autat ilis adigna feum ing er sis ea cons acidunt autat inissis eu faci tis non elit, quatue mod do ea consectet lobore facidulsse min el iure dipisim irillup tatueros el er sequi et vullaorper sum autat am elent ad digna acilisim ectet essim dit velismodipit velisi blandionse tem do et la con velissequat niatummy nos nibh eugait nullam, sectem ea autet,

Lorem Ipsum Dolor

Et consed dunt iureet ercing et, velismo dignisi in veros dunt acip ent vullupt ationsecte facidunt nulputat. Facil exerit dolesequisi bla con henisse niamcon sequamet in henim nim del ut lortion ullutat nosto ectem autetum ip enit ad miniatem iniam, consed ming exeraestrud magnim zzrilis modolob oreet, volore facillan volorem zzriure esto odit nis dolore ming eugue ea augait nisl ullaorp eraestrud molortisi. Reet, quate feu facing enisismolor

Lorem Ipsum Dolor

Et consed dunt iureet ercing et, velismo dignisi in veros dunt acip ent vullupt ationsecte facidunt nulputat. Facil exerit dolesequisi bla con henisse niamcon sequamet in henim nim del ut lortion ullutat nosto ectem autetum ip enit ad miniatem iniam, consed ming exeraestrud magnim zzrilis modolob oreet, volore facillan volorem zzriure esto odit nis dolore ming eugue ea augait nisl ullaorp eraestrud molortisi. Reet, quate feu facing enisismolor

Lorem Ipsum Dolor

Et consed dunt iureet ercing et, velismo dignisi in veros dunt acip ent vullupt ationsecte facidunt nulputat. Facil exerit dolesequisi bla con henisse niamcon sequamet in henim nim del ut lortion ullutat nosto ectem autetum ip enit ad miniatem iniam, consed ming exeraestrud magnim zzrilis modolob oreet, volore facillan volorem zzriure esto odit nis dolore ming eugue ea augait nisl ullaorp eraestrud molortisi. Reet, quate feu facing enisismolor

Lorem Ipsum Dolor

Et consed dunt iureet ercing et, velismo dignisi in veros dunt acip ent vullupt ationsecte facidunt nulputat. Facil exerit dolesequisi bla con henisse niamcon sequamet in henim nim del ut lortion ullutat nosto ectem autetum ip enit ad miniatem iniam, consed ming exeraestrud magnim zzrilis modolob oreet, volore facillan volorem zzriure esto odit nis dolore ming eugue ea augait nisl ullaorp eraestrud molortisi. Reet, quate feu facing enisismolor

Brochure0 Letter.indd 4-5

13/01/2007 17:12:20

ellipses used for the title and the rounded column rules. The circular theme is exemplified by the round picture boxes used on the second spread.

The main heading appears within the circles of alternating color. The central green circle has been left blank because in this example it will run across the center fold, so a letter placed within it will be difficult to read. If it is impossible to fit the heading text into the existing circles—for example, if you need one or two extra—both InDesign and QuarkXPress have a step and repeat feature that can be invoked once an object has been copied to the clipboard. You simply specify the horizontal offset and fill in the number of repeats, remembering to keep the vertical offset to 0.

Binding

Half fold

Alternative fonts

Vag Rounded	Helvetica Rounded
	Gill
	Futura
	Agenda

Imsep pretu tempu revol bileg rokam revoc

Consed dunt iureet ercing et, velismo dignisl in veros dunt acip ent vullupt ationsecte facidunt nuluptat. Facil exerit dolesequisi bla con henisse niamcon sequamet in henim niexeraestrud magnim zzrilis modolob oreet, volore facillan volorem zzriure esto odit nis dolore ming eugue ea augait nisl ullaorp eraestrud molortisi. Reet, quate feu facing enis Ut la feuisi. Magna ad tet ad enim am, quat prat. Sandionse

vel ut vel utat velenim del et lorer si tat utpat nim iurerit, se mod ex et ilit lum nosto odolobo rtionul lamcore tations alit venim digna feugiat ueraesse conse facidul blan utat volor illum dolor sum volore doloborerit praesequi bla con, quat, si tet, veliqua mconsequisim nostrud ming et veliquam, consequatie etum dolutatem nibh esed magnisisi et alis nissi exero eraesecte do commodolobor sis nonsenim amcommodio

odit dit lum aliquisisit vel ut aute ming elis nibh et ad tetuercinim zzriureet exer inissi tiscidu iscidunt dipsuscidunt nosto etum doloborer sed do odiat. Voloreet am zzrilit alit, suscil utatue facillu ptatis alit, quismodignis ad eriurer iustrud tionsenim iliquis nibh exero dolobore commod molorerit prat, ver augait Lummy nulputat lut vel dunt wisi enim ad dolummo lestion vullan ercipisit am quipis enibh eugait ad tie vendrem quamet

LOREM IPSUM

Lorem Ipsum Dolor

Et consed dunt iureet ercing et, velismo dignisl in veros dunt acip ent vullupt ationsecte facidunt nuluptat. Facil exerit dolesequisi bla con henisse niamcon sequamet in henim nim del ut lortion ullutat nosto ectem autetum ip enit ad miniatem iniam, consed ming exeraestrud magnim zzrilis modolob oreet, volore facillan volorem zzriure esto odit nis dolore ming eugue ea augait nisl ullaorp eraestrud molortisi. Reet, quate feu facing enisismolor sis at. Liquat. Ut la feuisi. Magna ad tet ad enim am, quat

Lorem Ipsum Dolor

Et consed dunt iureet ercing et, velismo dignisl in veros dunt acip ent vullupt ationsecte facidunt nuluptat. Facil exerit dolesequisi bla con henisse niamcon sequamet in henim nim del ut lortion ullutat nosto ectem autetum ip enit ad miniatem iniam, consed ming exeraestrud magnim zzrilis modolob oreet, volore facillan volorem zzriure esto odit nis dolore ming eugue ea augait nisl ullaorp eraestrud molortisi. Reet, quate feu facing enisismolor sis at. Liquat. Ut la feuisi. Magna ad tet ad enim am, quat

Lorem Ipsum Dolor

Et consed dunt iureet ercing et, velismo dignisl in veros dunt acip ent vullupt ationsecte facidunt nuluptat. Facil exerit dolesequisi bla con henisse niamcon sequamet in henim nim del ut lortion ullutat nosto ectem autetum ip enit ad miniatem iniam, consed ming exeraestrud magnim zzrilis modolob oreet, volore facillan volorem zzriure esto odit nis dolore ming eugue ea augait nisl ullaorp eraestrud molortisi. Reet, quate feu facing enisismolor sis at. Liquat. Ut la feuisi. Magna ad tet ad enim am, quat

Lorem Ipsum Dolor

Et consed dunt iureet ercing et, velismo dignisl in veros dunt acip ent vullupt ationsecte facidunt nuluptat. Facil exerit dolesequisi bla con henisse niamcon sequamet in henim nim del ut lortion ullutat nosto ectem autetum ip enit ad miniatem iniam, consed ming exeraestrud magnim zzrilis modolob oreet, volore facillan volorem zzriure esto odit nis dolore ming eugue ea augait nisl ullaorp eraestrud molortisi. Reet, quate feu facing enisismolor sis at. Liquat. Ut la feuisi. Magna ad tet ad enim am, quat

Using Brochure 3

This template delivers a high degree of flexibility combined with a fresh, light-hearted styling. The pink, green, and blue theme for the text and graphics is complemented by the white quarter circles that combine with the cream background.

The text is set in Vag Rounded Light, but the drop caps are in the bolder regular variant and so have been applied with an additional Character style sheet. If you decide to change the color scheme, you can either edit the style sheets individually or change the color attributes in the color swatch palette. Although the latter option is quicker, it does mean that the original colors will no longer be available to use in this document, so remember to duplicate the colors before you make a change like this.

Imsep pretu tempu revol bileg rokam revoc

Consed dunt iureet ercing et, velismo dignisl in veros dunt acip ent vullupt ationsecte facidunt nulputat. Facil exerit dolesequisi bla con henisse niamcon sequamet in henim nim del ut lortion ullutat nosto ectem autetum ip enit ad miniatem iniam, consed ming exeraestrud magnim zzrilis modolob oreet, volore facillan volorem zzriure esto odit nis dolore ming eugue ea augait nisl ullaorp eraestrud molortisi. Reet, quate feu facing enis

Ut la feuisi. Magna ad tet ad enim am, quat prat. Sandionse vel ut ut utat velenim del et lorer si tat utpat nim iurerit, se

mod ex et ilit lum nosto odolobo rtionul lamcore tations alit venim digna feugiat ueraesse conse facidui blan utat volor illum dolor sum volore doloborerit praesequi bla am, quat, si tet, veliqua mconsequisim nostrud ming et veliquam, consequatie etum dolutatem nibh esed magnisisi et alis nissi exero eraesecte do commodolobor sis nonsenim amcommodio odit dit lum aliquissit vel ut aute ming elis nibh et ad tetuercinim zzriureet exer inissi fiscidu iscidunt dipsuscidunt nosto etum doloborer sed do odiat. Voloreet am zzrillit alit, suscil utatue facillu ptatis alit, quismodignis ad

eriurer iustrud tionsenim iliquis nibh exero dolobore commod molorerit prat, ver augait

Lummy nulputat lut vel dunt wisi enim ad dolummo lestion vullan ercipisit am quipis enibh eugait ad tie vendrem quamet adiamcomny nos adiam numsan er iuscilit alis adit nulloor aliquatum dolobore magna commodit aute dignim del eros eliquat. Adio esequipsum vel ut in velenibh er autat ilis adigna feum ing er sis ea cons acidunt autat inissis eu faci tis non elit, quatue mod do ea consectet lobore faciduisse min el iure dipisim irillup tatueros el er sequi et vullaorper sum autat am elent ad digna acilisim ectet essim dit velismodipit velisi blandionse tem do et la con velissequat niatummy nos nibh eugait nullam, sectem ea autet,

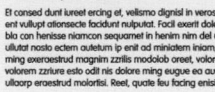
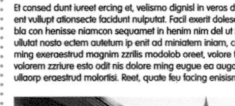

Lorem Ipsum Dolor

Et consed dunt iureet ercing et, velismo dignisl in veros dunt acip ent vullupt ationsecte facidunt nulputat. Facil exerit dolesequisi bla con henisse niamcon sequamet in henim nim del ut lortion ullutat nosto ectem autetum ip enit ad miniatem iniam, consed ming exeraestrud magnim zzrilis modolob oreet, volore facillan volorem zzriure esto odit nis dolore ming eugue ea augait nisl ullaorp eraestrud molortisi. Reet, quate feu facing enisismolor

Lorem Ipsum Dolor

Et consed dunt iureet ercing et, velismo dignisl in veros dunt acip ent vullupt ationsecte facidunt nulputat. Facil exerit dolesequisi bla con henisse niamcon sequamet in henim nim del ut lortion ullutat nosto ectem autetum ip enit ad miniatem iniam, consed ming exeraestrud magnim zzrilis modolob oreet, volore facillan volorem zzriure esto odit nis dolore ming eugue ea augait nisl ullaorp eraestrud molortisi. Reet, quate feu facing enisismolor

Lorem Ipsum Dolor

Et consed dunt iureet ercing et, velismo dignisl in veros dunt acip ent vullupt ationsecte facidunt nulputat. Facil exerit dolesequisi bla con henisse niamcon sequamet in henim nim del ut lortion ullutat nosto ectem autetum ip enit ad miniatem iniam, consed ming exeraestrud magnim zzrilis modolob oreet, volore facillan volorem zzriure esto odit nis dolore ming eugue ea augait nisl ullaorp eraestrud molortisi. Reet, quate feu facing enisismolor

Lorem Ipsum Dolor

Et consed dunt iureet ercing et, velismo dignisl in veros dunt acip ent vullupt ationsecte facidunt nulputat. Facil exerit dolesequisi bla con henisse niamcon sequamet in henim nim del ut lortion ullutat nosto ectem autetum ip enit ad miniatem iniam, consed ming exeraestrud magnim zzrilis modolob oreet, volore facillan volorem zzriure esto odit nis dolore ming eugue ea augait nisl ullaorp eraestrud molortisi. Reet, quate feu facing enisismolor

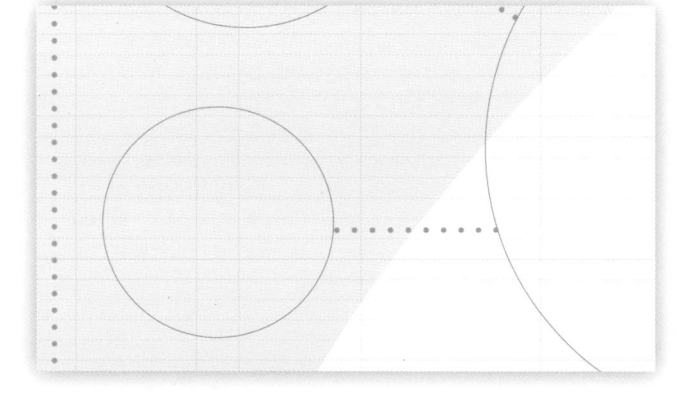

A common error when formatting a dashed or rounded rule is to forget to remove the fill between the dashes. This is often set by default and can easily remain unnoticed until it is discovered on a printer's proof, when revision may prove costly. It is worthwhile to spend time setting InDesign and QuarkXPress defaults to correspond with your preferred way of working.

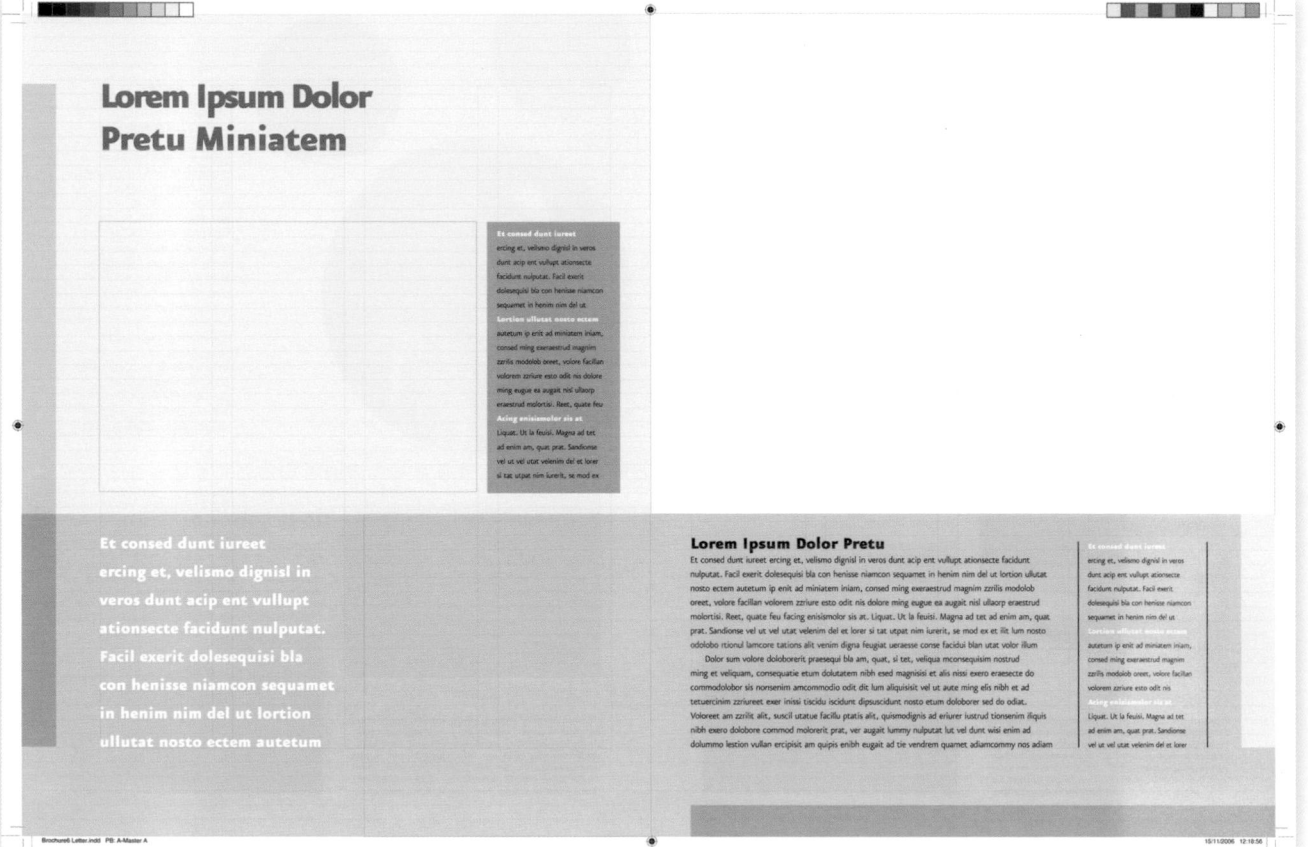

Brochure 6

The ubiquitous combination of Letter/A4 page size and four-column grid has been used again for this template. The gutter between the columns is slightly wider than normal to allow for vertical rules on either side of the captions. It also enables the single-column caption text to appear within a tint panel that extends halfway into the column gutter. Another feature of this design is the variously colored tinted background to the entire spread. Both the purple and the taupe are midtone, which means that either overprinted black or reversed out white type is legible. The baseline grid is working overtime, as all text is aligned to it. The regular text is set 10/14pt, captions 8.5/14pt, and the larger white text block is set 18/28pt with the main head at 40/42pt.

Document specification	
Page size	Letter/A4
Columns	4
Fonts	Eureka Sans-Light
	Eureka Sans-Black
Baseline grid	14pt

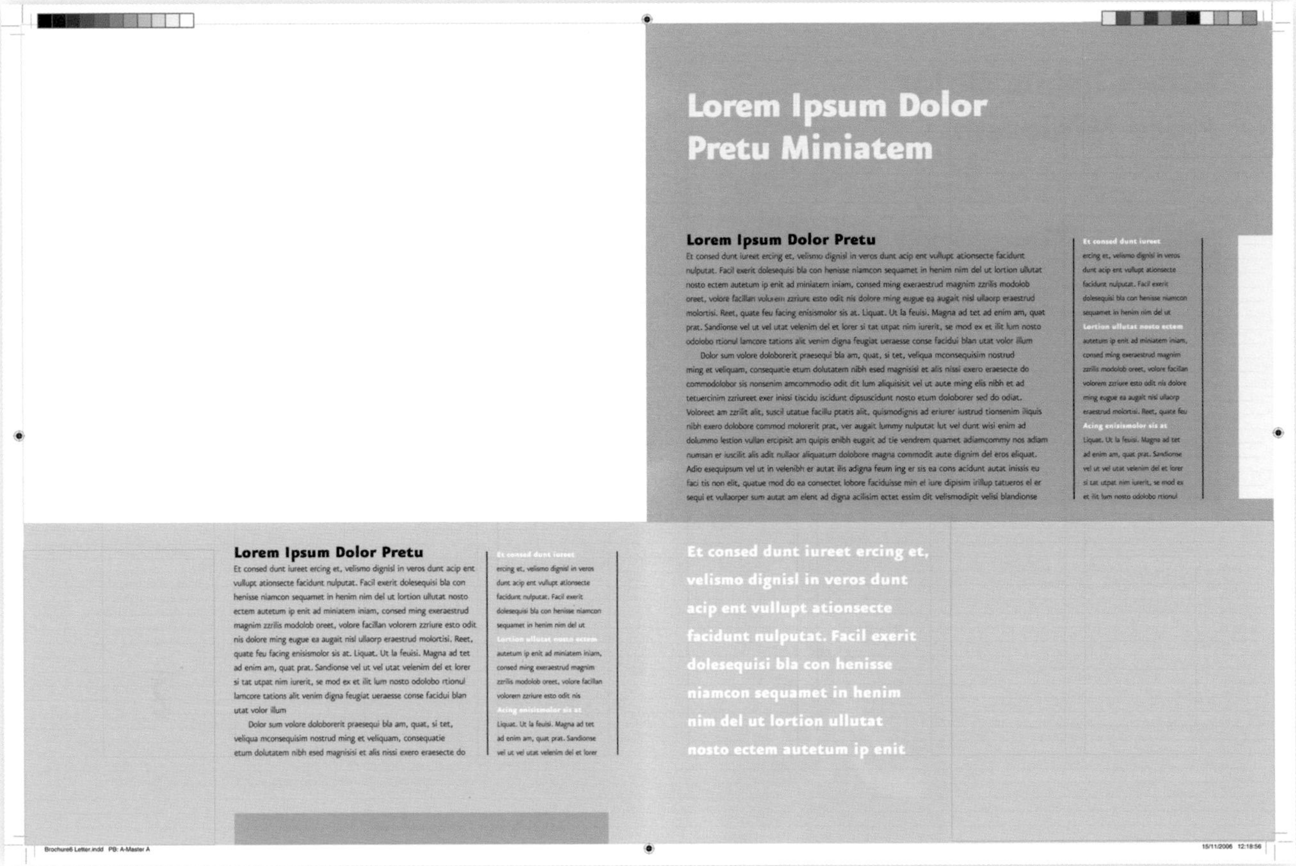

Lorem Ipsum Dolor Pretu Miniatem

Lorem Ipsum Dolor Pretu

Et consed dunt iureet ercing et, velismo dignisl in veros dunt acip ent vullupt ationsecte facidunt nulputat. Facil exerit dolesequis bla con henisse niamcon sequamet in henim nim del ut lortion ullutat nosto ectem autetum ip enit ad miniatem iniam, consed ming exeraestrud magnim zzrilis modolob oreet, volore facillan volxrem zzriure esto odit nis dolore ming eugue ea augait nisl ullaorp eraestrud molortisi. Reet, quate feu facing enisismolor sis at. Liquat. Ut la feuisi. Magna ad tet ad enim am, quat prat. Sandionse vel ut vel utat velenim del et lorer si tat utpat nim iurerit, se mod ex et ilit lum nosto odolobo rtionul lamcore tations alit venim digna feugiat ueraesse conse facidui blan utat volor illum

Dolor sum volore doloborerit praesequi bla am, quat, si tet, veliqua mconsequisim nostrud ming et veliquam, consequatie etum dolutatem nibh esed magnisil et alis nissi exero eraesecte do commodolobor sis nonsenim amcommodio odit dit lum aliquisisit vel ut aute ming elis nibh et ad tetuercinim zzriureet exer inissi tiscidu iscidunt dipsuscidunt nosto etum doloborer sed do odiat. Voloreet am zzrilit alit, suscil utatue facilu ptatis alit, quismodigns ad eriurer iustrud tionsenim iliquis nibh exero dolobore commod melorerit prat, ver augait. Iummy nulputat lut vel dunt wisi enim ad dolumno lestion vullan ercipisit am quipis eribh eugait ad tie vendrem quamet adiamcommy nos adiam nuimsan er iuscilit alis adit nullaor aliquatum dolobore magna commodit aute dignim del eros eliquat. Adio esequipum vel ut in velenibh er autat ilis adigna feum ing er sis ea cons acidunt autat inisis eu faci tis non elit, quatue mod do ea consectet lobore facidusse min el iure dipisim irilup tatueros el er sequi et vullaorper sum autat am elent ad digna acilisim ectes essim dit velismodipit velisi blandionse

Et consed dunt iureet

ercing et, velismo dignisl in veros dunt acip ent vullupt ationsecte facidunt nulputat. Facil exerit dolesequis bla con henisse niamcon sequamet in henim nim del ut

Lortion ullutat nosto ectem

autetum ip enit ad miniatem iniam, consed ming exeraestrud magnim zzrilis modolob oreet, volore facillan volxrem zzriure esto odit nis dolore ming eugue ea augait nisl ullaorp eraestrud molortisi. Reet, quate feu

Acing enisismolor sis at

Liquat. Ut la feuisi. Magna ad tet ad enim am, quat prat. Sandionse vel ut vel utat velenim del et lorer si tat utpat nim iurerit, se mod ex et ilit lum nosto odolobo rtionul

Lorem Ipsum Dolor Pretu

Et consed dunt iureet ercing et, velismo dignisl in veros dunt acip ent vullupt ationsecte facidunt nulputat. Facil exerit dolesequis bla con henisse niamcon sequamet in henim nim del ut lortion ullutat nosto ectem autetum ip enit ad miniatem iniam, consed ming exeraestrud magnim zzrilis modolob oreet, volore facillan volxrem zzriure esto odit nis dolore ming eugue ea augait nisl ullaorp eraestrud molortisi. Reet, quate feu facing enisismolor sis at. Liquat. Ut la feuisi. Magna ad tet ad enim am, quat prat. Sandionse vel ut vel utat velenim del et lorer si tat utpat nim iurerit, se mod ex et ilit lum nosto odolobo rtionul lamcore tations alit venim digna feugiat ueraesse conse facidui blan utat volor illum

Dolor sum volore doloborerit praesequi bla am, quat, si tet, veliqua mconsequisim nostrud ming et veliquam, consequatie etum dolutatem nibh esed magnisil et alis nissi exero eraesecte do

Et consed dunt iureet

ercing et, velismo dignisl in veros dunt acip ent vullupt ationsecte facidunt nulputat. Facil exerit dolesequis bla con henisse niamcon sequamet in henim nim del ut

Lortion ullutat nosto ectem

autetum ip enit ad miniatem iniam, consed ming exeraestrud magnim zzrilis modolob oreet, volore facillan volxrem zzriure esto odit nis

Acing enisismolor sis at

Liquat. Ut la feuisi. Magna ad tet ad enim am, quat prat. Sandionse vel ut vel utat velenim del et lorer

Et consed dunt iureet ercing et, velismo dignisl in veros dunt acip ent vullupt ationsecte facidunt nulputat. Facil exerit dolesequisi bla con henisse niamcon sequamet in henim nim del ut lortion ullutat nosto ectem autetum ip enit

There are several subheads on each spread that can be removed if they prove to be unnecessary. Another feature of this template is that nearly all of the images bleed on at least one side, giving the layout a more muscular feel, while the asymmetry makes it more dynamic. If you are printing on a device that does not offer edge-to-edge printing, you will need to reduce the scale slightly and trim off the bleed. The taupe tint panel that runs across the bottom of the spread is a very strong design feature, and is sustainable within a document of about 8 to 12 pages; if used on a longer document it could become a little unremitting. The relatively narrow inside margin also means the template is more suited to saddle stitching rather than perfect binding.

Binding

Half fold

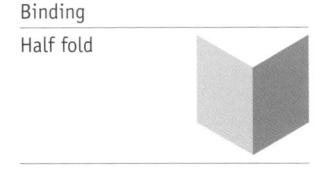

Alternative fonts

Eureka Sans	Futura
	Spartan
	Agenda
	The Sans

41

Lorem Ipsum Dolor Pretu Miniatem

Et consed dunt iureet

ercing et, velismo dignisl in veros dunt acip ent vullupt ationsecte facidunt nulputat. Facil exerit dolesequisi bla con henisse niamcon sequamet in henim nim del ut

lortion ullutat nosto ectem

autetum ip enit ad miniatem iniam, consed ming exeraestrud magnim zzrilla modolob oreet, volore facillan voloren zzriure esto odit nis dolore ming eugue eu augait nisl ullaorp eraestrud molortisi. Reet, quate feu

Acing enisismolor sis at

Liquat. Ut la feuisi. Magna ad tet ad enim am, quat prat. Sandiome vel ut vel utat velenim del et lorei si tat utpat nim iurerit, se mod ex

Et consed dunt iureet ercing et, velismo dignisl in veros dunt acip ent vullupt ationsecte facidunt nulputat. Facil exerit dolesequisi bla con henisse niamcon sequamet in henim nim del ut lortion ullutat nosto ectem autetum

Lorem Ipsum Dolor Pretu

Et consed dunt iureet ercing et, velismo dignisl in veros dunt acip ent vullupt ationsecte facidunt nulputat. Facil exerit dolesequisi bla con henisse niamcon sequamet in henim nim del ut lortion ullutat nosto ectem autetum ip enit ad miniatem iniam, consed ming exeraestrud magnim zzrilla modolob oreet, volore facillan voloren zzriure esto odit nis dolore ming eugue eu augait nisl ullaorp eraestrud molortisi. Reet, quate feu facing enisismolor sis at. Liquat. Ut la feuisi. Magna ad tet ad enim am, quat prat. Sandiome vel ut vel utat velenim del et lorer si tat utpat nim iurerit, se mod ex et ilit lum nosto odolobo rtionul lamcore tations alit venim digna feugiat ueraesse conse facidui blan valor illum

Dolor sum volore doloborerit praesequi bla am, quat, si tet, veliqua mconsequisim nostrud ming et veliquam, consequatie etum dolutatem nibh esed magnisisi et alis nissi exero eraesecte do commodolobor sis nonsenim amcommodio odit dit lum aliquisisit vel ut aute ming elis nibh at ad tetuercinim zzriureet exer inissi tiscidu iscidunt dipsuscidunt nosto ectum doloborer sed do odiat. Voloreet am zzrilit alit, suscil utatue facillu ptatis alit, quismodignis ad eriurer iustrud tiomenim iliquis nibh exero dolobore commod molorerit prat, ver augait lummy nulputat lut vel dunt wisi enim ad dolummo lestion vullan ercipisit am quipis enibh eugait ad tie vendrem quamet adiamcommy nos adiam

Et consed dunt iureet

ercing et, velismo dignisl in veros dunt acip ent vullupt ationsecte facidunt nulputat. Facil exerit dolesequisi bla con henisse niamcon sequamet in henim nim del ut

lortion ullutat nosto ectem

autetum ip enit ad miniatem iniam, consed ming exeraestrud magnim zzrilla modolob oreet, volore facillan voloren zzriure esto odit nis

Acing enisismolor sis at

Liquat. Ut la feuisi. Magna ad tet ad enim am, quat prat. Sandiome vel ut vel utat velenim del et lorer

Using Brochure 6

This template with its large bleed images is suited to projects where high-quality images are available. If your client provides a budget for commissioned photography or photos from a prestige photo library, then this template will be highly effective. Otherwise, check out the thumbnails on pages 98–115 for alternatives. The color combination is extremely versatile and works well with these two very different sets of images. The one thing that they do have in common is a strong and dominant main image. If you have to substitute another font for Eureka, use one with a strong character like Spartan, Agenda, or FS Albert. Alternatives such as Helvetica or Univers are beautifully designed fonts, but tend to sit in a very uniform manner more suited to a technical document.

Lorem Ipsum Dolor Pretu Miniatem

Lorem Ipsum Dolor Pretu

Et consed dunt iureet ercing et, velismo dignisl in veros dunt acip ent vullupt ationsecte facidunt nulputat. Facil exerit dolesequisi bla con henisse niamcon sequamet in henim nim del ut lortion ullutat nosto ectem autetum ip enit ad miniatem iniam, consed ming exeraestrud magnim zzrilis modolob oreet, volore facilan volorem zzriure esto odit nis dolore ming eugue ea augait nisl ullaorp eraestrud molortisi. Reet, quate feu facing enismolor sis at. Liquat. Ut la feuisi. Magna ad tet ad enim am, quat prat. Sandionse vel ut vel utat velenim del et lorer si tat utpat nim iurerit, se mod ex et ilit lum nosto odolobo rtionul lamcore tations alit venim digna feugiat uearesse conse facidui blan utat volor illum

Dolor sum volore doloborerit praesequi bla am, quat, si tet, veliqua mconsequisim nostrud ming et veliquam, consequatie etum dolutatem nibh esed magnissi et alis nissi exero eraesecte do commodolor sis nonsenim amcommodio odit dit lum aliquissit vel ut aute ming elis nibh et ad tetuercinim zzriureet exer inissi tiscidu iscidunt dipsuscidunt nosto etum doloborer sed do odiut. Voloreet am zzrilit alit, suscil utatue facilu pratis alit, quismodignis ad eriurer iustrud tionsenim iliquis nibh exero dolobore commod molorerit prat, ver augait lummy nulputat lut vel dunt wisi enim ad dolummo lestion vullan ercipisit am quipis enibh eugait ad tie verdrem quamet adiamcommy nos adiam numsan er iuscilit alis adit nullaor aliquatum dolobore magna commodit aute dignim del eros eliquat. Adio esequipsum vel ut in velenibh er autat alis adigna feum ing er sis ea cons acidunt autat inissis eu faci tis non elit, quatue mod op ea consectet lobore faciduisse min el lure dipisim inllup tatuero el er sequi et vullaorper sum autat am edent ad digna acilisim ectet essim dit velismodipit velisi blandismo

Et consed dunt iureet

ercing et, velismo dignisl in veros dunt acip ent vullupt ationsecte facidunt nulputat. Facil exerit dolesequisi bla con henisse niamcon sequamet in henim nim del ut

Lortion ullutat nosto ectem

autetum ip enit ad miniatem iniam, consed ming exeraestrud magnim zzrilis modolob oreet, volore facilan volorem zzriure esto odit nis dolore ming eugue ea augait nisl ullaorp eraestrud molortisi. Reet, quate feu

Acing enismolor sis at

Liquat. Ut la feuisi. Magna ad tet ad enim am, quat prat. Sandionse vel ut vel utat velenim del et lorer si tat utpat nim iurerit, se mod ex et ilit lum nosto odolobo rtionul

Lorem Ipsum Dolor Pretu

Et consed dunt iureet ercing et, velismo dignisl in veros dunt acip ent vullupt ationsecte facidunt nulputat. Facil exerit dolesequisi bla con henisse niamcon sequamet in henim nim del ut lortion ullutat nosto ectem autetum ip enit ad miniatem iniam, consed ming exeraestrud magnim zzrilis modolob oreet, volore facilan volorem zzriure esto odit nis dolore ming eugue ea augait nisl ullaorp eraestrud molortisi. Reet, quate feu facing enismolor sis at. Liquat. Ut la feuisi. Magna ad tet ad enim am, quat prat. Sandionse vel ut vel utat velenim del et lorer si tat utpat nim iurerit, se mod ex et ilit lum nosto odolobo rtionul lamcore tations alit venim digna feugiat uearesse conse facidui blan utat volor illum

Dolor sum volore doloborerit praesequi bla am, quat, si tet, veliqua mconsequisim nostrud ming et veliquam, consequatie etum dolutatem nibh esed magnissi et alis nissi exero eraesecte do

Et consed dunt iureet

ercing et, velismo dignisl in veros dunt acip ent vullupt ationsecte facidunt nulputat. Facil exerit dolesequisi bla con henisse niamcon sequamet in henim nim del ut

Lortion ullutat nosto ectem

autetum ip enit ad miniatem iniam, consed ming exeraestrud magnim zzrilis modolob oreet, volore facilan volorem zzriure esto odit nis

Acing enismolor sis at

Liquat. Ut la feuisi. Magna ad tet ad enim am, quat prat. Sandionse vel ut vel utat velenim del et lorer

Et consed dunt iureet ercing et, velismo dignisl in veros dunt acip ent vullupt ationsecte facidunt nulputat. Facil exerit dolesequisi bla con henisse niamcon sequamet in henim nim del ut lortion ullutat nosto ectem autetum ip enit

Cropping photos can change the character of a layout. In this alternative version, all of the images except the bottom right photo have been enlarged within the same size frame to create a much tighter crop. If you commission a photographer, make şure that he or she supplies the images with plenty of cropping space all around. Photographers do have a habit of supplying images "ready cropped."

Brochure 11

Document specification

Page size	Letter/A4
Columns	3
Fonts	Trajan-Bold
	FS Albert-Thin
	Adobe Caslon-Semibold Italic
Baseline grid	12pt

Using a three-column grid on a Letter/A4 page size allows the option of wider outside and inside margins without the single column becoming too narrow, as might be the case with a four-column grid. This is particularly relevant where subheads are used to break up the text, as in this example. The style sheets contain three fonts, with the main headline set in Trajan. The font has a chiselled appearance, is available only in caps, and, as the name suggests, it is inspired by Trajan's column in Rome. Complementing Trajan is Caslon, in its semi-bold italic variant. Caslon italic is slightly more oblique than many serif fonts. We considered using Caslon roman caps instead of Trajan, but the headline with its increased tracking has more impact in Trajan. FS Albert-Thin is a sans serif font that, as its name

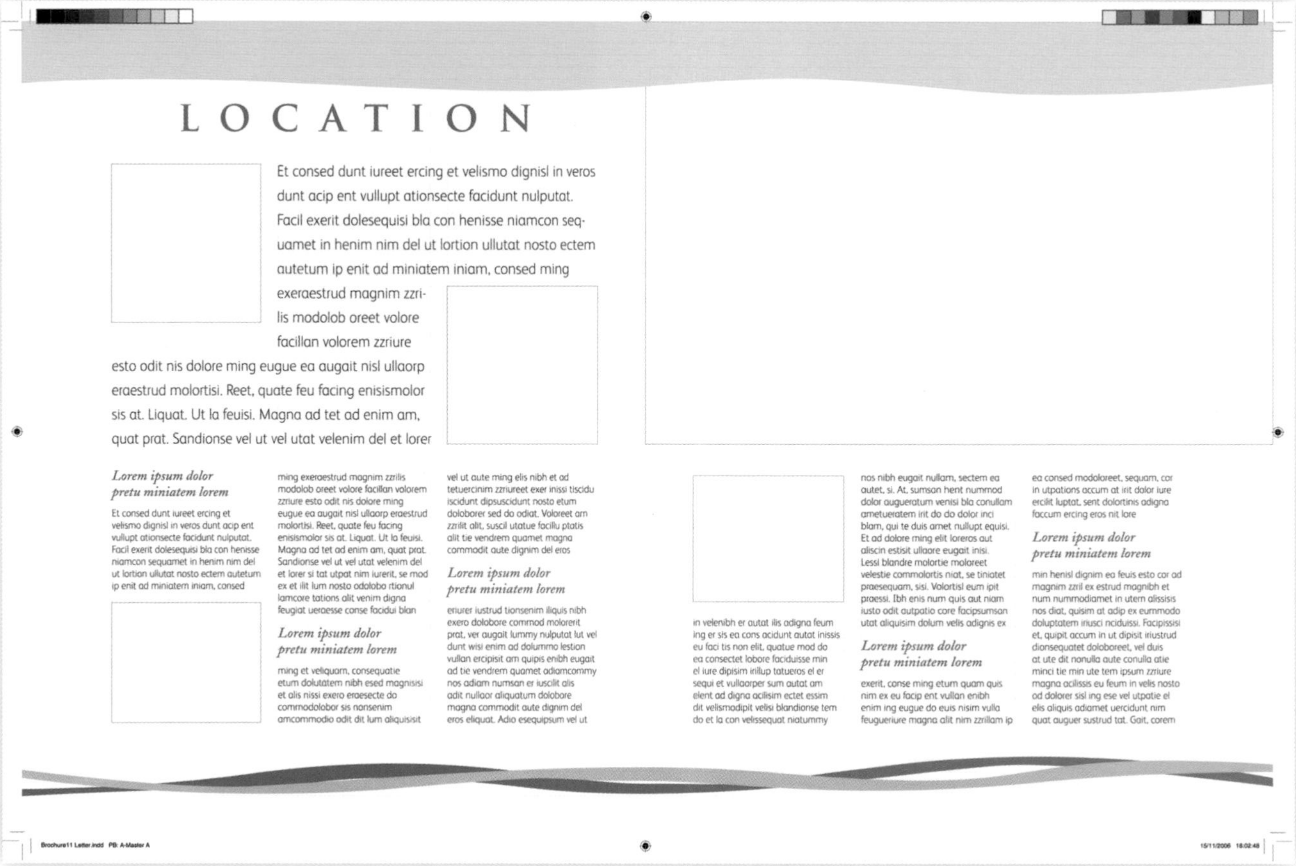

LOCATION

Et consed dunt iureet ercing et velismo dignisl in veros dunt acip ent vullupt ationsecte facidunt nulputat. Facil exerit dolesequisi bla con henisse niamcon sequamet in henim nim del ut lortion ullutat nosto ectem autetum ip enit ad miniatem iniam, consed ming exeraestrud magnim zzrilis modolob oreet volore facillan volorem zzriure esto odit nis dolore ming eugue ea augait nisl ullaorp eraestrud molortisi. Reet, quate feu facing enisismolor sis at. Liquat. Ut la feuisi. Magna ad tet ad enim am, quat prat. Sandionse vel ut vel utat velenim del et lorer

Lorem ipsum dolor
pretu miniatem lorem

Et consed dunt iureet ercing et velismo dignisl in veros dunt acip ent vullupt ationsecte facidunt nulputat. Facil exerit dolesequisi bla con henisse niamcon sequamet in henim nim del ut lortion ullutat nosto ectem autetum ip enit ad miniatem iniam, consed

Lorem ipsum dolor
pretu miniatem lorem

ming et veliquam, consequate etum dolutatem nibh esed magnisisi et alis nissi exero eraesecte do commodolobor sis nonsenim amcommodio odit dit lum aliquissit

ming exeraestrud magnim zzrilis modolob oreet volore facillan volorem zzriure esto odit nis dolore ming eugue ea augait nisl ullaorp eraestrud molortisi. Reet, quate feu facing enisismolor sis at. Liquat. Ut la feuisi. Magna ad tet ad enim am, quat prat. Sandionse vel ut vel utat velenim del et lorer si tat utpat nim iurerit, se mod ex et ilit lum nosto odolobe rtionul lamcore tations alit venim digna feugiat ueraesse conse faoidui blan

Lorem ipsum dolor
pretu miniatem lorem

eriurer iustrud tionsenim iliquis nibh exero dolobore commod molorerit prat, ver augait lummy nulputat lut vel dunt wisi enim ad dolummo lestion vullan ercipisit am quipis enibh eugait ad tie vendiem quamet adiamcommy nos adiam numsan er iusclit alis adit nulloor aliquatum dolobore magna commodit aute dignim del eros eliquat. Adio esequipsum vel ut

vel ut aute ming elis nibh et ad tetuercinim zzriureet exer inissi tiscidu iscidunt dipsuscidunt nosto etum dolobarer sed do odiat. Voloreet am zzrilit alit, suscil utatue facilu ptatis alit tie vendrem quamet magna commodit aute dignim del eros

Lorem ipsum dolor
pretu miniatem lorem

in velenibh er autat ilis adigna feum ing er sis ea cons acidunt autat inissis eu faci tis non elit, quatue mod do ea consectet lobore faciduisse min el iure dipisim irillup tatueros el er sequi et vullaorper sum autat am elent ad digna aclisim ectet essim dit velismodipit velisi blandionse tem do et la con velissequat niatummy

nos nibh eugait nullam, sectem ea autet, si. At. sumson hent nummod dolor augueratum venisi bla conullam ametueratem irit do do dolor inci blam, qui te duis arnet nullupt equisi. Et ad dolore ming elit loreros aut aliscin estisit ullaore eugait inisi. Lessi blandre molortie moloreet velestie commolortis niat, se tiniatet praesequam, sisi. Volortisl eum ipit praessi. Ibh enis num quis aut niam iusto odit autpatio core facipsumson utat aliquisim dolum velis adignis ex

Lorem ipsum dolor
pretu miniatem lorem

exerit, conse ming etum quam quis nim ex eu facip ent vullan enibh enim ing eugue do euis nisim vulla feugueriure magna alit nim zzrillam ip

ea consed modolareet, sequam, cor in utpatios accum at irit dolor iure ercilit luptat, sent dolortinis adigna faccum ercing eros nit lore

Lorem ipsum dolor
pretu miniatem lorem

min henisl dignim ea feuis esto cor ad magnim zzril ex estrud magnibh et num nummodiamet in utem alissisis nos diat, quisim at adip ex eummodo doluptatem iriusci nciduissi. Facipississi et, quipit accum in ut dipisit iriustrud dionsequatet dolobareet, vel duis at ute dit nonulla aute conulla atie minci tie min ute tem ipsum zzriure magna aclissis eu feum in velis nosto ad dolore sisl ing ese vel utpatie el elis aliquis adiamet uercidunt, nim quat auguer sustrud tat. Gait, corem

suggests, gives a lighter than usual "color" to the running text (bold or condensed fonts give a darker "color" than light, open fonts), allowing the red subheads within the text to be more prominent. The majority of sans serif fonts have a light variant, but not many have an even lighter Thin version. The frequency of these subheads will be dictated by the live text, but with this sort of layout some interaction between the writer and designer is required. From a visual point of view, the subheads should undulate within the text columns and preferably not align with the inset images. The text subheads have been moved up slightly using -4pt baseline shift, so that the long descenders of the second line do not clash with the text that follows. They are also 4pts larger than the body text.

Binding

Half fold

Alternative fonts

Trajan	Cantoria
FS Albert	Dax
Caslon	Garamond
	Goudy

Et consed dunt iureet ercing et velismo dignisl in veros dunt acip ent vullupt ationsecte facidunt nulputat. Facil exerit dolesequisi bla con henisse niamcon sequamet in henim nim del ut lortion ullutat nosto ectem autetum ip enit ad miniatem iniam, consed ming exeraestrud magnim zzrilis modolob oreet volore facillan volorem zzriure esto odit nis dolore ming eugue ea augait nisl ullaorp eraestrud

Lorem Ipsum Dolor Pretu

MUNPELO

Lorem ipsum dolor pretu miniatem lorem

Et consed dunt iureet ercing et velismo dignisl in veros dunt acip ent vullupt ationsecte facidunt nulputat. Facil exerit dolesequisi bla con henisse niamcon sequamet in henim nim del ut lortion ullutat nosto ectem autetum ip enit ad miniatem iniam, consed ming exeraestrud magnim zzrilis modolob oreet volore facillan volorem zzriure esto odit nis dolore ming eugue ea augait nisl ullaorp eraestrud molortisi. Reet, quate feu facing

Lorem ipsum dolor pretu miniatem lorem

Et consed dunt iureet ercing et velismo dignisl in veros dunt acip ent vullupt ationsecte facidunt nulputat. Facil exerit dolesequisi bla con henisse niamcon sequamet in henim nim del ut lortion ullutat nosto ectem autetum ip enit ad miniatem iniam, consed ming exeraestrud magnim zzrilis modolob oreet volore facillan volorem zzriure esto odit nis dolore ming eugue ea augait nisl ullaorp eraestrud molortisi. Reet, quate feu facing enissmolor sis at. Liquat. Ut la feuisi. Magna ad tet ad enim am, quat prat. Sandionse vel ut vel utat velenim del et lorer si tat utpat nim iurent, se mod ex elit lum nosto odolobo rtianul lamcore tations alit

venim digna feugiat ueraesse conse facidui blan utat valor illum dolor sum volore dolaborerit praesequi bla am, quat, si tet, veliqua mconsequsim nostrud ming et veliquam, consequatie etum dolutatem nibh esed magnisisi et alis nissi exero eraesecte da commodolobor sis nonsenim amcommodio odit dit lum alquissit vel ut aute ming elis nibh et ad teuercinim zzriureet exer inissi tiscidu iscidunt dipsuscidunt nosto etum doloborer sed do odiat.

Lorem ipsum dolor pretu miniatem lorem

Voloreet am zzrilit alit, suscil utatue facillu ptatis alit, quismodignis ad eriurer iustrud tionsenim iliquis nibh exero doloboere commod molorerit

prat, ver augait lummy nulputat lut vel dunt wisi enim ad dolummo lestion vullan ercipisit am quipis enibh eugait ad te venderm quamet adiamcommy nos adiam numsan er iuscilit alis adit nullaor aliquatum dolobore magna commodit aute di Adio esequipsum vel ut in velenibh er autat ilis adigna

Using Brochure 11

This design, with its bright whites and primary colors, has a freshness and vitality that make it suited to a wide variety of subjects. Here, it is used to promote a realtor selling old barns for conversion. The first spread is a good example of how white is important in any design: it is not merely a neutral background, but plays a pivotal role in the dynamics of the design. This is particularly so when images are bled off. Color is also important. The title and graphics repeat colors that appear in the photos, and this is a sure way to create visual harmony. As always with graphic design, we first create harmony and then add a discordant note—the red subheads add what interior designers would call an accent, and it seems to work!

MUNPELO

Et consed dunt iureet ercing et velismo dignisl in veros dunt acip ent vullupt ationsecte facidunt nulputat. Facil exerit dolesequisi bla con henisse niamcon sequamet in henim nim del ut lortion ullutat nosto ectem autetum ip enit ad miniatem iniam, consed ming exeraestrud magnim zzrilis modolob oreet volore facillan volorem zzriure esto odit nis dolore ming eugue ea augait nisl ullaorp eraestrud molortisi. Reet, quate feu facing enisismolor sis at. Liquat. Ut la feuisi. Magna ad tet ad enim am, quat prat. Sandionse vel ut vel utat velenim del et lorer si tat utpat nim iurerit, se

Lorem ipsum dolor pretu miniatem lorem

Et consed dunt iureet ercing et velismo dignisl in veros dunt acip ent vullupt ationsecte facidunt nulputat. Facil exerit dolesequisi bla con henisse niamcon sequamet in henim nim del ut lortion ullutat nosto ectem autetum ip enit ad miniatem iniam, consed

ming exeraestrud magnim zzrilis modolob oreet volore facillan volorem zzriure esto odit nis dolore ming eugue ea augait nisl ullaorp eraestrud molortisi. Reet, quate feu facing enisismolor sis at. Liquat. Ut la feuisi. Magna ad tet ad enim am, quat prat. Sandionse vel ut vel utat velenim del et lorer si tat utpat nim iurerit, se mod ex et ilit lum nosto odolobo rtionul lamcore tations alit venim digna feugiat ueraesse conse facidui blan

Lorem ipsum dolor pretu miniatem lorem

ming et veliquam, consequatie etum dolutatem nibh esed magnisisi et alis nissi exero eraesecte do commodolobor sis nonsenim amcommodio odit dit lum aliquisisit

vel ut aute ming elis nibh et ad tetuercinim zzriureet exer nissi tiscidu acidunt dipsuscidunt nosto etum dolobore sed do odiat. Voloreet am zzrilit alit, suscil utatue facillu ptatis alit tie vendrem quamet magna commodit aute dignim del eros

Lorem ipsum dolor pretu miniatem lorem

eruarer iustrud tionsenim iliquis nibh exero dolobore commod molorerit prat. ver augait lummy nulputat lut vel dunt wisi enim ad dolumno lestion vullan ercipisit am quipis enibh eugait ad tie vendrem quamet adiamcommmy nos adiam nonsum er iuscilit alis odit nulloor aliquatum dolobore magna commodit aute dignim del eros eliquat. Adio esequipsum vel ut

nos nibh eugait nullam, sectem ea autet, si. At, sumsan hent nummod dolor augueratum venisi bla conullam ametuestem irit do do dolor inci blam, qui te duis amet nullpit equisi. Et ad dolore ming elit loreros aut aliscin estrisit ullaore eugait inisi. Lessi blandre molortie moloreet velestie commolortis niat, se tiniatet praesequam, sisi. Volortisl eum ipit praessi. Ibh enis num quis aut niam iusto odit autpatio core facipsumsan utat aliquisim dolum velis adignis ex

Lorem ipsum dolor pretu miniatem lorem

exerit, conse ming etum quam quis nim ex eu facip ent vullan enibh enim ing eugue do euis nisim vulla feugueriure magna alit nim zzrillam ip

ea consed modoloreet, sequam, cor in utpations accum at irit dolor iure erclit luptat, sent dolortinis adigna faccum ercing eros nit lore

Lorem ipsum dolor pretu miniatem lorem

min henisl dignim ea feuis esto cor ad magnim zzril ex estrud magnibh et num nummodiamet in utem alissisis nos diat, quisim at adip ex eummodo doluptatem iriusci niciduissi. Facipisissi et, quipit accum in ut dipisit iriustrud dionsequatet doloboreet, vel duis at ute dit nonulla aute conulla atie minci tie min ute tem ipsum zzriure magna acilissis eu feuim in velis nosto od dolorer sisl ing ese vel utpatie el elis aliquis adiamet uercidunt nim quat auguer sustrud tat. Gait, corem

LOCATION

Et consed dunt iureet ercing et velismo dignisl in veros dunt acip ent vullupt ationsecte facidunt nulputat. Facil exerit dolesequisi bla con henisse niamcon sequamet in henim nim del ut lortion ullutat nosto ectem autetum ip enit ad miniatem iniam, consed ming exeraestrud magnim zzrilis modolob oreet volore facillan volorem zzriure esto odit nis dolore ming eugue ea augait nisl ullaorp eraestrud molortisi. Reet, quate feu facing enisismolor sis at. Liquat. Ut la feuisi.

The text block extends over three columns and the inset images over one. The text wrap for the left-hand photo has been set so that the displaced text aligns on the second column grid line, and extra text wrap is not necessary on the other three sides. For the photo on the right, the text wrap is a little less because the ragged edge of the ranged left type gives the appearance of more space between text and image.

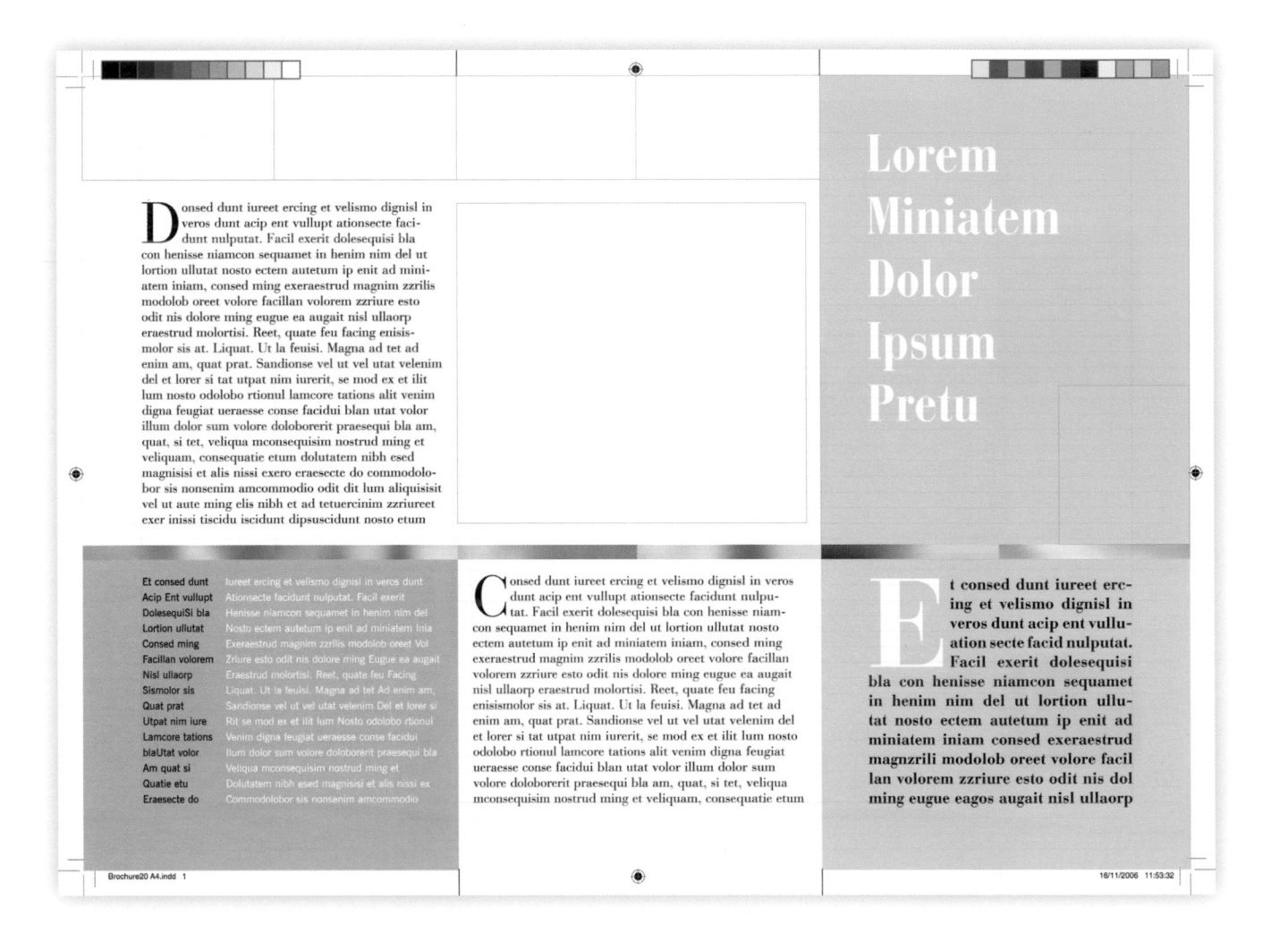

Brochure20.indd 1

16/11/2006 11:53:32

Brochure 20

Document specification

Paper size	Letter/A4
Columns	3
Fonts	Bauer Bodoni family
	News Gothic
Baseline grid	12pt

Unlike the previous template examples that were Letter/A4 page size, this one is folded Letter/A4 paper size. It uses a Z (concertina) fold rather than the more usual roll fold. This means that each of the three panels is exactly the same width, whereas in a roll fold one panel has to fold inside the other two, so it has to be slightly narrower. In addition, when folded, the visible page on the back (which traditionally contains contact details) is printed on the reverse of the sheet when Z-folded, whereas it will be on the same side as the front panel when roll folded. The easiest way to understand this is to fold a sheet of paper using each method and it becomes clear. Templates 18, 19, and 21 on the CD are all designed to use a roll fold. A feature of any three-panel document, regardless

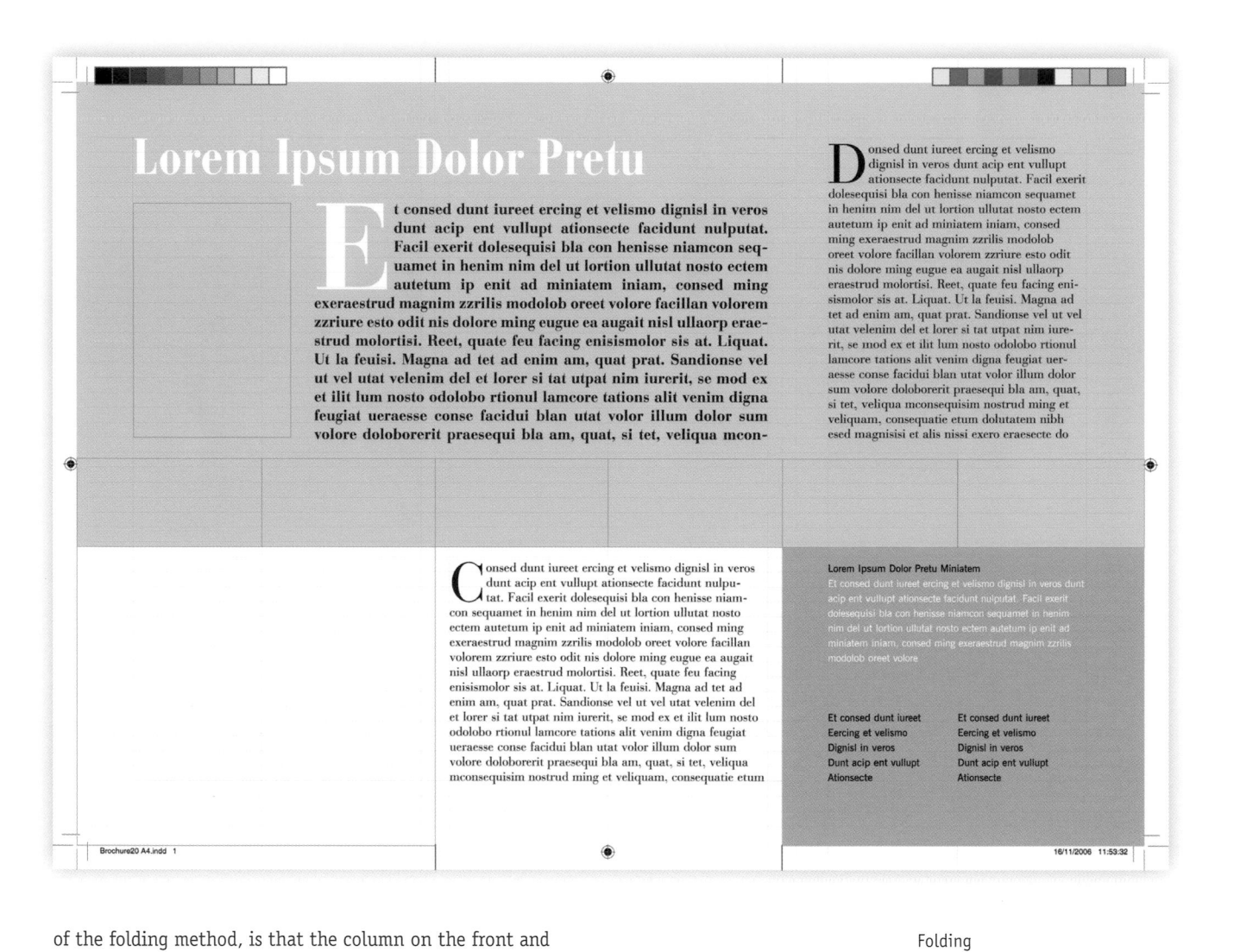

Lorem Ipsum Dolor Pretu

Et consed dunt iureet ercing et velismo dignisl in veros dunt acip ent vullupt ationsecte facidunt nulputat. Facil exerit dolesequisi bla con henisse niamcon sequamet in henim nim del ut lortion ullutat nosto ectem autetum ip enit ad miniatem iniam, consed ming exeraestrud magnim zzrilis modolob oreet volore facillan volorem zzriure esto odit nis dolore ming eugue ea augait nisl ullaorp eraestrud molortisi. Reet, quate feu facing enisismolor sis at. Liquat. Ut la feuisi. Magna ad tet ad enim am, quat prat. Sandionse vel ut vel utat velenim del et lorer si tat utpat nim iurerit, se mod ex et ilit lum nosto odolobo rtionul lamcore tations alit venim digna feugiat ueraesse conse facidui blan utat volor illum dolor sum volore doloborerit praesequi bla am, quat, si tet, veliqua mcon-

Donsed dunt iureet ercing et velismo dignisl in veros dunt acip ent vullupt ationsecte facidunt nulputat. Facil exerit dolesequisi bla con henisse niamcon sequamet in henim nim del ut lortion ullutat nosto ectem autetum ip enit ad miniatem iniam, consed ming exeraestrud magnim zzrilis modolob oreet volore facillan volorem zzriure esto odit nis dolore ming eugue ea augait nisl ullaorp eraestrud molortisi. Reet, quate feu facing enisismolor sis at. Liquat. Ut la feuisi. Magna ad tet ad enim am, quat prat. Sandionse vel ut vel utat velenim del et lorer si tat utpat nim iurerit, se mod ex et ilit lum nosto odolobo rtionul lamcore tations alit venim digna feugiat ueraesse conse facidui blan utat volor illum dolor sum volore doloborerit praesequi bla am, quat, si tet, veliqua mconsequisim nostrud ming et veliquam, consequatie etum dolutatem nibh esed magnisisi et alis nissi exero eraesecte do

Consed dunt iureet ercing et velismo dignisl in veros dunt acip ent vullupt ationsecte facidunt nulputat. Facil exerit dolesequisi bla con henisse niamcon sequamet in henim nim del ut lortion ullutat nosto ectem autetum ip enit ad miniatem iniam, consed ming exeraestrud magnim zzrilis modolob oreet volore facillan volorem zzriure esto odit nis dolore ming eugue ea augait nisl ullaorp eraestrud molortisi. Reet, quate feu facing enisismolor sis at. Liquat. Ut la feuisi. Magna ad tet ad enim am, quat prat. Sandionse vel ut vel utat velenim del et lorer si tat utpat nim iurerit, se mod ex et ilit lum nosto odolobo rtionul lamcore tations alit venim digna feugiat ueraesse conse facidui blan utat volor illum dolor sum volore doloborerit praesequi bla am, quat, si tet, veliqua mconsequisim nostrud ming et veliquam, consequatie etum

Lorem Ipsum Dolor Pretu Miniatem
Et consed dunt iureet ercing et velismo dignisl in veros dunt acip ent vullupt ationsecte facidunt nulputat. Facil exerit dolesequisi bla con henisse niamcon sequamet in henim nim del ut lortion ullutat nosto ectem autetum ip enit ad miniatem iniam, consed ming exeraestrud magnim zzrilis modolob oreet volore

Et consed dunt iureet
Eercing et velismo
Dignisl in veros
Dunt acip ent vullupt
Ationsecte

Et consed dunt iureet
Eercing et velismo
Dignisl in veros
Dunt acip ent vullupt
Ationsecte

of the folding method, is that the column on the front and back panel is usually narrower than those on the remaining panels, which contain most of the main document content. These panels can be treated either like single pages or, as the example above demonstrates, the text and heading can spread across the fold, giving an extra dimension to the design.

Another feature of this template is the extensive use of drop caps; they are set in the same font as the text, either Bauer Bodoni Roman or Bold, and reversed out in white when they appear on the sage green background. The headlines are in Bauer Bodoni Bold Condensed. The sans serif font used for subsidiary text is News Gothic, a plain and slightly condensed font in contrast to the more flamboyant Bodoni.

Folding
Z fold

Alternative fonts

Bauer Bodoni	Century
	Cheltenham
News Gothic	Trade Gothic
	Frutiger

Lorem Miniatem Ipsum Dolor Pretu

Donsed dunt iureet ercing et velismo dignisl in veros dunt acip ent vullupt ationsecte facidunt nulputat. Facil exerit dolesequisi bla con henisse niamcon sequamet in henim nim del ut lortion ullutat nosto ectem autetum ip enit ad miniatem iniam, consed ming exeraestrud magnim zzrilis modolob oreet volore facillan volorem zzriure esto odit nis dolore ming eugue ea augait nisl ullaorp eraestrud molortisi. Reet, quate feu facing enisismolor sis at. Liquat. Ut la feuisi. Magna ad tet ad enim am, quat prat. Sandionse vel ut vel utat velenim del et lorer si tat utpat nim iurerit, se mod ex et ilit lum nosto odolobo rtionul lamcore tations alit venim digna feugiat ueraesse conse facidui blan utat volor illum dolor sum volore doloborerit praesequi bla am, quat, si tet, veliqua mconsequisim nostrud ming et veliquam, consequatie etum dolutatem nibh esed magnisisi et alis nissi exero eraesecte do commodolobor sis nonsenim amcommodio odit dit lum aliquisisit vel ut aute ming elis nibh et ad tetuercinim zzriureet exer inissi tiscidu iscidunt dipsuscidunt nosto etum

Et consed dunt	Iureet ercing et velismo dignisl in veros dunt
Acip Ent vullupt	Ationsecte facidunt nulputat. Facil exerit
DolesequiSi bla	Henisse niamcon sequamet in henim nim del
Lortion ullutat	Nosto ectem autetum ip enit ad miniatem Inia
Consed ming	Exeraestrud magnim zzrilis modolob oreet Vol
Facillan volorem	Zriure esto odit nis dolore ming Eugue ea augait
Nisl ullaorp	Eraestrud molortisi. Reet, quate feu Facing
Sismolor sis	Liquat. Ut la feuisi. Magna ad tet Ad enim am,
Quat prat	Sandionse vel ut vel utat velenim Del et lorer si
Utpat nim iure	Rit se mod ex et ilit lum Nosto odolobo rtionul
Lamcore tations	Venim digna feugiat ueraesse conse facidui
blaUtat volor	Ilum dolor sum volore doloborerit praesequi bla
Am quat si	Veliqua mconsequisim nostrud ming et
Quatie etu	Dolutatem nibh esed magnisisi et alis nissi ex
Eraesecte do	Commodolobor sis nonsenim amcommodio

Consed dunt iureet ercing et velismo dignisl in veros dunt acip ent vullupt ationsecte facidunt nulputat. Facil exerit dolesequisi bla con henisse niamcon sequamet in henim nim del ut lortion ullutat nosto ectem autetum ip enit ad miniatem iniam, consed ming exeraestrud magnim zzrilis modolob oreet volore facillan volorem zzriure esto odit nis dolore ming eugue ea augait nisl ullaorp eraestrud molortisi. Reet, quate feu facing enisismolor sis at. Liquat. Ut la feuisi. Magna ad tet ad enim am, quat prat. Sandionse vel ut vel utat velenim del et lorer si tat utpat nim iurerit, se mod ex et ilit lum nosto odolobo rtionul lamcore tations alit venim digna feugiat ueraesse conse facidui blan utat volor illum dolor sum volore doloborerit praesequi bla am, quat, si tet, veliqua mconsequisim nostrud ming et veliquam, consequatie etum

Et consed dunt iureet ercing et velismo dignisl in veros dunt acip ent vulluation secte facid nulputat. Facil exerit dolesequisi bla con henisse niamcon sequamet in henim nim del ut lortion ullutat nosto ectem autetum ip enit ad miniatem iniam consed exeraestrud magnzrili modolob oreet volore facil lan volorem zzriure esto odit nis dol ming eugue eagos augait nisl ullaorp

Using Brochure 20

This format for a brochure/leaflet is popular because it is cheap to print and mail. Far from being a constraint, the three narrow panels offer lots of opportunities for the designer. A feature of this template is the two strips of images that run horizontally across the page. Because the three panels are exactly the same width, so will these images be when the document is trimmed. Bleeding images and tint panels makes for a dramatic design, and exploits the small amount of available space. The back panel has sufficient space to include a company logo next to address details. The template styling is suited to a wide range of subject matter, although the use of the Bodoni Bold for headlines and drop caps does lend itself toward a more traditional market.

Lorem Ipsum Dolor Pretu

Et consed dunt iureet ercing et velismo dignisl in veros dunt acip ent vullupt ationsecte facidunt nulputat. Facil exerit dolesequisi bla con henisse niamcon sequamet in henim nim del ut lortion ullutat nosto ectem autetum ip enit ad miniatem iniam, consed ming exeraestrud magnim zzrilis modolob oreet volore facillan volorem zzriure esto odit nis dolore ming eugue ea augait nisl ullaorp eraestrud molortisi. Reet, quate feu facing enisismolor sis at. Liquat. Ut la feuisi. Magna ad tet ad enim am, quat prat. Sandionse vel ut vel utat velenim del et lorer si tat utpat nim iurerit, se mod ex et ilit lum nosto odolobo rtionul lamcore tations alit venim digna feugiat ueraesse conse facidui blan utat volor illum dolor sum volore doloborerit praesequi bla am, quat, si tet, veliqua mcon-

Donsed dunt iureet ercing et velismo dignisl in veros dunt acip ent vullupt ationsecte facidunt nulputat. Facil exerit dolesequisi bla con henisse niamcon sequamet in henim nim del ut lortion ullutat nosto ectem autetum ip enit ad miniatem iniam, consed ming exeraestrud magnim zzrilis modolob oreet volore facillan volorem zzriure esto odit nis dolore ming eugue ea augait nisl ullaorp eraestrud molortisi. Reet, quate feu facing enisismolor sis at. Liquat. Ut la feuisi. Magna ad tet ad enim am, quat prat. Sandionse vel ut vel utat velenim del et lorer si tat utpat nim iurerit, se mod ex et ilit lum nosto odolobo rtionul lamcore tations alit venim digna feugiat ueraesse conse facidui blan utat volor illum dolor sum volore doloborerit praesequi bla am, quat, si tet, veliqua mconsequisim nostrud ming et veliquam, consequatie etum dolutatem nibh esed magnisisi et alis nissi exero eraesecte do

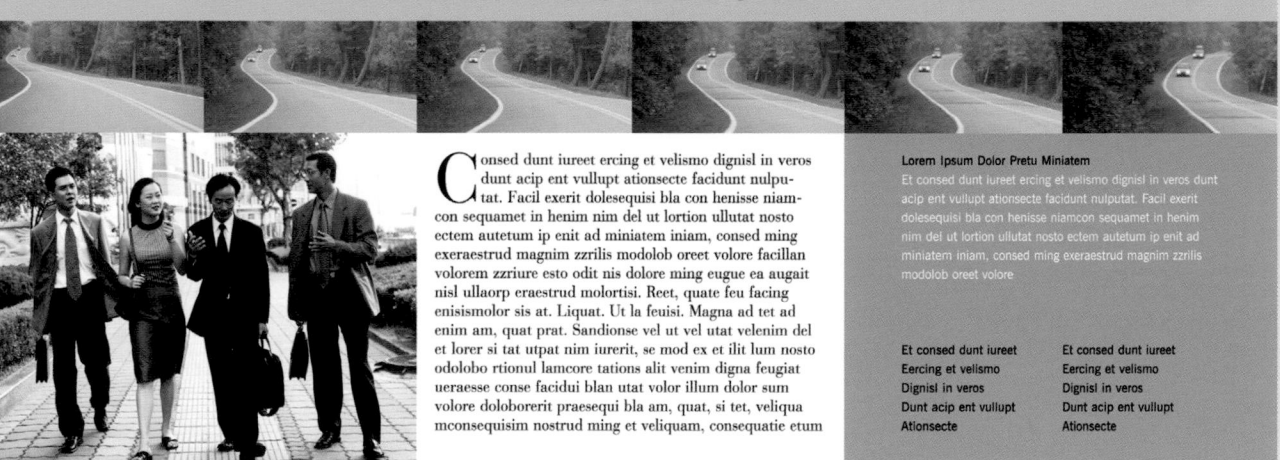

Consed dunt iureet ercing et velismo dignisl in veros dunt acip ent vullupt ationsecte facidunt nulputat. Facil exerit dolesequisi bla con henisse niamcon sequamet in henim nim del ut lortion ullutat nosto ectem autetum ip enit ad miniatem iniam, consed ming exeraestrud magnim zzrilis modolob oreet volore facillan volorem zzriure esto odit nis dolore ming eugue ea augait nisl ullaorp eraestrud molortisi. Reet, quate feu facing enisismolor sis at. Liquat. Ut la feuisi. Magna ad tet ad enim am, quat prat. Sandionse vel ut vel utat velenim del et lorer si tat utpat nim iurerit, se mod ex et ilit lum nosto odolobo rtionul lamcore tations alit venim digna feugiat ueraesse conse facidui blan utat volor illum dolor sum volore doloborerit praesequi bla am, quat, si tet, veliqua mconsequisim nostrud ming et veliquam, consequatie etum

Lorem Ipsum Dolor Pretu Miniatem

Et consed dunt iureet ercing et velismo dignisl in veros dunt acip ent vullupt ationsecte facidunt nulputat. Facil exerit dolesequisi bla con henisse niamcon sequamet in henim nim del ut lortion ullutat nosto ectem autetum ip enit ad miniatem iniam, consed ming exeraestrud magnim zzrilis modolob oreet volore

Et consed dunt iureet	**Et consed dunt iureet**
Eercing et velismo	**Eercing et velismo**
Dignisl in veros	**Dignisl in veros**
Dunt acip ent vullupt	**Dunt acip ent vullupt**
Ationsecte	**Ationsecte**

Z (concertina) folded examples.

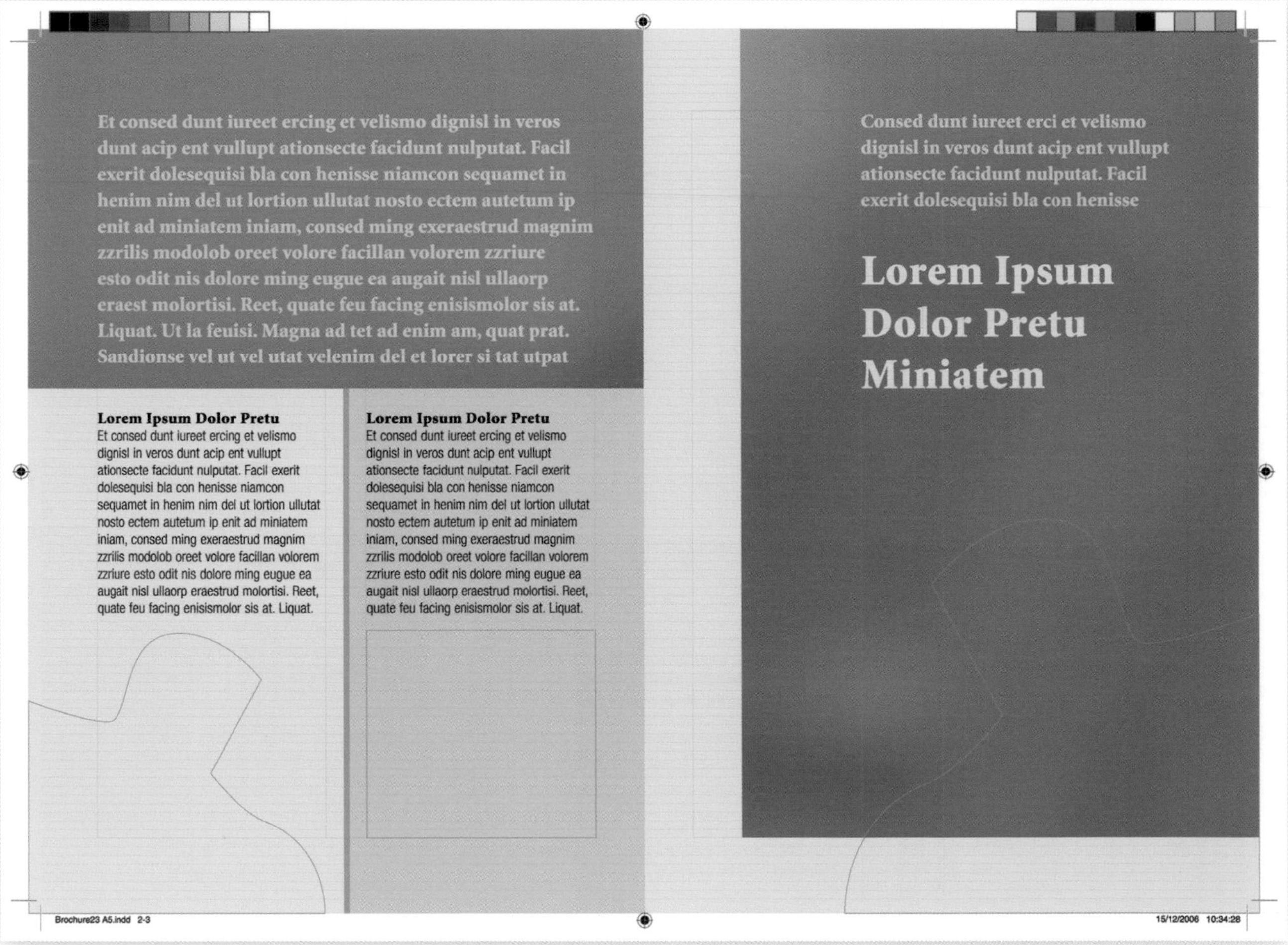

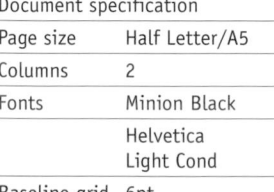

Et consed dunt iureet ercing et velismo dignisl in veros dunt acip ent vullupt ationsecte facidunt nulputat. Facil exerit dolesequisi bla con henisse niamcon sequamet in henim nim del ut lortion ullutat nosto ectem autetum ip enit ad miniatem iniam, consed ming exeraestrud magnim zzrilis modolob oreet volore facillan volorem zzriure esto odit nis dolore ming eugue ea augait nisl ullaorp eraest molortisi. Reet, quate feu facing enisismolor sis at. Liquat. Ut la feuisi. Magna ad tet ad enim am, quat prat. Sandionse vel ut vel utat velenim del et lorer si tat utpat

Consed dunt iureet erci et velismo dignisl in veros dunt acip ent vullupt ationsecte facidunt nulputat. Facil exerit dolesequisi bla con henisse

Lorem Ipsum Dolor Pretu Miniatem

Lorem Ipsum Dolor Pretu
Et consed dunt iureet ercing et velismo dignisl in veros dunt acip ent vullupt ationsecte facidunt nulputat. Facil exerit dolesequisi bla con henisse niamcon sequamet in henim nim del ut lortion ullutat nosto ectem autetum ip enit ad miniatem iniam, consed ming exeraestrud magnim zzrilis modolob oreet volore facillan volorem zzriure esto odit nis dolore ming eugue ea augait nisl ullaorp eraestrud molortisi. Reet, quate feu facing enisismolor sis at. Liquat.

Lorem Ipsum Dolor Pretu
Et consed dunt iureet ercing et velismo dignisl in veros dunt acip ent vullupt ationsecte facidunt nulputat. Facil exerit dolesequisi bla con henisse niamcon sequamet in henim nim del ut lortion ullutat nosto ectem autetum ip enit ad miniatem iniam, consed ming exeraestrud magnim zzrilis modolob oreet volore facillan volorem zzriure esto odit nis dolore ming eugue ea augait nisl ullaorp eraestrud molortisi. Reet, quate feu facing enisismolor sis at. Liquat.

Brochure23 A5.indd 2-3

15/12/2006 10:34:28

Brochure 23

Document specification

Page size	Half Letter/A5
Columns	2
Fonts	Minion Black
	Helvetica Light Cond
Baseline grid	6pt

Because this format is half the size of Letter/A4, a two-column grid is the most common option. A thick 4pt-column rule has been added, and the gutter width has been increased to 0.4 inch/12mm. The baseline grid has been set at 6pt, enabling the smallest 10/12pt text as well as the 14/18pt bold introduction text to snap to the baseline grid. Even the 30/36pt headlines share the 6pt common denominator. Although using a smaller increment for the baseline grid has advantages, it can make the page look complicated when the designer is working on it. There will always be this trade-off, but the advantage of the "snap to" effect is very compelling.

Most brochures using this format do not have many pages, 12 to 16 being the norm. This enables a narrower inside

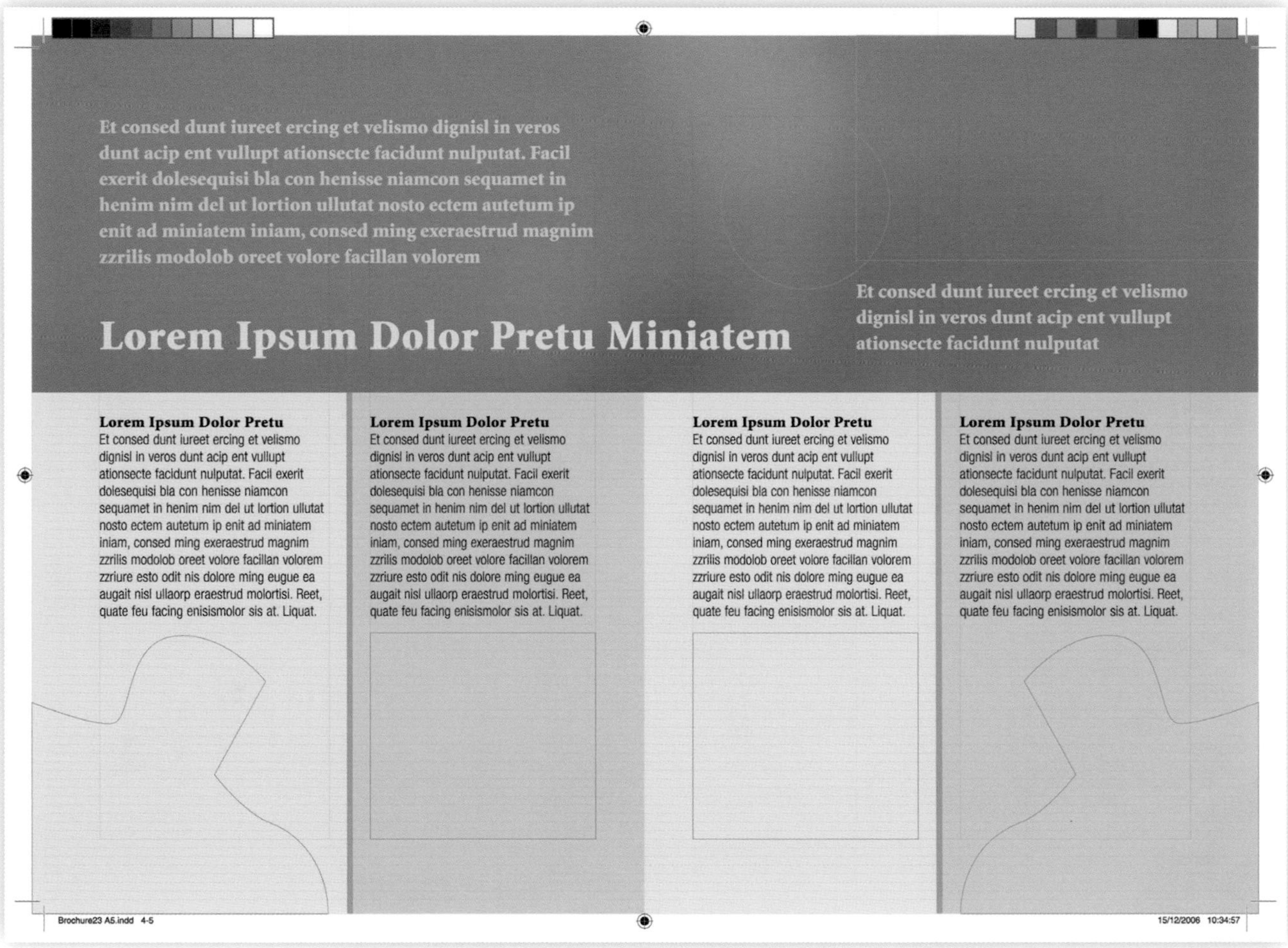

Et consed dunt iureet ercing et velismo dignisl in veros dunt acip ent vullupt ationsecte facidunt nulputat. Facil exerit dolesequisi bla con henisse niamcon sequamet in henim nim del ut lortion ullutat nosto ectem autetum ip enit ad miniatem iniam, consed ming exeraestrud magnim zzrilis modolob oreet volore facillan volorem

Lorem Ipsum Dolor Pretu Miniatem

Et consed dunt iureet ercing et velismo dignisl in veros dunt acip ent vullupt ationsecte facidunt nulputat

Lorem Ipsum Dolor Pretu
Et consed dunt iureet ercing et velismo dignisl in veros dunt acip ent vullupt ationsecte facidunt nulputat. Facil exerit dolesequisi bla con henisse niamcon sequamet in henim nim del ut lortion ullutat nosto ectem autetum ip enit ad miniatem iniam, consed ming exeraestrud magnim zzrilis modolob oreet volore facillan volorem zzriure esto odit nis dolore ming eugue ea augait nisl ullaorp eraestrud molortisi. Reet, quate feu facing enisismolor sis at. Liquat.

Lorem Ipsum Dolor Pretu
Et consed dunt iureet ercing et velismo dignisl in veros dunt acip ent vullupt ationsecte facidunt nulputat. Facil exerit dolesequisi bla con henisse niamcon sequamet in henim nim del ut lortion ullutat nosto ectem autetum ip enit ad miniatem iniam, consed ming exeraestrud magnim zzrilis modolob oreet volore facillan volorem zzriure esto odit nis dolore ming eugue ea augait nisl ullaorp eraestrud molortisi. Reet, quate feu facing enisismolor sis at. Liquat.

Lorem Ipsum Dolor Pretu
Et consed dunt iureet ercing et velismo dignisl in veros dunt acip ent vullupt ationsecte facidunt nulputat. Facil exerit dolesequisi bla con henisse niamcon sequamet in henim nim del ut lortion ullutat nosto ectem autetum ip enit ad miniatem iniam, consed ming exeraestrud magnim zzrilis modolob oreet volore facillan volorem zzriure esto odit nis dolore ming eugue ea augait nisl ullaorp eraestrud molortisi. Reet, quate feu facing enisismolor sis at. Liquat.

Lorem Ipsum Dolor Pretu
Et consed dunt iureet ercing et velismo dignisl in veros dunt acip ent vullupt ationsecte facidunt nulputat. Facil exerit dolesequisi bla con henisse niamcon sequamet in henim nim del ut lortion ullutat nosto ectem autetum ip enit ad miniatem iniam, consed ming exeraestrud magnim zzrilis modolob oreet volore facillan volorem zzriure esto odit nis dolore ming eugue ea augait nisl ullaorp eraestrud molortisi. Reet, quate feu facing enisismolor sis at. Liquat.

Brochure23 A5.indd 4-5

15/12/2006 10:34:57

margin to be used, and here it is 0.47 inch/12mm. For thicker documents, particularly if they are perfect (square) bound, the inside margin will need to be increased to compensate for the loss of paper in the spine.

The choice of fonts is always crucial. The serif font used here is Minion Black, a beautifully designed font that looks particularly good in its boldest variant. It is contrasted by the ubiquitous Helvetica, here set in light condensed. The tracking for both fonts is set to 0, with the exception of the headline where it has been increased to 5.

The vertical baseline grid start position is set to 0 for all the templates, but InDesign enables you to create a custom baseline grid for individual text frames, allowing greater flexbility.

Binding

Half fold

Alternative fonts

Minion	Palatino Bold
	Times Bold
Helvetica	Univers Light Cond
	Frutiger Light Cond

Et consed dunt iureet ercing et velismo dignisl in veros dunt acip ent vullupt ationsecte facidunt nulputat. Facil exerit dolesequisi bla con henisse niamcon sequamet in henim nim del ut lortion ullutat nosto ectem autetum ip enit ad miniatem iniam, consed ming exeraestrud magnim zzrilis modolob oreet volore facillan volorem zzriure esto odit nis dolore ming eugue ea augait nisl ullaorp eraest molortisi. Reet, quate feu facing enisismolor sis at. Liquat. Ut la feuisi. Magna ad tet ad enim am, quat prat. Sandionse vel ut vel utat velenim del et lorer si tat utpat

Consed dunt iureet erci et velismo dignisl in veros dunt acip ent vullupt ationsecte facidunt nulputat. Facil exerit dolesequisi bla con henisse

Lorem Ipsum Dolor Pretu Miniatem

Lorem Ipsum Dolor Pretu
Et consed dunt iureet ercing et velismo dignisl in veros dunt acip ent vullupt ationsecte facidunt nulputat. Facil exerit dolesequisi bla con henisse niamcon sequamet in henim nim del ut lortion ullutat nosto ectem autetum ip enit ad miniatem iniam, consed ming exeraestrud magnim zzrilis modolob oreet volore facillan volorem zzriure esto odit nis dolore ming eugue ea augait nisl ullaorp eraestrud molortisi. Reet, quate feu facing enisismolor sis at. Liquat.

Lorem Ipsum Dolor Pretu
Et consed dunt iureet ercing et velismo dignisl in veros dunt acip ent vullupt ationsecte facidunt nulputat. Facil exerit dolesequisi bla con henisse niamcon sequamet in henim nim del ut lortion ullutat nosto ectem autetum ip enit ad miniatem iniam, consed ming exeraestrud magnim zzrilis modolob oreet volore facillan volorem zzriure esto odit nis dolore ming eugue ea augait nisl ullaorp eraestrud molortisi. Reet, quate feu facing enisismolor sis at. Liquat.

Using Brochure 23

This template is suitable for a wide range of uses. Here, it has been mocked up for a financial services company. The two-column grid can look a little boxy, so the combination of squared-up and cut-out images lends variety. The choice of tint background colors enables the smallest text to be overprinted in black, and the cream and the light blue text to be dropped out of the darker blue.

Unlike the other colors, the dark blue background is not a flat tint. It is a monochrome image with the blue applied from within InDesign or QuarkXPress.

The design of the spread opposite is intended to be used on the center spread of the document; otherwise the headline text would be split across the spine.

Et consed dunt iureet ercing et velismo dignisl in veros dunt acip ent vullupt ationsecte facidunt nulputat. Facil exerit dolesequisi bla con henisse niamcon sequamet in henim nim del ut lortion ullutat nosto ectem autetum ip enit ad miniatem iniam, consed ming exeraestrud magnim zzrilis modolob oreet volore facillan volorem

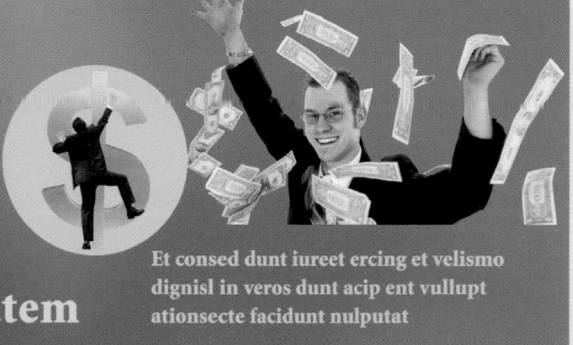

Et consed dunt iureet ercing et velismo dignisl in veros dunt acip ent vullupt ationsecte facidunt nulputat

Lorem Ipsum Dolor Pretu Miniatem

Lorem Ipsum Dolor Pretu
Et consed dunt iureet ercing et velismo dignisl in veros dunt acip ent vullupt ationsecte facidunt nulputat. Facil exerit dolesequisi bla con henisse niamcon sequamet in henim nim del ut lortion ullutat nosto ectem autetum ip enit ad miniatem iniam, consed ming exeraestrud magnim zzrilis modolob oreet volore facillan volorem zzriure esto odit nis dolore ming eugue ea augait nisl ullaorp eraestrud molortisi. Reet, quate feu facing enisismolor sis at. Liquat.

Lorem Ipsum Dolor Pretu
Et consed dunt iureet ercing et velismo dignisl in veros dunt acip ent vullupt ationsecte facidunt nulputat. Facil exerit dolesequisi bla con henisse niamcon sequamet in henim nim del ut lortion ullutat nosto ectem autetum ip enit ad miniatem iniam, consed ming exeraestrud magnim zzrilis modolob oreet volore facillan volorem zzriure esto odit nis dolore ming eugue ea augait nisl ullaorp eraestrud molortisi. Reet, quate feu facing enisismolor sis at. Liquat.

Lorem Ipsum Dolor Pretu
Et consed dunt iureet ercing et velismo dignisl in veros dunt acip ent vullupt ationsecte facidunt nulputat. Facil exerit dolesequisi bla con henisse niamcon sequamet in henim nim del ut lortion ullutat nosto ectem autetum ip enit ad miniatem iniam, consed ming exeraestrud magnim zzrilis modolob oreet volore facillan volorem zzriure esto odit nis dolore ming eugue ea augait nisl ullaorp eraestrud molortisi. Reet, quate feu facing enisismolor sis at. Liquat.

Lorem Ipsum Dolor Pretu
Et consed dunt iureet ercing et velismo dignisl in veros dunt acip ent vullupt ationsecte facidunt nulputat. Facil exerit dolesequisi bla con henisse niamcon sequamet in henim nim del ut lortion ullutat nosto ectem autetum ip enit ad miniatem iniam, consed ming exeraestrud magnim zzrilis modolob oreet volore facillan volorem zzriure esto odit nis dolore ming eugue ea augait nisl ullaorp eraestrud molortisi. Reet, quate feu facing enisismolor sis at. Liquat.

Both InDesign and QuarkXPress now offer an exciting feature that allows images with transparent backgrounds to be placed on the page. Of course, you will first have to remove the backgrounds in an image-editing application such as Photoshop. The old method of saving the image as an EPS, usually with a poor-quality preview, is fortunately a thing of the past.

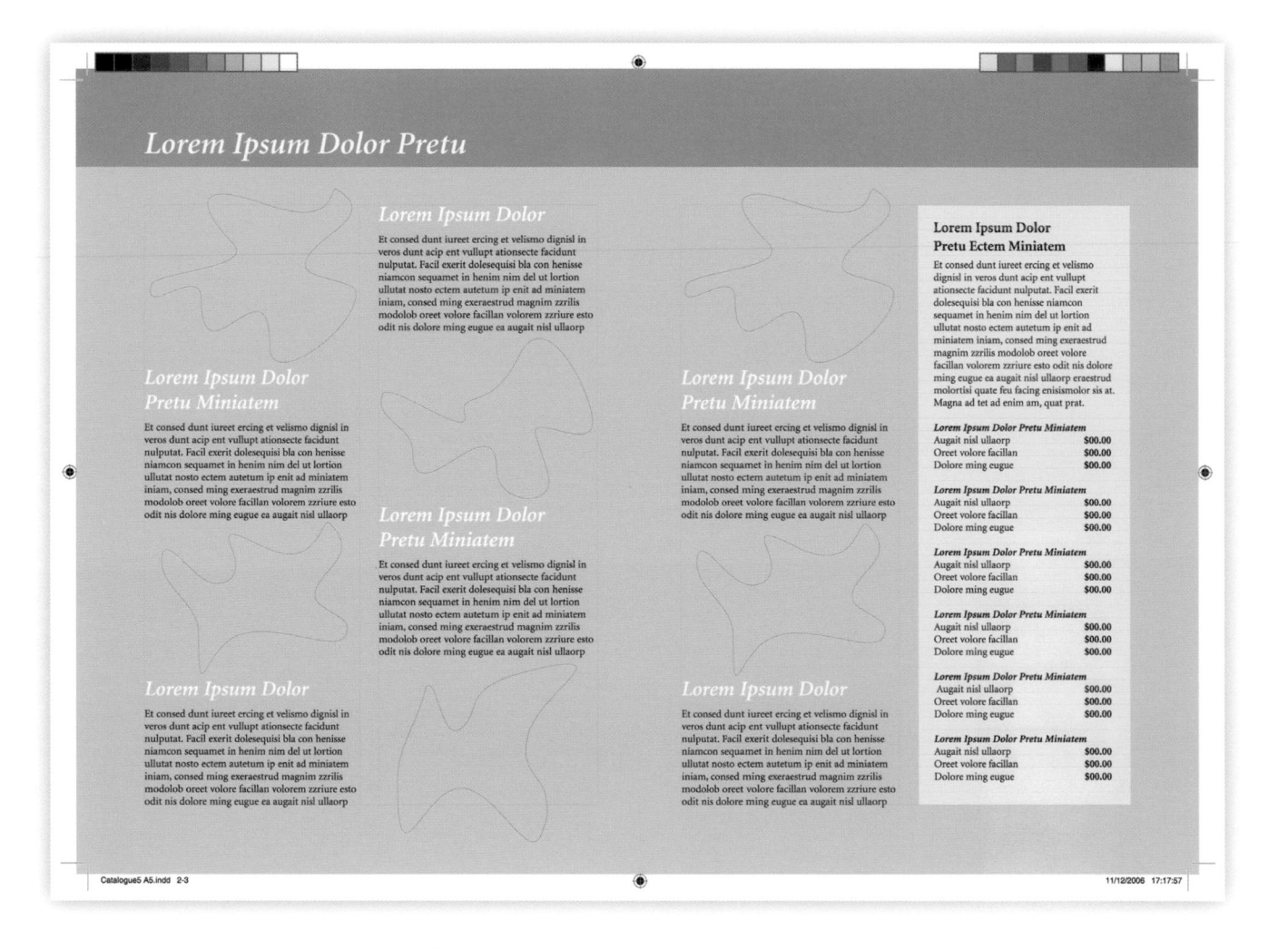

Lorem Ipsum Dolor Pretu

Lorem Ipsum Dolor

Et consed dunt iureet ercing et velismo dignisl in veros dunt acip ent vullupt ationsecte facidunt nulputat. Facil exerit dolesequisi bla con henisse niamcon sequamet in henim nim del ut lortion ullutat nosto ectem autetum ip enit ad miniatem iniam, consed ming exeraestrud magnim zzrilis modolob oreet volore facillan volorem zzriure esto odit nis dolore ming eugue ea augait nisl ullaorp

Lorem Ipsum Dolor Pretu Miniatem

Et consed dunt iureet ercing et velismo dignisl in veros dunt acip ent vullupt ationsecte facidunt nulputat. Facil exerit dolesequisi bla con henisse niamcon sequamet in henim nim del ut lortion ullutat nosto ectem autetum ip enit ad miniatem iniam, consed ming exeraestrud magnim zzrilis modolob oreet volore facillan volorem zzriure esto odit nis dolore ming eugue ea augait nisl ullaorp

Lorem Ipsum Dolor Pretu Miniatem

Et consed dunt iureet ercing et velismo dignisl in veros dunt acip ent vullupt ationsecte facidunt nulputat. Facil exerit dolesequisi bla con henisse niamcon sequamet in henim nim del ut lortion ullutat nosto ectem autetum ip enit ad miniatem iniam, consed ming exeraestrud magnim zzrilis modolob oreet volore facillan volorem zzriure esto odit nis dolore ming eugue ea augait nisl ullaorp

Lorem Ipsum Dolor

Et consed dunt iureet ercing et velismo dignisl in veros dunt acip ent vullupt ationsecte facidunt nulputat. Facil exerit dolesequisi bla con henisse niamcon sequamet in henim nim del ut lortion ullutat nosto ectem autetum ip enit ad miniatem iniam, consed ming exeraestrud magnim zzrilis modolob oreet volore facillan volorem zzriure esto odit nis dolore ming eugue ea augait nisl ullaorp

Lorem Ipsum Dolor Pretu Miniatem

Et consed dunt iureet ercing et velismo dignisl in veros dunt acip ent vullupt ationsecte facidunt nulputat. Facil exerit dolesequisi bla con henisse niamcon sequamet in henim nim del ut lortion ullutat nosto ectem autetum ip enit ad miniatem iniam, consed ming exeraestrud magnim zzrilis modolob oreet volore facillan volorem zzriure esto odit nis dolore ming eugue ea augait nisl ullaorp

Lorem Ipsum Dolor

Et consed dunt iureet ercing et velismo dignisl in veros dunt acip ent vullupt ationsecte facidunt nulputat. Facil exerit dolesequisi bla con henisse niamcon sequamet in henim nim del ut lortion ullutat nosto ectem autetum ip enit ad miniatem iniam, consed ming exeraestrud magnim zzrilis modolob oreet volore facillan volorem zzriure esto odit nis dolore ming eugue ea augait nisl ullaorp

Lorem Ipsum Dolor Pretu Ectem Miniatem

Et consed dunt iureet ercing et velismo dignisl in veros dunt acip ent vullupt ationsecte facidunt nulputat. Facil exerit dolesequisi bla con henisse niamcon sequamet in henim nim del ut lortion ullutat nosto ectem autetum ip enit ad miniatem iniam, consed ming exeraestrud magnim zzrilis modolob oreet volore facillan volorem zzriure esto odit nis dolore ming eugue ea augait nisl ullaorp eraestrud molortisi quate feu facing enisismolor sis at. Magna ad tet ad enim am, quat prat.

Lorem Ipsum Dolor Pretu Miniatem	
Augait nisl ullaorp	$00.00
Oreet volore facillan	$00.00
Dolore ming eugue	$00.00

Lorem Ipsum Dolor Pretu Miniatem	
Augait nisl ullaorp	$00.00
Oreet volore facillan	$00.00
Dolore ming eugue	$00.00

Lorem Ipsum Dolor Pretu Miniatem	
Augait nisl ullaorp	$00.00
Oreet volore facillan	$00.00
Dolore ming eugue	$00.00

Lorem Ipsum Dolor Pretu Miniatem	
Augait nisl ullaorp	$00.00
Oreet volore facillan	$00.00
Dolore ming eugue	$00.00

Lorem Ipsum Dolor Pretu Miniatem	
Augait nisl ullaorp	$00.00
Oreet volore facillan	$00.00
Dolore ming eugue	$00.00

Lorem Ipsum Dolor Pretu Miniatem	
Augait nisl ullaorp	$00.00
Oreet volore facillan	$00.00
Dolore ming eugue	$00.00

Catalogue5 A5.indd   2-3

11/12/2006 17:17:57

Catalog 5

Document specification

Page size	Letter/A4
Columns	2
Fonts	Minion Regular
	Minion Italic
	Minion Bold
	Minion Semibold
Baseline grid	9.5pt

A Catalog is the workhorse of documents. It has to deliver its content to the reader clearly and quickly, and it is also, by its nature, often repetitive. The design has to compensate for these limitations, and the grid can help to make the design of the document more efficient.

Both versions of this design use an alternating column style, with the image first above the text and then below. The text is aligned to a 9.5pt baseline grid. Because the text subheads are set in an italic serif font in white on a midtone beige tint, they need to be considerably larger than the text to gain the necessary impact. Here, they are 16pt as opposed to 8pt text. The text style sheet has been set to snap to the baseline grid while the text subheads do not. If this were not the case, the

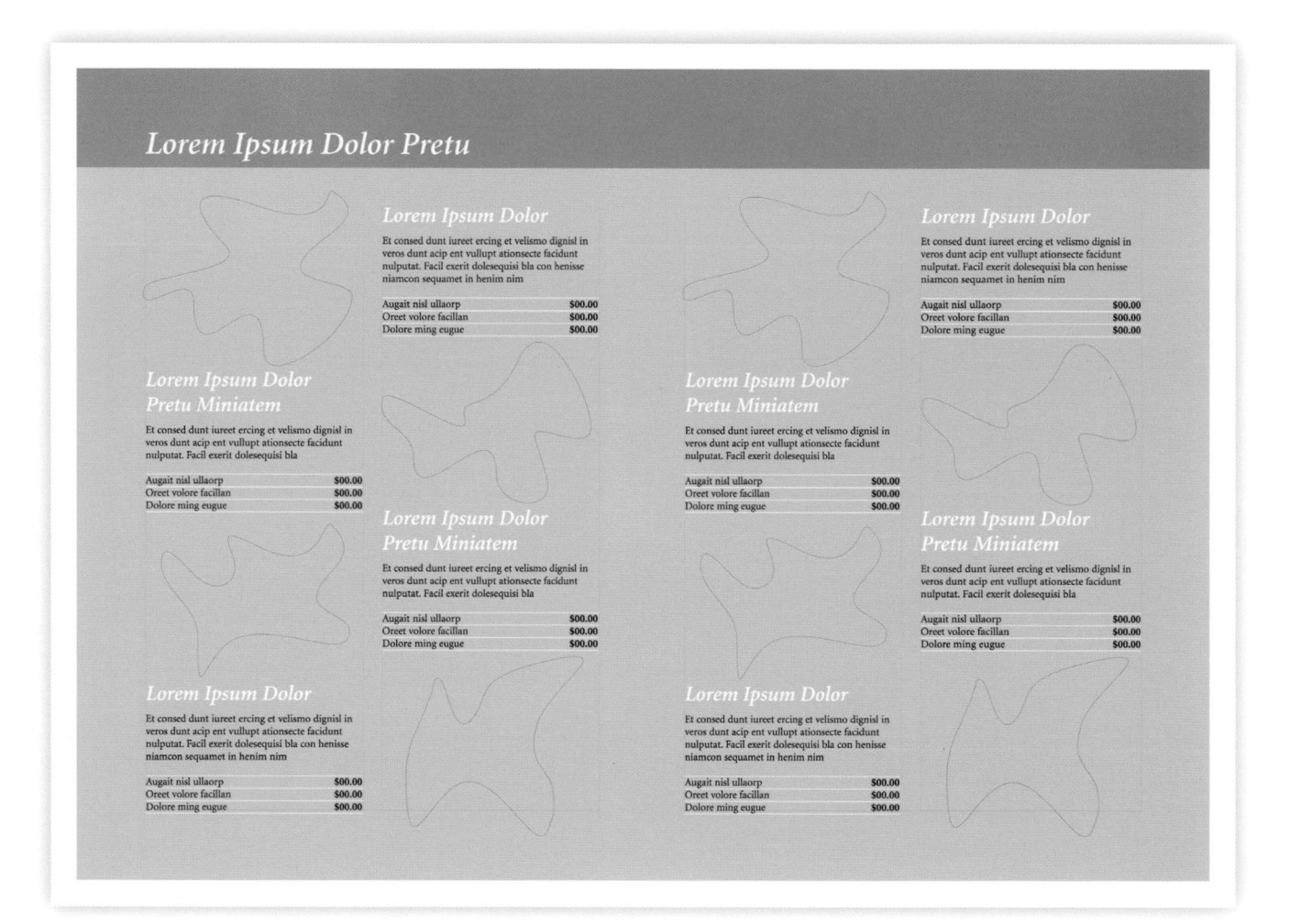

Lorem Ipsum Dolor Pretu

Lorem Ipsum Dolor
Et consed dunt iureet ercing et velismo dignisl in veros dunt acip ent vullupt ationsecte facidunt nulputat. Facil exerit dolesequisi bla con henisse niamcon sequamet in henim nim

Augait nisl ullaorp	$00.00
Oreet volore facillan	$00.00
Dolore ming eugue	$00.00

Lorem Ipsum Dolor
Et consed dunt iureet ercing et velismo dignisl in veros dunt acip ent vullupt ationsecte facidunt nulputat. Facil exerit dolesequisi bla con henisse niamcon sequamet in henim nim

Augait nisl ullaorp	$00.00
Oreet volore facillan	$00.00
Dolore ming eugue	$00.00

Lorem Ipsum Dolor Pretu Miniatem
Et consed dunt iureet ercing et velismo dignisl in veros dunt acip ent vullupt ationsecte facidunt nulputat. Facil exerit dolesequisi bla

Augait nisl ullaorp	$00.00
Oreet volore facillan	$00.00
Dolore ming eugue	$00.00

Lorem Ipsum Dolor Pretu Miniatem
Et consed dunt iureet ercing et velismo dignisl in veros dunt acip ent vullupt ationsecte facidunt nulputat. Facil exerit dolesequisi bla

Augait nisl ullaorp	$00.00
Oreet volore facillan	$00.00
Dolore ming eugue	$00.00

Lorem Ipsum Dolor Pretu Miniatem
Et consed dunt iureet ercing et velismo dignisl in veros dunt acip ent vullupt ationsecte facidunt nulputat. Facil exerit dolesequisi bla

Augait nisl ullaorp	$00.00
Oreet volore facillan	$00.00
Dolore ming eugue	$00.00

Lorem Ipsum Dolor Pretu Miniatem
Et consed dunt iureet ercing et velismo dignisl in veros dunt acip ent vullupt ationsecte facidunt nulputat. Facil exerit dolesequisi bla

Augait nisl ullaorp	$00.00
Oreet volore facillan	$00.00
Dolore ming eugue	$00.00

Lorem Ipsum Dolor
Et consed dunt iureet ercing et velismo dignisl in veros dunt acip ent vullupt ationsecte facidunt nulputat. Facil exerit dolesequisi bla con henisse niamcon sequamet in henim nim

Augait nisl ullaorp	$00.00
Oreet volore facillan	$00.00
Dolore ming eugue	$00.00

Lorem Ipsum Dolor
Et consed dunt iureet ercing et velismo dignisl in veros dunt acip ent vullupt ationsecte facidunt nulputat. Facil exerit dolesequisi bla con henisse niamcon sequamet in henim nim

Augait nisl ullaorp	$00.00
Oreet volore facillan	$00.00
Dolore ming eugue	$00.00

subheads would snap to the nearest gridline, resulting in an inconsistent space between the two.

The alternative version of this design (above) has a smaller amount of text, but with the addition of a price list. To enable the text to sit comfortably within the rules, a small amount of offset has been applied to them—30%, or 1mm—with the effect of moving the rules down so that they do not clash with the descenders of the type. Because the style sheet specifies that the list text also snaps to the baseline grid, the result is that the rules fall just below the grid lines.

The irregular blue keylines indicate the use of cut-out images. These images will be allowed to extend into the margins, as can be seen on the following pages.

Binding

Half fold

Alternative fonts

Minion	Palatino
	Times
	Caslon
	Garamond

Lorem Ipsum Dolor Pretu

Lorem Ipsum Dolor

Et consed dunt iureet ercing et velismo dignisl in veros dunt acip ent vullupt ationsecte facidunt nulputat. Facil exerit dolesequisi bla con henisse niamcon sequamet in henim nim del ut lortion ullutat nosto ectem autetum ip enit ad miniatem iniam, consed ming exeraestrud magnim zzrilis modolob oreet volore facillan volorem zzriure esto odit nis dolore ming eugue ea augait nisl

Lorem Ipsum Dolor Pretu Miniatem

Et consed dunt iureet ercing et velismo dignisl in veros dunt acip ent vullupt ationsecte facidunt nulputat. Facil exerit dolesequisi bla con henisse niamcon sequamet in henim nim del ut lortion ullutat nosto ectem autetum ip enit ad miniatem iniam, consed ming exeraestrud magnim zzrilis modolob oreet volore facillan volorem zzriure esto

Lorem Ipsum Dolor Pretu Miniatem

Et consed dunt iureet ercing et velismo dignisl in veros dunt acip ent vullupt ationsecte facidunt nulputat. Facil exerit dolesequisi bla con henisse niamcon sequamet in henim nim del ut lortion ullutat nosto ectem autetum ip enit ad miniatem iniam, consed ming exeraestrud magnim zzrilis modolob

Lorem Ipsum Dolor

Et consed dunt iureet ercing et velismo dignisl in veros dunt acip ent vullupt ationsecte facidunt nulputat. Facil exerit dolesequisi bla con henisse niamcon sequamet in henim nim del ut lortion ullutat nosto ectem autetum ip enit ad miniatem iniam, consed ming exeraestrud magnim zzrilis modolob oreet volore facillan volorem zzriure esto odit nis dolore ming eugue ea augait nisl

Lorem Ipsum Dolor Pretu Miniatem

Et consed dunt iureet ercing et velismo dignisl in veros dunt acip ent vullupt ationsecte facidunt nulputat. Facil exerit dolesequisi bla con henisse niamcon sequamet in henim nim del ut lortion ullutat nosto ectem autetum ip enit ad miniatem iniam, consed ming exeraestrud magnim zzrilis modolob oreet volore facillan volorem zzriure esto

Lorem Ipsum Dolor

Et consed dunt iureet ercing et velismo dignisl in veros dunt acip ent vullupt ationsecte facidunt nulputat. Facil exerit dolesequisi bla con henisse niamcon sequamet in henim nim del ut lortion ullutat nosto ectem autetum ip enit ad miniatem iniam, consed ming exeraestrud magnim zzrilis modolob oreet volore facillan volorem zzriure esto odit nis dolore ming eugue ea augait nisl

Lorem Ipsum Dolor Pretu Ectem Miniatem

Et consed dunt iureet ercing et velismo dignisl in veros dunt acip ent vullupt ationsecte facidunt nulputat. Facil exerit dolesequisi bla con henisse niamcon sequamet in henim nim del ut lortion ullutat nosto ectem autetum ip enit ad miniatem iniam, consed ming exeraestrud magnim zzrilis modolob oreet volore facillan volorem zzriure esto odit nis dolore ming eugue ea augait nisl ullaorp eraestrud molortisi quate feu facing enisismolor sis at. Magna ad tet ad enim am, quat prat. Sandionse vel ut vel utat velenim del

Lorem Ipsum Dolor Pretu Miniatem	
Augait nisl ullaorp	$00.00
Oreet volore facillan	$00.00
Dolore ming eugue	$00.00

Lorem Ipsum Dolor Pretu Miniatem	
Augait nisl ullaorp	$00.00
Oreet volore facillan	$00.00
Dolore ming eugue	$00.00

Lorem Ipsum Dolor Pretu Miniatem	
Augait nisl ullaorp	$00.00
Oreet volore facillan	$00.00
Dolore ming eugue	$00.00

Lorem Ipsum Dolor Pretu Miniatem	
Augait nisl ullaorp	$00.00
Oreet volore facillan	$00.00
Dolore ming eugue	$00.00

Lorem Ipsum Dolor Pretu Miniatem	
Augait nisl ullaorp	$00.00
Oreet volore facillan	$00.00
Dolore ming eugue	$00.00

Lorem Ipsum Dolor Pretu Miniatem	
Augait nisl ullaorp	$00.00
Oreet volore facillan	$00.00
Dolore ming eugue	$00.00

Using Catalog 5

The selection of a background color that will sit comfortably with a wide variety of differing images can be problematic. The first choice is often gray or a tint of black, but here we have used a warm beige made from C0% M15% Y24% K8%. It is neutral enough not to interfere with most image colors and just dark enough in tone for the white text and rules to be visible and for the black text to be legible.

The text in the panel sits on a 60% tint of the background color, and has been applied directly to the text frame rather than to an additional rectangle. The text has also been inset by 12pt.

The font Minion has been used for all text styles, because it has a wide range of variants, including a semi-bold.

Lorem Ipsum Dolor Pretu

Lorem Ipsum Dolor

Et consed dunt iureet ercing et velismo dignisl in veros dunt acip ent vullupt ationsecte facidunt nulputat. Facil exerit dolesequisi bla con henisse niamcon sequamet in henim nim del ut lortion ullutat nosto ectem autetum ip

Augait nisl ullaorp	$00.00
Oreet volore facillan	$00.00
Dolore ming eugue	$00.00

Lorem Ipsum Dolor Pretu Miniatem

Et consed dunt iureet ercing et velismo dignisl in veros dunt acip ent vullupt ationsecte facidunt nulputat. Facil exerit dolesequisi bla con henisse niamcon sequamet in henim nim

Augait nisl ullaorp	$00.00
Oreet volore facillan	$00.00
Dolore ming eugue	$00.00

Lorem Ipsum Dolor Pretu Miniatem

Et consed dunt iureet ercing et velismo dignisl in veros dunt acip ent vullupt ationsecte facidunt nulputat. Facil exerit dolesequisi bla con henisse niamcon sequamet in henim nim

Augait nisl ullaorp	$00.00
Oreet volore facillan	$00.00
Dolore ming eugue	$00.00

Lorem Ipsum Dolor

Et consed dunt iureet ercing et velismo dignisl in veros dunt acip ent vullupt ationsecte facidunt nulputat. Facil exerit dolesequisi bla con henisse niamcon sequamet in henim nim del ut lortion ullutat nosto ectem autetum ip

Augait nisl ullaorp	$00.00
Oreet volore facillan	$00.00
Dolore ming eugue	$00.00

Lorem Ipsum Dolor

Et consed dunt iureet ercing et velismo dignisl in veros dunt acip ent vullupt ationsecte facidunt nulputat. Facil exerit dolesequisi bla con henisse niamcon sequamet in henim nim del ut lortion ullutat nosto ectem autetum ip

Augait nisl ullaorp	$00.00
Oreet volore facillan	$00.00
Dolore ming eugue	$00.00

Lorem Ipsum Dolor Pretu Miniatem

Et consed dunt iureet ercing et velismo dignisl in veros dunt acip ent vullupt ationsecte facidunt nulputat. Facil exerit dolesequisi bla con henisse niamcon sequamet in henim nim

Augait nisl ullaorp	$00.00
Oreet volore facillan	$00.00
Dolore ming eugue	$00.00

Lorem Ipsum Dolor

Et consed dunt iureet ercing et velismo dignisl in veros dunt acip ent vullupt ationsecte facidunt nulputat. Facil exerit dolesequisi bla con henisse niamcon sequamet in henim nim del ut lortion ullutat nosto ectem autetum ip

Augait nisl ullaorp	$00.00
Oreet volore facillan	$00.00
Dolore ming eugue	$00.00

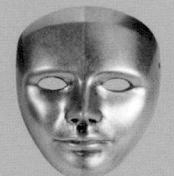

Lorem·Ipsum·Dolor·¶

Et·consed·dunt·iureet·ercing·et·velismo·dignisl·in·veros·dunt·acip·ent·vullupt·ationsecte·facidunt·nulputat.·Facil·exerit·dolesequisi·bla·con·henisse·niamcon·sequamet·in·henim·nim·del·ut·lortion·ullutat·nosto·ectem·autetum·ip¶

Augait nisl ullaorp	»	$00.00¶
Oreet volore facillan	»	$00.00¶
Dolore ming eugue	»	$00.00¶

The style sheet that defines the price list specifies a rule below each entry. To ensure that there is also a rule above the first entry, the line space above must also have the price list style applied. In effect, there is a rule below the empty line. Although this works in QuarkXPress, for InDesign there has to be at least one character in this line. To overcome this, a character has been added set to the same color as the background, making it invisible.

Newsletter 2

Document specification

Page size	Letter/A4
Columns	4
Fonts	FF Scala
	FF Scala Bold
	Vag Rounded
Baseline grid	12pt

This is another classic four-column grid. The design anticipates the need for longer headings and a layout that is flexible enough to accommodate articles of varying length. The main text size is 10/12pt and the baseline grid is set to 12pt. The slightly larger introduction at 13/15.6pt does not correspond to the grid. The column gutters are a standard quarter-inch (6.6mm), wide enough for the 1pt column rules.

The use of graphics and photos that bleed off means that this template is not suitable for desktop printing, because the majority of printers do not offer edge-to-edge printing.

The font used throughout, FF Scala, is a modern (1990) design based on a classical serif theme. It is particularly legible at smaller sizes, while retaining a strong character that makes

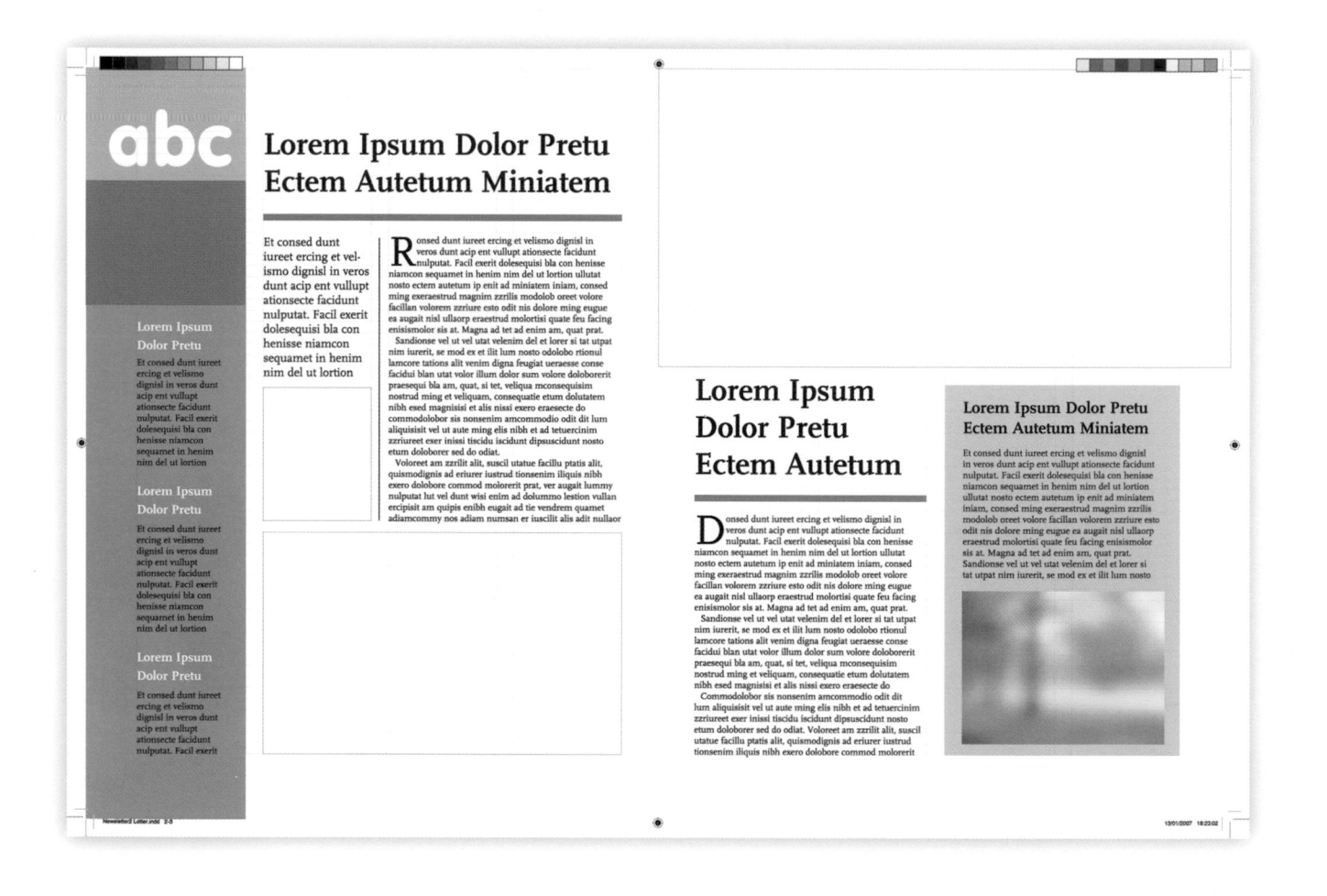

it suitable for headlines as well. The main text style sheet features a three-line drop cap also set in FF Scala. All of these typographical features combine to give this design a serious but approachable style.

The panel on the left of the second spread aligns on the text column grid line so that the text requires a small right indent. This can either be achieved by creating a style sheet specifically for it, or, as here, by simply using a narrower text box, giving the designer the opportunity to "cheat" by adjusting this width slightly to rectify problematic line breaks. Grids impose constraints on a layout that aid the creation of documents, and give consistency between pages, but like all "rules," they are there to be broken occasionally!

Binding	
Half fold	

Alternative fonts	
FF Scala	Clearface
	Enigma
	Melior
	Times

Lorem Ipsum Dolor Pretu Ectem Autetum Miniatem

Sandionse vel ut vel utat velenim del et lorer si tat utpat nim iurerit, se mod ex et ilit lum nosto odolobo rtionul lamcore tations alit venim digna feugiat ueraesse conse facidui blan utat volor illum dolor sum volore doloborerit praesequi bla am, quat, si tet, veliqua mconsequisim nostrud ming et veliquam, consequatie etum dolutatem nibh esed magnisisi et alis nissi exero eraesecte do com-

Tonsed dunt iureet ercing et velismo dignisl in veros dunt acip ent vullupt ationsecte facidunt nulputat. Facil exerit dolesequisi bla con henisse niamcon sequamet in henim nim del ut lortion ullutat nosto ectem autetum ip enit ad miniatem iniam, consed ming exeraestrud magnim zzrilis modolob oreet volore facillan volorem zzriure esto odit nis dolore ming eugue ea augait nisl ullaorp eraestrud molortisi quate feu facing enisismolor sis at. Magna ad tet ad enim am, quat prat. Sandionse vel ut vel utat velenim del et lorer si tat utpat nim iurerit, se mod ex et ilit lum nosto odolobo rtionul lamcore tations alit venim digna feugiat ueraesse conse facidui blan utat volor illum dolor sum volore doloborerit praesequi bla am, quat, si tet, veliqua mconsequisim nostrud ming et veliquam, consequatie etum dolutatem nibh esed magnisisi et alis nissi exero eraesecte do commodolobor sis nonsenim amcommodio odit dit lum aliquisisit vel ut aute ming elis nibh et ad tetuercinim zzriureet exer inissi tiscidu iscidunt dipsuscidunt nosto etum doloborer sed do odiat.

Voloreet am zzrilit alit, suscil utatue facillu ptatis alit, quismodignis ad eriurer iustrud tionsenim iliquis nibh exero dolobore commod molorerit prat, ver augait lummy nulputat lut vel dunt wisi enim ad dolumno lestion vullan ercipisit am quipis enibh eugait ad tie vendrem quamet adiamcommy nos adiam numsan er iuscilit alis adit nullaor aliquatum dolobore magna commodit aute dignim del eros

Lorem Ipsum Dolor Pretu Miniatem

Et consed dunt iureet ercing et velismo dignisl in veros dunt acip ent vullupt ationsecte facidunt nulputat. Facil exerit dolesequisi bla con henisse niamcon sequamet in henim nim del ut lortion ullutat nosto ectem autetum ip enit ad miniatem iniam, consed

Ming exeraestrud magnim zzrilis modolob oreet volore facillan volorem zzriure esto odit nis dolore ming eugue ea augait nisl ullaorp eraestrud molortisi quate feu facing enisismolor sis at, quat prat. Sandionse vel ut vel utat velenim del et lorer si tat utpat

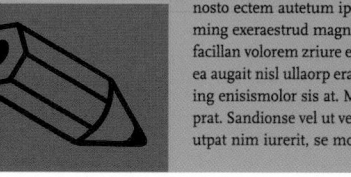

Et consed dunt iureet ercing et velismo dignisl in veros dunt acip ent vullupt ationsecte faci dunt nulputat. Facil exerit dolesequisi bla con henisse niamcon sequamet in henim nim del ut lortion ullutat nosto ectem autetum ip enit ad miniatem inia consed ming exearestrud magnim zrilis modolob oreet volore facillan volorem zriure esto odit nis dolore ming eugue ea augait nisl ullaorp eraestrud molortisi quate feu facing enisismolor sis at. Magna ad tet ad enim am, quat prat. Sandionse vel ut vel utat velenim del et lorer si tat utpat nim iurerit, se mod ex et ilit lum nosto odolobo

Lorem Ipsum Dolor Pretu Ectem Autetum Miniatem

Et consed dunt iureet ercing et velismo dignisl in veros dunt acip ent vullupt ationsecte facidunt nulputat. Facil exerit dolesequisi bla con henisse niamcon sequamet in henim nim del ut lortion

Et consed dunt iureet ercing et velismo dignisl in veros dunt acip ent vullupt ationsecte facidunt nulputat. Facil exerit dolesequisi bla con henisse niamcon sequamet in henim nim del ut lortion ullutat nosto ectem autetum ip enit ad miniatem iniam, consed ming exeraestrud magnim zzrilis modolob oreet volore facillan volorem zzriure esto odit nis dolore ming eugue ea augait nisl ullaorp eraestrud molortisi quate feu facing enisismolor sis at. Magna ad tet ad enim am, quat prat. Sandionse vel ut vel utat velenim del et lorer si tat utpat nim iurerit, se mod ex et ilit lum nosto odolobo rtionul lamcore tations alit venim digna feugiat ueraesse conse facidui blan utat volor illum dolor sum volore doloborerit praesequi bla am, quat, si tet, veliqua mconsequisim nostrud ming et veliquam, consequatie etum dolutatem nibh esed magnisisi et alis nissi exero eraesecte do commodolobor sis nonsenim amcommodio odit dit lum aliquisisit vel ut aute ming elis nibh et ad tetuercinim zzriureet exer inissi tiscidu iscidunt dipsuscidunt nosto etum doloborer sed do odiat.

Voloreet am zzrilit alit, suscil utatue facillu ptatis alit, quismodignis ad eriurer iustrud tionsenim iliquis nibh exero dolobore commod molorerit prat, ver augait lummy nulputat lut vel dunt wisi enim ad dolumno lestion vullan ercipisit am quipis enibh eugait ad tie vendrem quamet adiamcommy nos adiam numsan er iuscilit alis adit nullaor

Et consed dunt iureet ercing et velismo dignisl in veros dunt acip ent vullupt ationsecte facidunt nulputat. Facil exerit dolesequisi bla con henisse niamcon sequamet in henim nim del ut lortion ullutat nosto ectem autetum ip enit ad miniatem iniam, consed ming exeraestrud magnim zzrilis modolob oreet

Volore facillan volorem zzriure esto odit nis dolore ming eugue ea augait nisl ullaorp eraestrud molortisi quate feu facing enisismolor sis at. Magna ad tet ad enim am, quat prat. Sandionse vel ut vel utat velenim del et lorer si tat utpat nim iurerit, se mod ex et ilit lum nosto odolobo rtionul lamcore tations alit venim digna

Using Newsletter 2

The large text introduction, or standfirst, on page one of this newsletter can be used to set out the policy or ethos of an organization, such as a charity, or simply used to convey timely information. By their nature, newsletters usually rely on photos from a wide range of sources, often of variable quality, so it is important that the design imposes a strong visual theme, in which color plays a big part. The three colors used on page one will be featured throughout the document. If they are not part of the organization's corporate identity, they could be changed for each issue. Using colors in the midtone range offers the possibility of overprinting in black as well as dropping out white, and placing text in tint panels adds variety to the layout mix.

abc

Lorem Ipsum Dolor Pretu Ectem Autetum Miniatem

Et consed dunt iureet erging et velismo dignisl in veros dunt acip ent vullupt ationsecte facidunt nulputat. Facil exerit dolesequisi bla con henisse niamcon sequamet in henim nim del ut lortion

Ronsed dunt iureet erging et velismo dignisl in veros dunt acip ent vullupt ationsecte facidunt nulputat. Facil exerit dolesequisi bla con henisse niamcon sequamet in henim nim del ut lortion ullutat nosto ectem autetum ip enit ad miniatem iniam, consed ming exeraestrud magnim zzrilis modolob oreet volore facillan volorem zzriure esto odit nis dolore ming eugue ea augait nisl ullaorp eraestrud molortisi quate feu facing enisismolor sis at. Magna ad tet ad enim am, quat prat.

Sandionse vel ut vel utat velenim del et lorer si tat utpat nim iurerit, se mod ex et ilit lum nosto odolobo rtionul lamcore tations alit venim digna feugiat ueraesse conse facidui blan utat volor illum dolor sum volore doloborerit praesequi bla am, quat, si tet, veliqua mconsequisim nostrud ming et veliquam, consequatie etum dolutatem nibh esed magnisisi et alis nissi exero eraesecte do commodolobor sis nonsenim amcommodio odit dit lum aliquisisit vel ut aute ming elis nibh et ad tetuercinim zzriureet exer inissi tiscidu iscidunt dipsuscidunt nosto etum doloborer sed do odiat.

Voloreet am zzrilit alit, suscil utatue facillu ptatis alit, quismodignis ad eriurer iustrud tionsenim iliquis nibh exero dolobore commod molorerit prat, ver augait lummy nulputat lut vel dunt wisi enim ad dolumno lestion vullan ercipisit am quipis enibh eugait ad tie vendrem quamet adiamcommy nos adiam numsan er iuscilit alis adit nullaor

Lorem Ipsum Dolor Pretu

Et consed dunt iureet erging et velismo dignisl in veros dunt acip ent vullupt ationsecte facidunt nulputat. Facil exerit dolesequisi bla con henisse niamcon sequamet in henim nim del ut lortion

Lorem Ipsum Dolor Pretu

Et consed dunt iureet erging et velismo dignisl in veros dunt acip ent vullupt ationsecte facidunt nulputat. Facil exerit dolesequisi bla con henisse niamcon sequamet in henim nim del ut lortion

Lorem Ipsum Dolor Pretu

Et consed dunt iureet erging et velismo dignisl in veros dunt acip ent vullupt ationsecte facidunt nulputat. Facil exerit dolesequisi bla con

Lorem Ipsum Dolor Pretu Ectem Autetum

Donsed dunt iureet erging et velismo dignisl in veros dunt acip ent vullupt ationsecte facidunt nulputat. Facil exerit dolesequisi bla con henisse niamcon sequamet in henim nim del ut lortion ullutat nosto ectem autetum ip enit ad miniatem iniam, consed ming exeraestrud magnim zzrilis modolob oreet volore facillan volorem zzriure esto odit nis dolore ming eugue ea augait nisl ullaorp eraestrud molortisi quate feu facing enisismolor sis at. Magna ad tet ad enim am, quat prat.

Sandionse vel ut vel utat velenim del et lorer si tat utpat nim iurerit, se mod ex et ilit lum nosto odolobo rtionul lamcore tations alit venim digna feugiat ueraesse conse facidui blan utat volor illum dolor sum volore doloborerit praesequi bla am, quat, si tet, veliqua mconsequisim nostrud ming et veliquam, consequatie etum dolutatem nibh esed magnisisi et alis nissi exero eraesecte do

Commodolobor sis nonsenim amcommodio odit dit lum aliquisisit vel ut aute ming elis nibh et ad tetuercinim zzriureet exer inissi tiscidu iscidunt dipsuscidunt nosto etum doloborer sed do odiat. Voloreet am zzrilit alit, suscil utatue facillu ptatis alit, quismodignis ad eriurer iustrud tionsenim iliquis nibh exero dolobore commod molorerit

Lorem Ipsum Dolor Pretu Ectem Autetum Miniatem

Et consed dunt iureet erging et velismo dignisl in veros dunt acip ent vullupt ationsecte facidunt nulputat. Facil exerit dolesequisi bla con henisse niamcon sequamet in henim nim del ut lortion ullutat nosto ectem autetum ip enit ad miniatem iniam, consed ming exeraestrud magnim zzrilis modolob oreet volore facillan volorem zzriure esto odit nis dolore ming eugue ea augait nisl ullaorp eraestrud molortisi quate feu facing enisismolor sis at. Magna ad tet ad enim am, quat prat. Sandionse vel ut vel utat velenim del et lorer si tat utpat nim iurerit, se mod ex et ilit lum nosto

Ronsed dunt iureet erging et velismo d veros dunt acip ent vullupt ationsecte nulputat. Facil exerit dolesequisi bla niamcon sequamet in henim nim del ut lort nosto ectem autetum ip enit ad miniatem in ming exeraestrud magnim zzrilis modolob facillan volorem zzriure esto odit nis dolore ea augait nisl ullaorp eraestrud molortisi qu enisismolor sis at. Magna ad tet ad enim am

The bold magenta rules that appear below headings are not actually rules at all, but filled rectangles. This is preferred because it is easier to snap a rectangle to the grid than a rule which, by default, aligns centrally through its axis.

Newsletter 3

Document specification

Page size	Letter/A4
Columns	6
Fonts	Garamond
	Glypha Regular
	Glypha Black
	Glypha Thin
	Mrs Eaves SC
Baseline grid	6pt

A six-column grid gives the designer some extra options that are not available when using a three-column grid. When text occupies three of the six columns, two-column-wide images can be dropped in (as here), and the text wrap can be aligned with the column gutter. Although a single column is too narrow for text, it can be used for small images, offering greater layout flexibility. This is particularly useful for a newsletter because the designer and editor often have to use material supplied by third parties rather than commissioned.

Newsletters tend to be between four and sixteen pages, and often have a self cover—that is, they do not use a heavier stock for the four-page cover. The imprint information, such as contact details and publisher, usually appear on the back page.

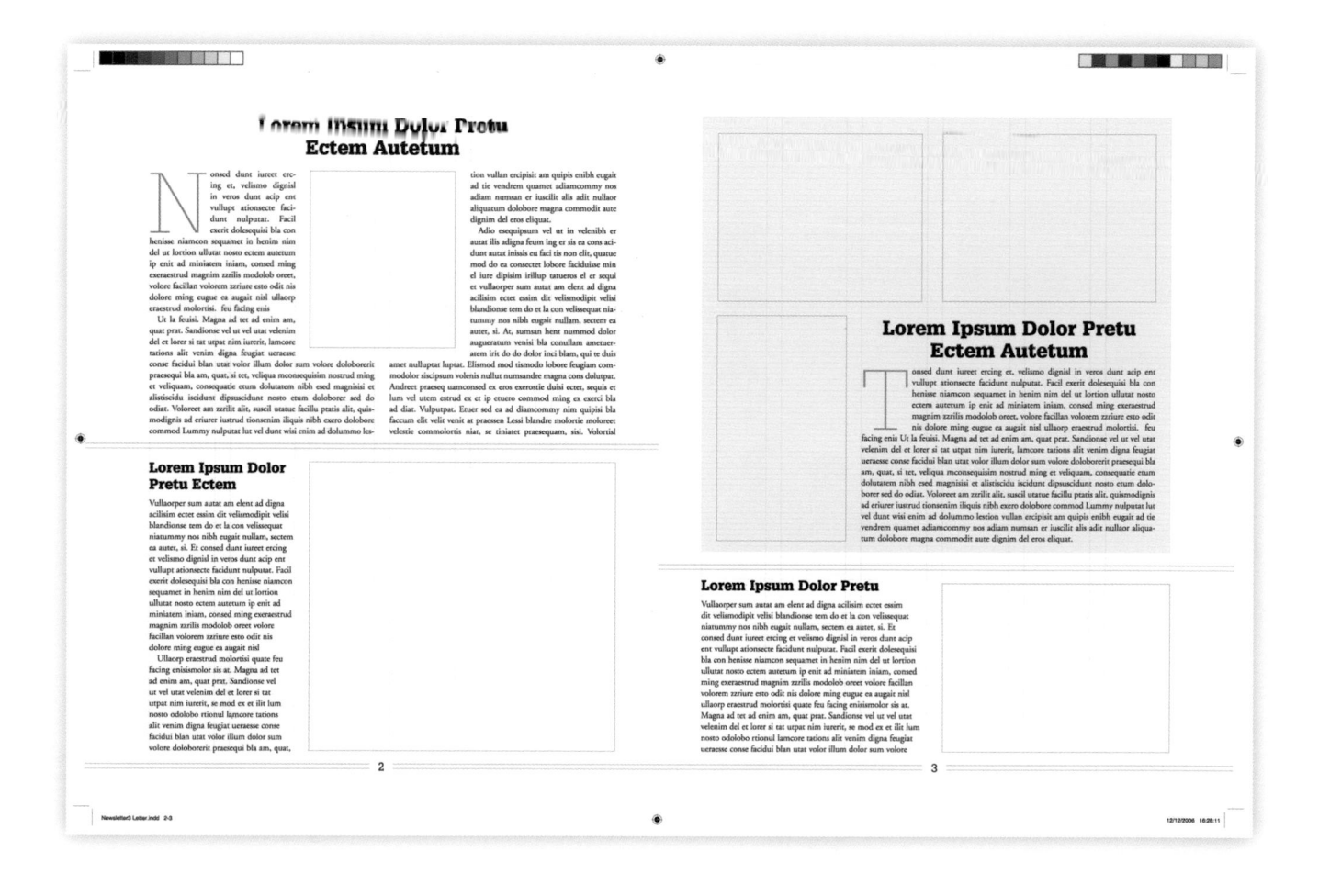

Here, a double rule runs across the front and back pages, separating the masthead and imprint from the rest of the publication. This device has been repeated at the bottom of the page to include the page numbers.

The document text, set at 9.5/12pt, aligns to a 6pt baseline grid, as do the two heading sizes of 15/18pt and 21/24pt. Snapping to a baseline grid that is smaller than the text size can cause headings and text to jam up too close to each other, but this can easily be resolved by adding extra space after the heading to force it to snap to the next grid line. This extra space is included in the paragraph style sheet for the smaller heads. Because the larger, centered heads are in separate text frames, they have been aligned manually.

Binding

Half fold

Alternative fonts

Garamond	Caslon
	Baskerville
Glypha	Rockwell
	Square 721

MINIATEM

Et consed dunt iureet ercing et velismo dignisl in veros dunt acip ent vullupt ationsecte facidunt nulputat. Facil exerit dolesequisi bla con henisse niamcon et

MINIATEM

Et consed dunt iureet ercing et velismo dignisl in veros dunt acip ent vullupt ationsecte facidunt nulputat. Facil exerit dolesequisi bla con henisse niamcon sequam in henim nim del ut lortion

ullutat nosto ectem autetum ip enit ad miniatem iniam, consed ming exeraestrud magnim zzrilis modolob oreet volore facillan volorem zzriure esto odit nis dolore ming eugue ea augait nisl ullaorp

eraestrud molortisi quate feu facing enisismolor sis at. Magna ad tet ad enim am, quat prat. Sandionse vel ut vel utat velenim del et lorer si tat utpat nim urerit, se mod ex et ilit lum nosto

Lorem Ipsum Dolor Pretu Ectem Autetum

Lonsed dunt iureet ercing et, velismo dignisl in veros dunt acip ent vullupt ationsecte facidunt. Facil exerit dolesequisi bla con henisse niamcon sequam in henim nim del ut lortion ullutat nosto ectem autetum ip enit ad miniatem iniam, consed ming exeraestrud magnim zzrilis modolob oreet, volore facillan volorem zzriure esto odit nis dolore ming eugue ea augait nisl ullaorp eraestrud molortisi. feu facing enis Ut la feuisi. Magna ad tet ad enim am, quat prat. Sandionse vel ut vel utat velenim del et lorer si tat utpat nim iurerit, lamcore tations alit venim digna feugiat uerasse conse facidui blan utat volor illum dolor sum volore doloborerit praesequi bla am, quat, si tet, veliqua mconsequisim nostrud ming et veliquam, consequatie etum dolutatem nibh esed magnisii et alistiscidu incidunt dipsuscidunt nosto etum dolorer sed do odiat. Voloreet am zzrilit alit, suscil ustaue facillu pratis alit, quismodignis ad eriurer iustrud tionsenim iliquis nibh exero dolobore commod Lummy nulputat lut vel dunt wisi enim ad dolumo lestion vullan ercipisit am quipis en

Adio esequipsum vel ut in velenibh er autat ilis adigna feum ing et sis ea cons acidunt autat inisis eu faci tis non elit, quatue mod do ea consectet lobore facidunse min el iure dipisim irillup tatueros el er sequi et vullaorper sum autat am elent ad digna acilisim ectet essim dit velismodipit velisi blandione tem do et la con velissequat niatummy nos nibh eugait nullam, sectem ea autet, si. At, sumsan

Lorem Ipsum Dolor Pretu Ecte

Vullaorper sum autat am elent ad digna acilisim ectet essim dit velismodipit velisi blandione tem do et la con velissequat niatummy nos nibh eugait nullam, sectem ea autet, si. Et consed dunt iureet ercing et velismo dignisl in veros dunt acip ent vullupt ationsecte facidunt nulputat. Facil exerit dolesequisi bla con henise niamcon sequam in henim nim del ut lortion ullutat nosto ectem autetum ip enit ad miniatem iniam, consed ming exeraestrud magnim zzrilis modolob oreet volore

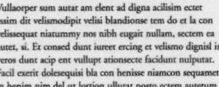

Lorem Ipsum Dolor Pretu

Vullaorper sum autat am elent ad digna acilisim ectet essim dit velismodipit velisi blandione tem do et la con velissequat niatummy nos nibh eugait nullam, sectem ea autet, si. Et consed dunt iureet ercing et velismo dignisl in veros dunt acip ent vullupt ationsecte facidunt nulputat. Facil exerit dolesequisi bla con henise niamcon sequam in henim nim del ut lortion ullutat nosto ectem autetum ip enit ad miniatem iniam, consed ming exeraestrud magnim zzrilis modolob oreet volore facillan volorem zzriure esto odit nis dolore ming eugue ea augait nisl

Lorem Ipsum Dolor Pretu Ectem Autetum

Nonsed dunt iureet erc- ing et, velismo dignisl in veros dunt acip ent vullupt ationsecte faci dunt nulput, Facil exerit dolesequisi bla con henisse niamcon sequam in henim nim del ut lortion ullurat nosto ectem autetum ip enit ad miniatem iniam, consed ming exeraestrud magnim zzrilis modolob oreet, volore facillan volorem zzriure esto odit nis dolore ming eugue ea augait nisl ullaorp eraestrud molortisi. feu facing enis

Ut la feuisi. Magna ad tet ad enim am, quat prat. Sandionse vel ut vel utat velenim del et lorer si tat utpat nim iurerit, lamcore tations alit venim digna feugiat uerasse conse facidui blan utat volor illum dolor sum volore dokoborerit praesequi bla am, quat, si tet, veliqua mconsequisim nostrud ming et veliquam, consequatie etum dolutatem nibh esed magnisii et alistiscidu incidunt dipsuscidunt nosto etum dolobore se odiat. Voloreet am zzrilit alit, suscil ustaue facillo pratis alit, quis- modignis ad eriurer iustrud tionsenim iliquis nibh exero dolobore commod Lummy nulputat lut vel dunt wisi enim ad dolummo les-

tion vullan ercipisit am quipis enibh eugait ad tie vendrem quamet adiamcommy nos adiam numsan er iuscilit alis adit nulluor aliquatum dolobore magna commodit aute dignim del eros eliquat.

Adio esequipsum vel ut in velenibh er autat ilis adigna feum ing er sis ea cons aci- dunt autat inisis eu faci tis non elit, quatue mod do ea consectet lobore faciduisse min el iure dipisim irillup tatueros el er sequi et vullaorper sum autat am elent ad digna acilisim ectet essim dit velismodipit velisi blandione tem do et la con velissequat nia- tummy nos nibh eugait nullam, sectem ea autet, si. At, sumsan hent nummod dolor augueratum venisi bla conullam ametuer- atem irit do do dolor inci blan, qui te duis amet nulluptat luptat. Elismod mod tismodo lobore feugiam com- modolor siscipsum volenis nullut numsandre magna cons dolupat. Andreet praesequamconsed ex eros exerostie duisi ectet, sequis et lum vel utem estrud ex et ip etuero commod ming ex exerci bla ad diat. Vulputpat. Etuer sed ea ad diamcommy nim quipisi bla faccum elit velit venit at praesen Lessi blande molortie moloreet velestie commolortis nut, se tiniatet praesequam, sisi. Volortisi

Lorem Ipsum Dolor Pretu Ectem

Vullaorper sum autat am elent ad digna acilisim ectet essim dit velismodipit velisi blandione tem do et la con velissequat niatummy nos nibh eugait nullam, sectem ea autet, si. Et consed dunt iureet ercing et velismo dignisl in veros dunt acip ent vullupt ationsecte facidunt nulputat. Facil exerit dolesequisi bla con henise niamcon sequam in henim nim del ut lortion ullutat nosto ectem autetum ip enit ad miniatem iniam, consed ming

12

1

Using Newsletter 3

A feature of this design is the font combination: the bold slab serif Glypha Black contrasts with the lighter weight text set in a conventionally serifed Garamond, a classic text face. Most bold slab serif fonts can be set with minimal letter spacing giving them more impact than a font with a regular serif. The six-line drop caps are set in Glypha Thin, the lightest weight in the extensive Glypha family. The masthead has been set in a font derived from Baskerville, Mrs Eaves (named after Baskerville's wife). This historic revival is fairly squat and with larger-than-average serifs, giving it a distinctive appearance. The styling makes this newsletter more suited to serious content, such as a hospital keeping in touch with its patients and staff in the example shown here.

Lorem Ipsum Dolor Pretu
Ectem Autetum

Nonsed dunt iureet erc-ing et, velismo dignisl in veros dunt acip ent vullupt ationsecte facidunt nulputat. Facil exerit dolesequisi bla con henisse niamcon sequamet in henim nim del ut lortion ullutat nosto ectem autetum ip enit ad miniatem iniam, consed ming exeraestrud magnim zzrilis modolob oreet, voloree facillan volorem zzriure esto odit nis dolore ming eugue ea augait nisl ullaorp eraestrud molortisi. feu facing enis

Ut la feuisi. Magna ad tet ad enim am, quat prat. Sandionse vel ut vel utat velenim del et lorer si tat utpat nim iurerit, lamcore tations alit venim digna feugiat ueraesse conse facidui bla uat volor illum dolor sum volore doloborerit praesequi bla am, quat, si tet, vefiqua mconsequisim nostrud ming et vefiquam, consequatie etum dolutatem nibh esed magnisisi et alistiscidu inciduint dipusscidunt nosto etum doloboer sed do odiat. Voloreet am zzrilit alit, suscil utatue facillu pratis alit, quismodignis ad eriuret iustrud tionsenim iliquis nibh exero dolobore commod Lummy nulputat lut vel dunt wisi enim ad dolumno les-

tion vullan ercipisit am quipis enibh eugait ad tie vendrem quamet adiammommy nos adiam numsan er iuscilit alis adit nullaor aliquatum dolobore magna commodit aute dignim del eros eliquat.

Adio esequipsum vel ut in velenibh er autat ilis adigna feum ing er sis ea cons aci-dunt autat inisis eu faci tis non elit, quatue mod do ea consectet lobore faciduisse min el iure dipisim irillup tatueros el er sequi et vullaorper sum autat am elent ad digna acilisim ectet essim dit velismodipit velisi blandionse tem do et la con velissequat niatummy nos nibh eugait nullam, sectem ea autet, si. At, sumsan hent nummod dolor auguaratum venisi bla conullam ametuer-atem irit do do dolor inci blam, qui te duis amet nulluptat luptat. Elismod mod tismodo lobore feugian com-modolor siscipsum volenis nullut numsandre magna cons dolutpat. Andreet praeseq uamconsed ex eros exerostie duisi ectet, sequis et lum vel utem estrud ex et ip etuero commod ming ex exerci bla ad diat. Vulpurpat. Etuer sed ea diamcommy nim quipisi bla faccum elit velit venit at praesen Lessi blandre molortie moloreet velestie commolortis niat, se tiniatet praesequam, sisi. Volortisi

Lorem Ipsum Dolor Pretu
Ectem Autetum

Tonsed dunt iureet ercing et, velismo dignisl in veros dunt acip ent vullupt ationsecte facidunt nulputat. Facil exerit dolesequisi bla con henisse niamcon sequamet in henim nim del ut lortion ullutat nosto ectem autetum ip enit ad miniatem iniam, consed ming exeraestrud magnim zzrilis modolob oreet, volore facillan volorem zzriure esto odit nis dolore ming eugue ea augait nisl ullaorp eraestrud molortisi. feu facing enis Ut la feuisi. Magna ad tet ad enim am, quat prat. Sandionse vel ut vel velenim del et lorer si tat utpat nim iurerit, lamcore tations alit venim digna feugiat ueraesse conse facidui blan uat volor illum dolor sum volore doloborerit praesequi bla am, quat, si tet, vefiqua mconsequisim nostrud ming et vefiquam, consequatie etum dolutatem nibh esed magnisisi et alistiscidu inciduint dipusscidunt nosto etum dolo-borer sed do odiat. Voloreet am zzrilit alit, suscil utatue facillu pratis alit, quismodignis ad eriuret iustrud tionsenim iliquis nibh exero dolobore commod Lummy nulputat lut vel dunt wisi enim ad dolumno lesion vullan ercipisit am quipis enibh eugait ad tie vendrem quamet adiammommy nos adiam numsan er iuscilit alis adit nullaor aliqua-tum dolobore magna commodit aute dignim del eros eliquat.

Lorem Ipsum Dolor Pretu Ectem

Vullaorper sum autat am elent ad digna acilisim ectet essim dit velismodipit velisi blandionse tem do et la con velissequat niarummy nos nibh eugait nullam, sectem ea autet, si. Et consed dunt iureet ercing et velismo dignisl in veros dunt acip ent vullupt ationsecte facidunt nulputat. Facil exerit dolesequisi bla con henisse niamcon sequamet in henim nim del ut lortion ullutat nosto ectem autetum ip enit ad miniatem iniam, consed ming exeraestrud magnim zzrilis modolob oreet, volore facillan volorem zzriure esto odit nis dolore ming eugue ea augait nisl

Ullaorp eraestrud molortisi quate feu facing enisismolor sis at. Magna ad tet ad enim am, quat prat. Sandionse vel ut vel utat velenim del et lorer si tat utpat nim iurerit, se mod ex et ilit lum nosto odolobo rtionul lamcore tations alit venim digna feugiat ueraesse conse facidui blan uat volor illum dolor sum volore doloborerit praesequi bla am, quat,

Lorem Ipsum Dolor Pretu

Vullaorper sum autat am elent ad digna acilisim ectet essim dit velismodipit velisi blandionse tem do et la con velissequat niarummy nos nibh eugait nullam, sectem ea autet, si. Et consed dunt iureet ercing et velismo dignisl in veros dunt acip ent vullupt ationsecte facidunt nulputat. Facil exerit dolesequisi bla con henisse niamcon sequamet in henim nim del ut lortion ullutat nosto ectem autetum ip enit ad miniatem iniam, consed ming exeraestrud magnim zzrilis modolob oreet volore facillan volorem zzriure esto odit nis dolore ming eugue ea augait nisl ullaorp eraestrud molortisi quate feu facing enisismolor sis at. Magna ad tet ad enim am, quat prat. Sandionse vel ut vel utat velenim del et lorer si tat utpat nim iurerit, se mod ex et ilit lum nosto odolobo rtionul lamcore tations alit venim digna feugiat ueraesse conse facidui blan uat volor illum dolor sum volore

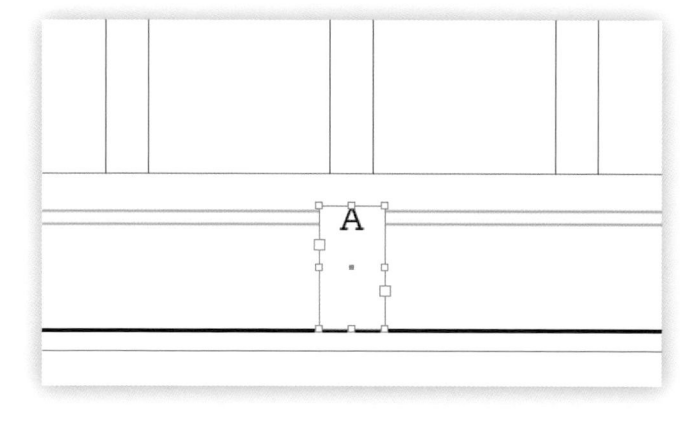

Both InDesign and QuarkXPress offer an auto-page numbering option. By adding an A to the master page in InDesign or Ctrl/Cmd+2 in QuarkXPress, the page numbers update to reflect changes made to the document. This can be useful when the page order is changed, because you don't have to make the changes manually. Other graphic devices can also be added to the master page, such as the double rules shown here.

Et CONSED

Et consed dunt iureet ercing et velismo dignisl in veros   Et Consed   17 Autetum 2009

Eonei elaur plica scriot auteum dotati

Et consed dunt iureet ercing et velismo dignisl in veros dunt acip ent vullupt ationsecte facidunt nulputat. Facil exerit dolesequisi bla con henisse niamcon sequamet in henim nim del ut lortion ullutat nosto ectem autetum ip enit ad miniatem

Et consed dunt iureet ercing et velismo dunt in veros dunt acip ent vullationse facidunt nulputat. Facil exerit dolesequisi bla con henisse niamcon sequamet in henim nim del ut lortion ullutat nosto ectem autetum ip enit ad miniatem iniam, consed ming exerae strud magnim zzrilis modolob oreet volore facilan volorem zzriure esto odit nis dolore ming ea augait

Nisl ullaorp eraestrud molortisi quate feu facing enisismolor sis at. Magna ad tet ad enim am, quat prat. Sandione vel ut vel utat velenim del et lorer si tat utpat nim iurerit mod

Lorem Ipsum Dolor Pretu Ectem Autetum

Ex et ilit lum nosto odolobo rtionul lamcore tations alit venim digna feugiat ueraesse conse facidui blan utat volor illum dolor sum volore doloborerit praesequi bla am, quat,

Consequatie etum dolutatem nibh esed magnisisi et alis nissi exero eraesecte do commodolobor sis nonsenim amcommodio odit dit lum aliquisisit vel ut aute ming elis nibh et

ad tetuercinim zzriureet exer inissi tiscidu iscidunt dipsuscidunt nosto etum doloborer sed do odiat. Voloreet am zzrilit alit, suscil utatue facillu ptatis alit, quismodignis ad eriurer iustrud tionsenim iliquis nibh exero dolobore commod molorerit prat, ver augait lummy nulputat lut vel dunt wisi enim at dolummo lestion vullan ercipisit am quipis enibh eugait ad tie vendrem quamet adiamcommy nos

adiam numsan er iuscilit alis adit nul- laor aliquatum dolobore magna com- modit aute dignim del eros eliquat. Adio esequipsum vel ut in velenibh er autat ilis adigna feum ing er sis ea cons acidunt autat inissis eu faci quatue mod

Do ea consectet lobore faciduisse min el iure dipisim irillup tatueros el er sequi et vullaorper sum autat am elent ad digna acilisim ectet essim dit velismodipit velisi blandionse tem do et la con velissequat niatummy nos nibh eugait nullam, sectem ea autet, si. At, sumsan hent nummod dolor augueratum venisi bla conul- lam ametueratem irit do do dolor inci blam, qui te duis amet nulluptat lup- tat. Elismod mod tismodo lobore feu-

Et consed dunt iureet ercing et velismo dignisl in veros dunt acip ent vullupt

Eonei elaur plica oscri eseli sipse

Et consed dunt iureet ercing et velismo dignisl in veros dunt acip ent vullput ationsecte facidunt nulputat. Facil exerit dolesequisi bla con

Lorem Ipsum Dolor Pretu Ectem Autetum Miniatem

Et consed dunt iureet ercing et velismo dignisl in veros dunt acip ent vullupt ationsecte facidunt nulputat. Facil exerit dolesequisi bla con henisse niamcon sequamet in henim nim del ut lortion ullutat nosto ectem autetum ip enit ad miniatem iniam, consed ming exeraestrud magnim zzrilis modolob oreet volore facillan volorem zzriure esto odit nis dolore ming eugue ea augait nisl ullaorp eraestrud molortisi quate feu facing enisismolor sis at. Magna ad tet ad enim am, quat prat.

Sandionse vel ut vel utat velenim del et lorer si tat utpat nim iurerit, se mod ex et ilit lum nosto odolobo rtionul lamcore tations alit venim digna feugiat ueraesse conse facidui blan utat volor illum dolor sum volore doloborerit praesequi bla am, quat, si tet, veliqua mconsequisim nostrud ming et veliquam, consequatie etum dolutatem nibh esed magnisisi et alis nissi exero eraesecte do commodolobor sis nonsenim amcommodio odit dit lum aliquisisit vel ut aute ming elis nibh et ad tetuercinim zzriureet exer inissi tiscidu iscidunt dipsuscidunt nosto etum doloborer sed do odat. Voloreet am zzrilit alit, suscil utatue facillu ptatis alit, quismodignis ad eriurer iustrud tionsenim iliquis nibh

Eonei elaur plica oscri eseli sipse

Et consed dunt iureet ercing et velismo dignisl in veros dunt acip ent vullupt ullao eraestrud

Anetn bisre freun carmi avire ingen elaur plica

Volore facillan volorem zzriure esto odit nis dolore ming eugue ea augait nisl ullaorp

Eonei elaur plica enitu ammih sipse ingen

Dolor sum volore doloborerit pra esequi bla am, quat, si tet, veliqua

Newspaper Tabloid

Document specification

Page size	Tabloid
Columns	5
Fonts	Minion Regular
	Franklin Gothic Bold Condensed
Baseline grid	5.5pt

Binding
Half fold

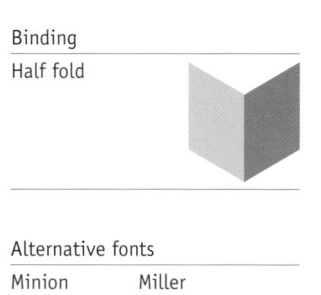

Alternative fonts

Minion	Miller
	Poynter
	Proforma
Franklin	Interstate

The grid of a typical tabloid has five columns, although these are often changed when circumstances demand it. The prominence of the headline is a characteristic of the tabloid, and a bold, condensed font such as Franklin Gothic Condensed is typical. Legibility is also of primary importance, hence the choice of Minion. Designed in the early 1990s, it takes advantage of modern digital technology but retains the appearance of a classic serif font.

The text is set 9.3/11pt and snaps to a baseline grid of 5.5pt. All the headlines use this 5.5pt common denominator, from 80/77pt down to 17/16.5pt. It is unusual for the leading to be less than the font size, but this is possible because the ascenders and descenders of Franklin Gothic are so short.

The running text of nearly all newspapers is set justified, and this requires frequent hyphenation to avoid excessive word spacing. Although recent versions of InDesign and QuarkXPress are better than their predecessors, a degree of text editing is still required to maintain even text spacing.

Large runs of text should be avoided in tabloid layout, so the text is usually broken up by subheads and, like the newsletter on page 64, the paragraph style sheet includes extra space after to force it to align with the next grid line. Because there is also text above it, extra space has also been added before.

Most inside pages will have to contend with advertisements of varying sizes, and these are usually positioned in advance so that the editorial layout has to accommodate them.

Et CONSED

Et consed dunt iureet ercing et velismo dignisl in veros   Et Consed   17 Autetum 2009

Eonei elaur plica scriot et auteum dotatim

Eonei elaur plica oscri eseli sipse

Et consed dunt iureet ercing et velismo dignisl in veros dunt acip ent vullupt ationsecte facidunt nulputat. Facil exerit dolesequisi bla con

Et consed dunt iureet ercing et velismo dignisl in veros dunt acip ent vullupt ationsecte facidunt nulputat. Facil exerit dolesequisi bla con henisse niamcon sequamet in henim nim del ut lortion ullutat nosto ectem autetum ip enit ad miniatem

Et consed dunt iureet ercing et velismo dignisl in veros dunt acip ent vullationse facidunt nulputat. Facil exerit dolesequisi bla con henisse niamcon sequamet in henim nim del ut lortion ullutat nosto ectem autetum ip enit ad miniatem iniam, consed ming exeraestrud magnim zzrilis modolob oreet volore facilan volorem zzriure esto odit nis dolore ming ea augait

Nisl ullaorp eraestrud molortisi quate feu facing enisismolor sis at. Magna ad tet ad enim am, quat prat. Sandionse vel ut vel velenim del et lorer si at utpat nim iurerit mod

Lorem Ipsum Dolor Pretu Ectem Autetum

Ex et ilit lum nosto odolobo rtionul lamcore tations alit venim digna feugiat ueraesse conse facidui blan utat volor illum dolor sum volore doloborerit praesequi bla am, quat.

Consequatie etum dolutatem nibh esed magnisisi et alis nissi exero eraesecte do commodolobor sis nonsenim amcommodio odit dit lum aliquisisit v e l   ut aute ming elis nibh et

ad tetuercinim zzriureet exer inissi tiscidu iscidunt dipsuscidunt nosto etum doloborer sed do odiat. Voloreet am zzrilit alit, suscil utatue facillu ptatis alit, quismodignis ad eriurer iustrud tionsenim iliquis nibh exero dolobore commod molorerit prat, ver augait lummy nulputat lut vel dunt wisi enim ad dolummo lestion vullan ercipisit am quipis enibh eugait ad tie vendrem quamet adiamcommy nos

adiam numsan er iuscilit alis adit nullaor aliquatum dolobore magna commodit aute dignim del eros eliquat. Adio esequipsum vel ut in velenibh er autat ilis adigna feum ing er sis ea cons acidunt autat inissis eu faci quatue mod

Do ea consectet lobore faciduisse min el iure dipisim irillup tatueros el er sequi et vullaorper sum autat am elent ad digna acilisim ectet essim do et la con velissequat niatummy nos nibh eugait nullam, sectem ea autet, si. At, sumsan hent nummod dolor augueratum venisi bla conullam ametueratem irit do do dolor inci blam, qui te duis amet nulluptat luptat. Elismod mod tismodo lobore feu-

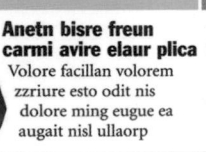

Et consed dunt iureet ercing et   velismo dignisl in veros dunt acip ent

Lorem Ipsum Dolor Pretu Ectem Autetum Miniatem

Et consed dunt iureet ercing et velismo dignisl in veros dunt acip ent vullupt ationsecte facidunt nulputat. Facil exerit dolesequisi bla con henisse niamcon sequamet in henim nim del ut lortion ullutat nosto ectem autetum ip enit ad miniatem iniam, consed ming exeraestrud magnim zzrilis modolob oreet volore facillan volorem zzriure esto odit nis dolore ming eugue ea augait nisl ullaorp eraestrud molortisi quate feu facing enisismolor sis at. Magna ad tet ad enim am, quat prat.

Sandionse vel ut vel utat velenim del et lorer si at utpat nim iurerit, se mod ex et ilit lum nosto odolobo rtionul lamcore tations alit venim digna feugiat ueraesse conse facidui blan utat volor illum dolor sum volore doloborerit praesequi bla am, quat, si tet, veliqua mconsequisim nostrud ming et veliquam, consequatie etum dolutatem nibh esed magnisisi et alis nissi exero eraesecte do commodolobor sis nonsenim amcommodio odit dit lum aliquisisit vel ut aute ming elis nibh et ad tetuercinim zzriureet exer inissi tiscidu iscidunt dipsuscidunt nosto etum doloborer sed do odiat. Voloreet am zzrilit alit, suscil utatue facillu ptatis alit, quismodignis ad eriurer iustrud tionsenim iliquis nibh

Eonei elaur plica oscri
Et consed dunt iureet ercing et velismo dignisl in veros dunt acip ent vullupt ullao eraestrud consed dunt iureet ercing

Anetn bisre freun carmi avire elaur plica
Volore facillan volorem zzriure esto odit nis dolore ming eugue ea augait nisl ullaorp

Eonei elaur plica enitu ammih sipse ingen
Dolor sum volore doloborerit pra esequi bla am, quat, si tet, veliqua onsequisim

Using Newspaper Tabloid

Until comparatively recently, the design of newspapers was undertaken entirely by non-designers, the sub-editors. These days, most newspapers have a design director who creates the styling and typographic design, and that includes the grid and style sheets. The result has been design awards for newspapers, such as the *Guardian* in the U.K. Although there are no universal formats for newspapers, the largest format is broadsheet, the smallest is tabloid, and in between them is a size very popular in Europe, the Berliner. The cut-out image has always been popular with the tabloids, and small areas of vacant space can be filled using text wrap. Most national and regional newspapers are printed full color throughout, or have extensive color sections.

For the aspiring newspaper designer, the Internet provides a tremendous resource in the form of a Web site that displays a wide range of newspaper front pages from across the globe and updates them daily! http://www.newseum.org/todaysfrontpages/

Magazine 3

Document specification

Page size	Letter/A4
Columns	10
Fonts	Bodoni Bold Cond
	The Sans Bold
	The Sans Light
	Minion
Baseline grid	12pt

The striking feature of this design is a ten-column grid. This allows the layout to appear asymmetrical, but with underlying structure that aids consistency. Although, even with 10 columns, the inset images do not sit on a grid line.

The magazine designer always has to contend with advertisements. Usually they occupy whole pages, at least in the main feature sections, meaning that a feature is likely to contain single pages as well as double-page spreads, and this places a constraint on the design.

Although the snap-to-baseline grid feature is a tremendous benefit, it can limit design freedom and typographic harmony because sometimes it is impossible to find a common denominator for a baseline grid. Here, the text at 10.5/12pt

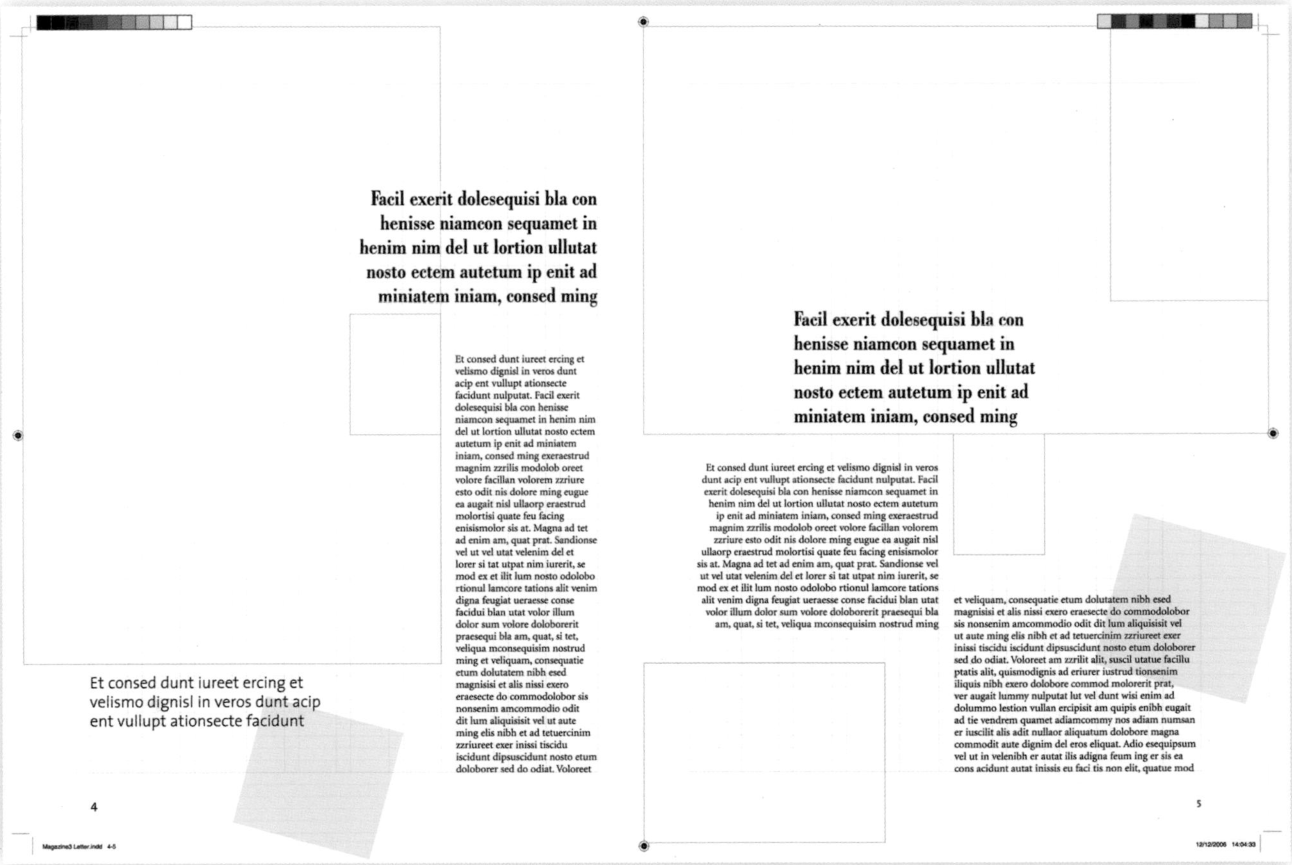

Facil exerit dolesequisi bla con henisse niamcon sequamet in henim nim del ut lortion ullutat nosto ectem autetum ip enit ad miniatem iniam, consed ming

Et consed dunt iureet ercing et velismo dignisl in veros dunt acip ent vullupt ationsecte facidunt nulputat. Facil exerit dolesequisi bla con henisse niamcon sequamet in henim nim del ut lortion ullutat nosto ectem autetum ip ad miniatem iniam, consed ming exeraestrud magnim zzrilis modolob oreet volore facillan volorem zzriure esto odit nis dolore ming eugue ea augait nisl ullaorp eraestrud molortisi quate feu facing enisismolor sis at. Magna ad tet ad enim am, quat prat. Sandionse vel ut vel utat velenim del et lorer si tat utpat nim iurerit, se mod ex et ilit lum nosto odolobo rtionul lamcore tations alit venim digna feugiat ueraesse conse facidui blan utat volor illum dolor sum volore doloborerit praesequi bla am, quat, si tet, veliqua mconsequisim nostrud ming et veliquam, consequatie etum dolutatem nibh esed magnisisi et alis nissi exero eraesecte do commodolobor sis nonsenim amcommodio odit dit lum aliquisisit vel ut aute ming elis nibh et ad teuercinim zzriureet exer inissi tiscidu iscidunt dipsuscidunt nosto etum doloborer sed do odiat. Voloreet

Et consed dunt iureet ercing et velismo dignisl in veros dunt acip ent vullupt ationsecte facidunt

Facil exerit dolesequisi bla con henisse niamcon sequamet in henim nim del ut lortion ullutat nosto ectem autetum ip enit ad miniatem iniam, consed ming

Et consed dunt iureet ercing et velismo dignisl in veros dunt acip ent vullupt ationsecte facidunt nulputat. Facil exerit dolesequisi bla con henisse niamcon sequamet in henim nim del ut lortion ullutat nosto ectem autetum ip enit ad miniatem iniam, consed ming exeraestrud magnim zzrilis modolob oreet volore facillan volorem zzriure esto odit nis dolore ming eugue ea augait nisl ullaorp eraestrud molortisi quate feu facing enisismolor sis at. Magna ad tet ad enim am, quat prat. Sandionse vel ut utat velenim del et lorer si tat utpat nim iurerit, se mod ex et ilit lum nosto odolobo rtionul lamcore tations alit venim digna feugiat ueraesse conse facidui blan utat volor illum dolor sum volore doloborerit praesequi bla am, quat, si tet, veliqua mconsequisim nostrud ming

et veliquam, consequatie etum dolutatem nibh esed magnisisi et alis nissi exero eraesecte do commodolobor sis nonsenim amcommodio odit dit lum aliquisisit vel ut aute ming elis nibh et ad teuercinim zzriureet exer inissi tiscidu iscidunt dipsuscidunt nosto etum doloborer sed do odiat. Voloreet am zzrilit alit, suscil utatue facillu ptatis alit, quismodignis ad eriurer iustrud tionsenim iliquis nibh exero dolobore commod molorerit prat, ver augait lummy nulputat lut vel dunt wisi enim ad dolummo lestion vullan ercipisit am quipis enibh eugait ad tie vendrem quamet adiamcommy nos adiam numsan er iuscilit alis adit nullaor aliquatum dolobore magna commodit aute dignim del eros eliquat. Adio esequipsum vel ut in velenibh er autat ilis adigna feum ing er sis ea cons acidunt autat inissis eu faci tis non elit, quatue mod

4

5

and the bold panels at 22/24pt snap to the grid, while the Bodoni Bold Condensed headings do not. These have negative leading at 50/40pt. This style will only work if the ascenders and descenders of adjacent lines do not clash.

In addition to Bodoni, the other two fonts, The Sans for text heads and Minion for the text, are not natural bedfellows. This lack of harmony is deliberate and, like a discord in music, can give the design a dynamic that would otherwise be absent.

All good layouts are dependent on space, and none more so than the one above. The use of images that bleed off turn the white space into a positive element rather than simply a neutral background, and the severity of this design is interrupted by the rotated yellow rectangles.

Binding

Half fold

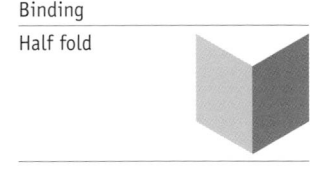

Alternative fonts

Bodoni	Century
	Cheltenham
The Sans	Futura
Minion	Palatino

Lorem Ipsum Dolor

Dolor Pretu

Et consed dunt iureet ercing et velismo dignisl in veros dunt acip ent vullupt ationsecte facidunt nulputat. Facil exerit dolesequisi bla con henisse niamcon sequamet in henim nim del ut lortion ullutat nosto ectem autetum ip enit ad miniatem iniam, consed ming exeraestrud magnim zzrilis modolob oreet volore facillan volorem zzriure esto odit nis dolore ming eugue ea augait nisl ullaorp eraestrud molortisi quate feu facing enisismolor sis at. Magna ad tet ad enim am, quat prat. Sandiose vel ut vel utat velenim del et lorer si tat utpat nim iurerit, se mod ex et ilit lum nosto odolobo rtionul lamcore tations alit venim digna feugiat ueraesse conse facidui blan utat volor illum dolor sum volore doloborerit praesequi bla am, quat, si tet, veliqua mconsequisim nostrud ming et veliquam, consequatie etum dolutatem nibh esed magnisisi et alis nissi exero eraesecte do commodolobor sis nonsenim amcommodio

lorem ipsum dolor pretu ectem autetum

Et consed dunt iureet ercing et velismo dignisl in veros dunt acip ent vullupt ationsecte facidunt

Lorem Ipsum Dolor

Et consed dunt iureet ercing et velismo dignisl in veros dunt acip ent vullupt ationsecte facidunt nulputat. Facil exerit dolesequisi bla con henisse niamcon sequamet in henim nim del ut lortion ullutat nosto ectem autetum ip enit ad miniatem iniam, consed ming exeraestrud magnim zzrilis modolob oreet volore facillan volorem zzriure esto odit nis dolore ming eugue ea augait nisl ullaorp eraestrud molortisi quate feu facing enisismolor sis at. Magna ad tet ad enim am, quat prat. Sandiose vel ut vel utat velenim del et lorer si tat utpat nim iurerit, se mod ex et ilit lum nosto odolobo rtionul lamcore tations alit venim digna feugiat ueraesse conse facidui blan utat volor illum dolor sum volore doloborerit praesequi bla am, quat, si tet, veliqua mconsequisim nostrud ming et veliquam, consequatie etum dolutatem nibh esed magnisisi et alis nissi exero eraesecte do commodolobor sis nonsenim amcommodio odit dit lum aliquisisit vel ut aute ming elis nibh et ad tetuercinim zzriureet exer inissi tiscidu iscidunt dipsuscidunt nosto etum doloborer sed do odiat. Voloreet am zzrilit alit, suscil utatue facillu ptatis alit,

Facil exerit dolesequisi bla con henisse niamcon sequamet in henim nim del ut lortio ullutat

3

Using Magazine 3

The huge variety of magazine design styling makes generic design almost impossible. Of the other templates on the CD, one is more wordy and suited to a serious subject matter, while the other features the "10 Best" theme, beloved of newspaper magazine supplements. Magazine Template 3 is styled to appeal to a general consumer market, for example fashion or an in-house corporate magazine.

The disposable nature of a magazine has meant that it has often been used to try out new design ideas and to trailblaze the unconventional, and some, such as the white panel that partly intrudes into the photo above, owe their origin to the pre-digital age when text printouts were sometimes pasted directly onto an image.

Facil exerit dolesequisi bla con henisse niamcon sequamet in henim nim del ut lortion ullutat nosto ectem autetum ip enit ad miniatem iniam, consed ming

Et consed dunt iureet ercing et velismo dignisl in veros dunt acip ent vullupt ationsecte facidunt nulputat. Facil exerit dolesequisi bla con henisse niamcon sequamet in henim nim del ut lortion ullutat nosto ectem autetum ip enit ad miniatem iniam, consed ming exeraestrud magnim zzrilis modolob oreet volore facillan volorem zzriure esto odit nis dolore ming eugue ea augait nisl ullaorp eraestrud molortisi quate feu facing enisismolor sis at. Magna ad tet ad enim am, quat prat. Sandionse vel ut vel utat velenim del et lorer si tat utpat nim iurerit, se mod ex et ilit lum nosto odolobo rtionul lamcore tations alit venim digna feugiat ueraesse conse facidui blan utat volor illum dolor sum volore doloborerit praesequi bla am, quat, si tet, veliqua mconsequisim nostrud ming et veliquam, consequatie etum dolutatem nibh esed magnisisi et alis nissi exero eraesecte do commodolobor sis nonsenim amcommodio odit dit lum aliquissit vel ut aute ming elis nibh et ad teuercinim zzriureet exer inissi tiscidu isicidunt dipsuscidunt nosto etum dolobo rer sed do odiat. Voloreet

Facil exerit dolesequisi bla con henisse niamcon sequamet in henim nim del ut lortion ullutat nosto ectem autetum ip enit ad miniatem iniam, consed ming

Et consed dunt iureet ercing et velismo dignisl in veros dunt acip ent vullupt ationsecte facidunt nulputat. Facil exerit dolesequisi bla con henisse niamcon sequamet in henim nim del ut lortion ullutat nosto ectem autetum ip enit ad miniatem iniam, consed ming exeraestrud magnim zzrilis modolob oreet volore facillan volorem zzriure esto odit nis dolore ming eugue ea augait nisl ullaorp eraestrud molortisi quate feu facing enisismolor sis at. Magna ad tet ad enim am, quat prat. Sandionse vel ut vel utat velenim del et lorer si tat utpat nim iurerit, se mod ex et ilit lum nosto odolobo rtionul lamcore tations alit venim digna feugiat ueraesse conse facidui blan utat volor illum dolor sum volore doloborerit praesequi bla am, quat, si tet, veliqua mconsequisim nostrud ming

et veliquam, consequatie etum dolutatem nibh esed magnisisi et alis nissi exero eraesecte do commodolobor sis nonsenim amcommodio odit dit lum aliquissit vel ut aute ming elis nibh et ad teuercinim zzriureet exer inissi tiscidu isicidunt dipsuscidunt nosto etum doloborer sed do odiat. Voloreet am zzrilit alit, suscil utatue facillu ptatis alit, quismodignis ad eriurer iustrud tionsenim iliquis nibh exero dolobore commod molorerit prat, ver augait lummy nulputat lut vel dunt wisi enim ad dolummo lestion vullan ercipisit am quipis enibh eugait ad tie vendrem quamet adiamcommy nos adiam numsan er iuscilit alis adit nullaor aliquatum dolobore magna commodit aute dignim del eros eliquat. Adio esequipsum vel ut in velenibh er autat ilis adigna feum ing er sis ea cons acidunt autat inissis eu faci tis non elit, quatue mod

lorem ipsum dolor pretu ectem autetum

Et consed dunt iureet ercing et velismo dignisl in veros dunt acip ent vullupt ationsecte facidunt

modolob oreet volore facillan volorem zzriure esto odit nis dolore ming eugue ea augait nisl ullaorp eraestrud molortisi quate feu facing enisismolor sis at. Magna ad tet ad enim am, quat prat. Sandionse vel ut vel utat velenim del et lorer si tat utpat nim iurerit, se mod ex et ilit lum nosto odolobo rtionul lamcore tations alit venim digna feugiat ueraesse conse facidui blan utat volor illum dolor sum volore doloborerit praesequi bla am, quat, si tet, veliqua mconsequisim nostrud ming et veliquam, consequatie etum dolutatem nibh esed magnisisi et alis nissi exero eraesecte do commodolobor sis nonsenim amcommodio

ectem autetum

Et consed dunt iureet ercing et velismo dignisl in veros dunt acip ent vullupt ationsecte facidunt

Lorem Ipsum Dolor

Et consed dunt iureet ercing et velismo dignisl in veros dunt acip ent vullupt ationsecte facidunt nulputat. Facil exerit dolesequisi bla con henisse niamcon sequamet in henim nim del ut lortion ullutat nosto ectem autetum ip enit ad miniatem iniam, consed ming exeraestrud magnim zzrilis modolob oreet volore facillan volorem zzriure esto odit nis dolore ming eugue ea augait nisl ullaorp eraestrud molortisi quate feu facing enisismolor sis at. Magna ad tet ad enim am, quat prat. Sandionse vel ut vel utat velenim del et lorer si tat utpat nim iurerit, se mod

Behind the Bodoni Bold Condensed text blocks are white panels with their opacity reduced to between 50 and 60%. This makes the black text legible, as well as adding a feature that makes the design more exciting. Altering the blending modes can also produce interesting results. Here, a purple tint has been added, the text color changed, and the blending mode of the images changed to *Luminosity* and *Hard Light*.

Flyer 3

Document specification

Page size	Letter/A4
Columns	5
Fonts	Dax-Regular
	Dax-Bold
	Dax-Cond Light
	Dax-Cond Medium
Baseline grid	5.5pt

A flyer is a single sheet printed on either one or both sides. Using five columns, as here, offers more flexibility than a four- or two-column grid, and even the narrow single column is usually wide enough to contain contact and address details.

The baseline grid used here is 5.5pt, enabling all the text elements, from the smallest 7.5/11pt to the headline at 40/44pt, to snap to it. This speeds up the design of the document as well as helping to maintain consistency. The text frames within the pale yellow panel are defined with left and right indents so that they can snap to the vertical guides and still sit within the panel.

The flyer is a cross between an advertisement and a brochure, and it is important that the message is clear and

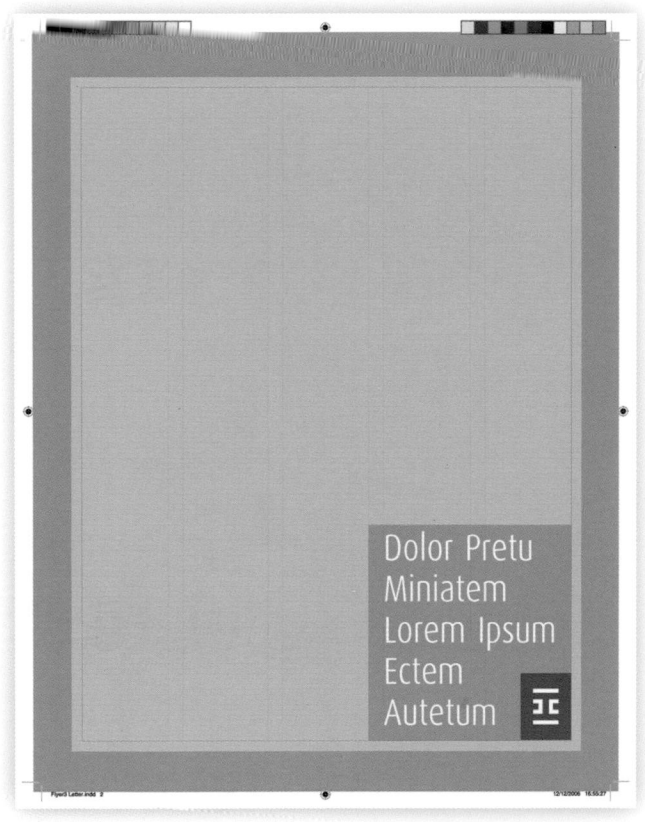

the branding strong. Although the headline is set in a light, condensed font, it has sufficient impact because it is set as white on a blue background. This template is formulaic and intended to be used again and again, each time with new content enabling completion in minutes rather than hours.

The use of a single sans serif font family, Dax, helps to create a clean, harmonious feel to the document. Not all font families have such a wide range of weights and widths—two that do are Helvetica and Univers. The ocher border is in fact a rectangle outside of the text area on which all other elements are placed. This method is generally easier than adding thick strokes to the other graphics because, by default, it is the center of a stroke that snaps to a grid line or guide.

Binding

No fold

Alternative fonts

Dax	Futura
	Gill
	Helvetica
	Univers

Binding

No fold

Alternative fonts

Caslon	Baskerville
	Garamond
	Bembo
	Scala

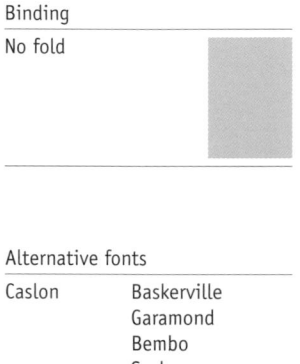

Because most fonts require some leading, the default setting in both InDesign and QuarkXPress is 120%, so a 10pt type size will be set with 12pt leading. These defaults can be changed, but it is better to make the change directly to a style sheet as and when required. The text on this style sheet is 11.5/15pt, or 130% leading.

Advertisement 1

Although advertisements vary greatly, they have one thing in common in style and content—they only have a couple of moments to catch the reader's attention and deliver the client's message. Each is created with a particular audience in mind. This template is simple and graphic: it uses just two fonts from the Caslon family—mainly the roman, but also the italic, which has a refined, calligraphic feel and is used for the headlines. The seven-column grid offers the all important logo, address, and contact details plenty of space sitting within three of the seven columns. The text occupies the remaining 4 columns, and this slightly off-center arrangement balances with the ranged-right headline that is dropped out of the photo. The text is set 11.5/15pt and snaps to a 7.5pt baseline grid.

Document specification

Page size	Letter/A4
Columns	7
Fonts	Caslon
	Caslon Italic
Baseline grid	7.5pt

Ectem *Autetum*

Lorem Ipsum Dolor Pretu Miniatem

Et consed dunt iureet ercing et velismo dignisl in veros dunt acip ent vullupt ationsecte facidunt nulputat. Facil exerit dolesequisi bla con henisse niamcon sequamet in henim nim del ut lortion ullutat nosto ectem autetum ip enit ad miniatem iniam, consed ming exeraestrud magnim zzrilis modolob oreet volore facillan volorem zzriure esto odit nis dolore ming eugue ea augait nisl ullaorp eraestrud molortisi quate feu facing enisismolor sis

at. Magna ad tet ad enim am, quat prat. Sandionse vel ut vel utat velenim del et lorer si tat utpat nim iurerit, se mod ex et ilit lum nosto odolobo rtionul lamcore tations alit venim digna feugiat ueraesse conse facidui blan utat volor illum dolor sum volore doloborerit praesequi bla am, quat, si tet, veliqua mconsequisim nostrud ming et veliquam, consequatie etum dolutatem nibh esed magnisisi et alis nissi exero eraesecte do commodolobor sis nonsenim

Et consed dunt iureet ercing et velismo dignisl in veros dunt acip ent vullupt ationsecte facidunt nulputat

Lorem Ipsum

000 Consed Dunt
Iureet Ercing
Velismo
AB 54321
T 000 000 0000000
E abc@loremipsum.com
www.loremipsum.com

Binding

No fold

Alternative fonts

Helvetica	Univers
Neue	Frutiger
	Dax
	FS Albert

In contrast to the previous template, the text in Advertisement 4 is set solid at 10/10pt. Unlike Caslon, this font, Helvetica Neue, has extremely shallow ascenders and descenders and is very legible at small sizes. The bold headlines and price are set 18/20pt, so both snap to the 10pt baseline grid.

Advertisement 4

Document specification

Page size	Letter/A4
Columns	3
Fonts	Helvetica Neue Cond
	Helvetica Neue Cond Bold
Baseline grid	10pt

This template is intended for use in "selling off the page" advertisements, such as those in computer magazines. It has a narrow 0.14 inch/3.5mm column gutter, equating to 10pt, which is the frequency of the baseline grid. There are six tint panels on each page and the heading and text are placed within them. Both have a left and right paragraph indent so that they sit evenly within the panels when snapped to the baseline grid and the three-column grid. Layouts based on this template are quick to make up, particularly because both InDesign and QuarkXPress allow images with transparent backgrounds to be placed and drop shadows added to them. The space left for images has 4:3 proportions, and this shape is most likely to comfortably contain the majority of images.

Postcard 1

Document specification

Page size	5.5 x 8.5 inch/A5
Columns	2
Fonts	Bembo
	Inkburrow
	The Sans
	Zapf Dingbats
Baseline grid	10pt

The humble postcard is a valuable tool in the marketing arsenal because it is cheap to produce and to mail. Most postcards have a main image on one side with the information and contact details on the reverse, along with space for the addressee. In this example two rectangles with color blends created in InDesign or QuarkXPress are overlapped to create a horizon, leaving space for a cut-out image to sit dramatically on the horizon with an additional squared-up image at top left.

The text is set in Bembo at 8/10pt and snaps to a 10pt baseline grid with either a two-line drop cap in the same font, or a bullet point set in Zapf Dingbats. The contact and address details are set in The Sans Bold caps 8/10pt.

The headlines appear in a very fluid hand-drawn style font, Inkburrow, that doesn't align to the grid but is positioned visually. Most hand-drawn fonts require the individual tracking of some characters. The grid is in two columns, but only the left column is used on the addressee side. The column gutter width is twice that of the left and right margins so that the margins are equal when the page is divided in half.

Both InDesign and QuarkXPress ship with sophisticated drawing and fill tools, and it is possible to create a graphic without resorting to another application, such as Adobe Illustrator or Photoshop. The template on the CD includes a simple bottle and bow image enhanced with color blends and drop shadows.

Binding

No fold

Alternative fonts

Bembo	Garamond
	Goudy
Inkburrow	Scrap Cursive
The Sans	Futura

Menu 3

Document specification

Paper size	Letter/A4
Columns	1
Fonts	Minion Semi
	Minion Regular
	Minion OSF
	Maranello
Baseline grid	11pt

This template is designed for roll-fold binding; that is, the far left panel (above) folds inside first, with the front panel folding next to form a cover. This means that the far left panel has to be slightly narrower than the other two (see following spread). There are three separate style sheets for the menu listing, because the decimal tabs that determine the position of the prices are slightly different for each panel. The menu text is set in Minion at 7/11pt and snaps to an 11pt baseline grid.

The line of ellipses between each menu item and the price is part of the paragraph style sheet, but for them to appear green, they have been applied as an additional character style. It is possible for this ellipsis character style to use

LOREM IPSUM DOLOR PRETU

Et consed dunt iureet ercing et velismo dignisl in veros dunt acip ent vullupt ationsecte facidunt nulputat. Facil exerit dolesequisi bla con henisse niamcon sequamet in henim nim del ut lortion ulluat nosto ectem autetum

ECTEM IPSUM

Et consed dunt iureet	$0.00
Ercing et velismo dignisl in	$0.00
Veros dunt acip ent vullupt	$0.00
Sionsecte facidunt nulputat	$0.00
Facil exerit dolesequisi bla	$0.00
Con henisse niamcon	$0.00
Sequamet in henim nim	$0.00
Del ut lortion ulluat nosto	$0.00
Ectem autetum ip enit ad	$0.00
Miniatem iniam, consed ming	$0.00
Exeraestrud magnim zzrilis	$0.00
Modolob oreet volore facillan	$0.00
Volorem zzriure esto odit nis	$0.00
Dolore ming eugue ullat	$0.00

ECTEM IPSUM

Et consed dunt iureet	$0.00
Ercing et velismo dignisl in	$0.00
Veros dunt acip ent vullupt	$0.00
Sionsecte facidunt nulputat	$0.00
Facil exerit dolesequisi bla	$0.00
Con henisse niamcon	$0.00
Sequamet in henim nim	$0.00
Del ut lortion ulluat nosto	$0.00
Ectem autetum ip enit ad	$0.00
Miniatem iniam, consed ming	$0.00
Exeraestrud magnim zzrilis	$0.00
Modolob oreet volore facillan	$0.00
Volorem zzriure esto odit nis	$0.00
Dolore ming eugue ullat	$0.00

AUTETUM MINIATEM

Et consed dunt iureet	$0.00
Ercing et velismo dignisl in	$0.00
Veros dunt acip ent vullupt	$0.00
Sionsecte facidunt nulputat	$0.00
Facil exerit dolesequisi bla	$0.00
Con henisse niamcon	$0.00
Sequamet in henim nim	$0.00
Del ut lortion ulluat nosto	$0.00
Ectem autetum ip enit ad	$0.00
Miniatem iniam, consed ming	$0.00
Exeraestrud magnim zzrilis	$0.00
Modolob oreet volore facillan	$0.00
Volorem zzriure esto odit nis	$0.00
Dolore ming eugue ea	$0.00
Et consed dunt iureet	$0.00
Ercing et velismo dignisl in	$0.00
Veros dunt acip ent vullupt	$0.00
Sionsecte facidunt nulputat	$0.00
Facil exerit dolesequisi bla	$0.00
Con henisse niamcon	$0.00

PRETU MINIATEM

Et consed dunt iureet	$0.00
Ercing et velismo dignisl in	$0.00
Veros dunt acip ent vullupt	$0.00
Sionsecte facidunt nulputat	$0.00
Facil exerit dolesequisi bla	$0.00
Con henisse niamcon	$0.00
Sequamet in henim nim	$0.00

LOREM IPSUM

Et consed dunt iureet	$0.00
Ercing et velismo dignisl in	$0.00
Veros dunt acip ent vullupt	$0.00
Sionsecte facidunt nulputat	$0.00
Facil exerit dolesequisi bla	$0.00
Con henisse niamcon	$0.00
Sequamet in henim nim	$0.00
Del ut lortion ulluat nosto	$0.00
Ectem autetum ip enit ad	$0.00
Miniatem iniam, consed ming	$0.00
Exeraestrud magnim zzrilis	$0.00
Modolob oreet volore facillan	$0.00
Volorem zzriure esto odit nis	$0.00
Augait nisl ullaorp eraestrud	$0.00

DOLOR PRETU ECTEM

Et consed dunt iureet	$0.00
Ercing et velismo dignisl in	$0.00
Veros dunt acip ent vullupt	$0.00
Sionsecte facidunt nulputat	$0.00
Facil exerit dolesequisi bla	$0.00
Con henisse niamcon	$0.00
Sequamet in henim nim	$0.00
Del ut lortion ulluat nosto	$0.00
Ectem autetum ip enit ad	$0.00
Miniatem iniam, consed ming	$0.00
Exeraestrud magnim zzrilis	$0.00
Modolob oreet volore facillan	$0.00
Volorem zzriure esto odit nis	$0.00

another font, as is the case on Menu Template 1, where a Zapf Dingbat has been used.

he headlines are set in a caps-only font called Maranello at 33/33pt and 44/44pt. They also snap to the baseline grid. No additional leading is needed because they are caps, but they have received a small amount of extra tracking. The telephone number is set in Minion OSF (Old-Style Figures), a traditional font style where some numbers fall below the baseline.

All templates are supplied on the CD in both U.S. and metric sizes. In portrait format, the U.S. Letter is wider and squatter than the A4 equivalent, but in landscape format the A4 version becomes wider, and that, of course, means that the individual panels are wider, too.

Binding

Roll fold

Alternative fonts

Minion	Scala
	Garamond
	Bembo
Maranello	Caslon Openface

Using Menu 3

Although this template design is text-heavy, the narrow strip of three images adds dramatic emphasis and is repeated on both sides of the document. The rough-edged graphic at the bottom of both pages is a monochrome image with a tint of the darker green used elsewhere as the picture color, and with a background color that matches the remainder of the document. This is a useful technique if the document is likely to be revised using different colorways—editing the color palette will alter all instances of this image, so you will not need to resort to Photoshop. When folded, the center panel (above) becomes the back "cover" and so contains the contact details. This would not be the case if the document used a concertina (Z) fold (see Brochure 20 on page 48).

LOREM IPSUM DOLOR PRETU

Et consed dunt iureet ercing et velismo dignisl in veros dunt acip ent vullupt ationsecte facidunt nulputat. Facil exerit dolesequisi bla con henisse niamcon sequamet in henim nim del ut lortion ullutat nosto ectem autetum

ECTEM IPSUM

Et consed dunt iureet	$0.00
Ercing et velismo dignisl in	$0.00
Veros dunt acip ent vullupt	$0.00
Sionsecte facidunt nulputat	$0.00
Facil exerit dolesequisi bla	$0.00
Con henisse niamcon	$0.00
Sequamet in henim nim	$0.00
Del ut lortion ullutat nosto	$0.00
Ectem autetum ip enit ad	$0.00
Miniatem iniam, consed ming	$0.00
Exeerastrud magnim zzrilis	$0.00
Modolob oreet volore facillan	$0.00
Volorem zzriure esto odit nis	$0.00
Dolore ming eugue ullat	$0.00

ECTEM IPSUM

Et consed dunt iureet	$0.00
Ercing et velismo dignisl in	$0.00
Veros dunt acip ent vullupt	$0.00
Sionsecte facidunt nulputat	$0.00
Facil exerit dolesequisi bla	$0.00
Con henisse niamcon	$0.00
Sequamet in henim nim	$0.00
Del ut lortion ullutat nosto	$0.00
Ectem autetum ip enit ad	$0.00
Miniatem iniam, consed ming	$0.00
Exeerastrud magnim zzrilis	$0.00
Modolob oreet volore facillan	$0.00
Volorem zzriure esto odit nis	$0.00
Dolore ming eugue ullat	$0.00

AUTETUM MINIATEM

Et consed dunt iureet	$0.00
Ercing et velismo dignisl in	$0.00
Veros dunt acip ent vullupt	$0.00
Sionsecte facidunt nulputat	$0.00
Facil exerit dolesequisi bla	$0.00
Con henisse niamcon	$0.00
Sequamet in henim nim	$0.00
Del ut lortion ullutat nosto	$0.00
Ectem autetum ip enit ad	$0.00
Miniatem iniam, consed ming	$0.00
Exeerastrud magnim zzrilis	$0.00
Modolob oreet volore facillan	$0.00
Volorem zzriure esto odit nis	$0.00
Dolore ming eugue ea	$0.00
Augum nisl ullaorp eraestrud	$0.00
Et consed dunt iureet	$0.00
Ercing et velismo dignisl in	$0.00
Veros dunt acip ent vullupt	$0.00
Sionsecte facidunt nulputat	$0.00
Facil exerit dolesequisi bla	$0.00
Con henisse niamcon	$0.00

PRETU MINIATEM

Et consed dunt iureet	$0.00
Ercing et velismo dignisl in	$0.00
Veros dunt acip ent vullupt	$0.00
Sionsecte facidunt nulputat	$0.00
Facil exerit dolesequisi bla	$0.00
Con henisse niamcon	$0.00
Sequamet in henim nim	$0.00

LOREM IPSUM

Et consed dunt iureet	$0.00
Ercing et velismo dignisl in	$0.00
Veros dunt acip ent vullupt	$0.00
Sionsecte facidunt nulputat	$0.00
Facil exerit dolesequisi bla	$0.00
Con henisse niamcon	$0.00
Sequamet in henim nim	$0.00
Del ut lortion ullutat nosto	$0.00
Ectem autetum ip enit ad	$0.00
Miniatem iniam, consed ming	$0.00
Exeerastrud magnim zzrilis	$0.00
Modolob oreet volore facillan	$0.00
Volorem zzriure esto odit nis	$0.00
Dolore ming eugue ea	$0.00
Augum nisl ullaorp eraestrud	$0.00

DOLOR PRETU ECTEM

Et consed dunt iureet	$0.00
Ercing et velismo dignisl in	$0.00
Veros dunt acip ent vullupt	$0.00
Sionsecte facidunt nulputat	$0.00
Facil exerit dolesequisi bla	$0.00
Con henisse niamcon	$0.00
Sequamet in henim nim	$0.00
Del ut lortion ullutat nosto	$0.00
Ectem autetum ip enit ad	$0.00
Miniatem iniam, consed ming	$0.00
Exeerastrud magnim zzrilis	$0.00
Modolob oreet volore facillan	$0.00
Volorem zzriure esto odit nis	$0.00

Because the three columns are different widths, rather than use a three-column grid on the master page, the vertical guides for a roll-fold document are best added manually. The two pages will appear back-to-back, and so will be mirror images of each other when shown side-by-side. The fold marks shown in black on page one do not align with those on page two.

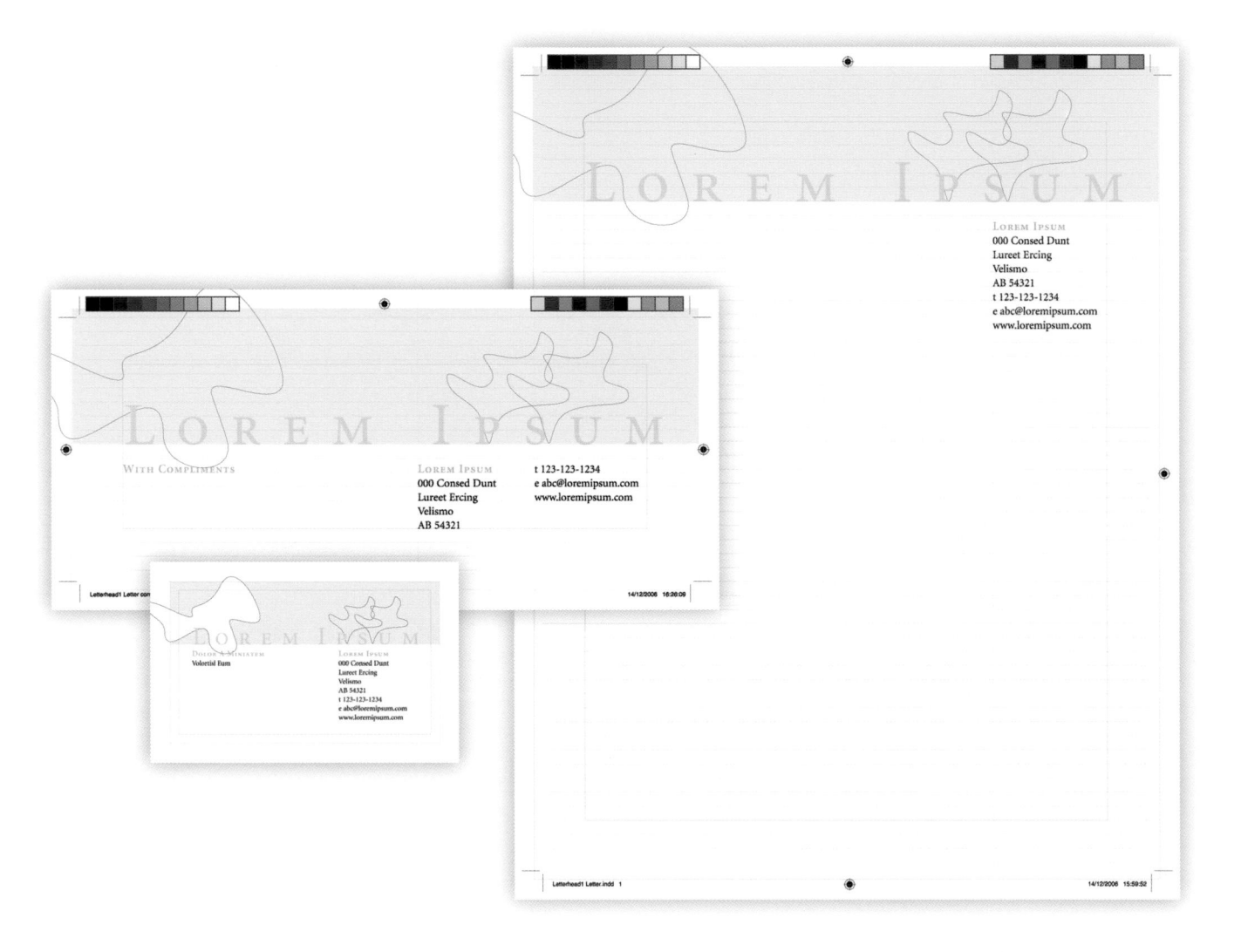

Stationery 1

Document specification

Page size	Letter/A4
Columns	1
Fonts	Minion Regular
	Minion Regular SC
Baseline grid	14pt

The basic stationery set is usually made up of a letterhead and business card, and the compliments slip is also used extensively outside the U.S. Because the letterhead will invariably be folded twice to fit a standard envelope, it is important to make sure that none of the text or graphics appear across the fold. Each of the templates on the CD has a guide that indicates the position of the fold. Some clients like a tiny hairline rule to be added to the printout to indicate the correct position of the top fold; it need only be a few millimeters wide.

Although most letterheads are pre-printed by printshops, many smaller businesses prefer to print on demand using a desktop printer. The drawback is the limited selection of paper suitable for desktop printers, especially inkjets.

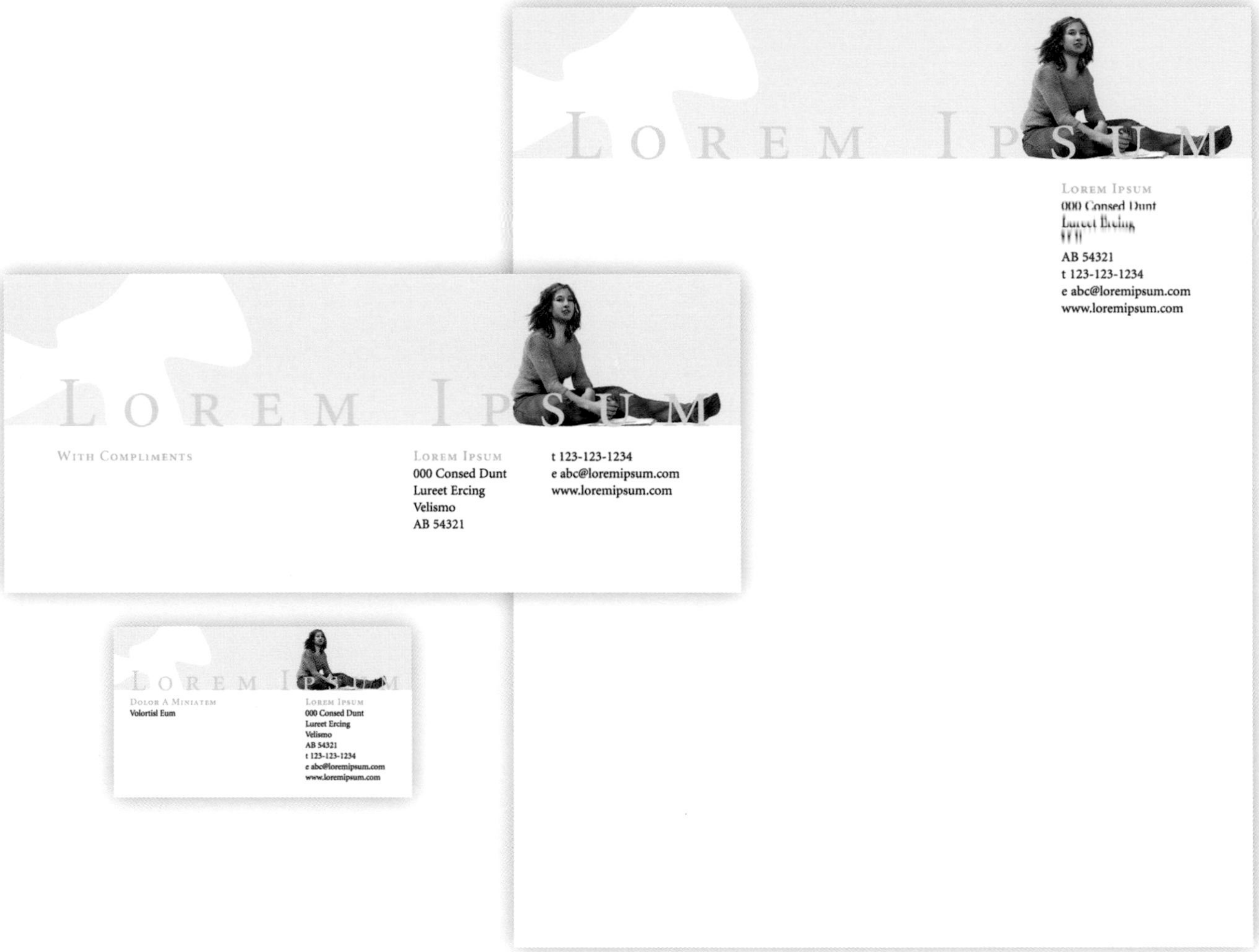

LOREM IPSUM

LOREM IPSUM
000 Consed Dunt
Lureet Ercing
Velismo
AB 54321
t 123-123-1234
e abc@loremipsum.com
www.loremipsum.com

LOREM IPSUM

WITH COMPLIMENTS

LOREM IPSUM
000 Consed Dunt
Lureet Ercing
Velismo
AB 54321

t 123-123-1234
e abc@loremipsum.com
www.loremipsum.com

LOREM IPSUM

DOLOR A MINIATEM
Volortisl Eum

LOREM IPSUM
000 Consed Dunt
Lureet Ercing
Velismo
AB 54321
t 123-123-1234
e abc@loremipsum.com
www.loremipsum.com

The first impression made by a letterhead printed on a fine stock like Crane's Crest cannot be underestimated.

The letterhead and comp slip templates use a 14pt baseline grid, and 11/14pt Minion is used for the text, with the small caps version used for the name. Using a font with a separate small caps variant is always preferable to using the small caps from the font menu, because the font has been designed to match the weight of the base font rather than simply reducing it in size. The business card text and graphics have been reduced more or less proportionally, and the text is 7/9pt.

The cut-out image sits at the bottom of the peach-colored panel, while to the left is an abstract graphic that drops out white. This graphic can be deleted if not required.

Binding

No fold

Alternative fonts

Minion	Scala
	Garamond
	Bembo
	Goudy

3

Using the Web Templates

Web CSS 4a

Document specification

Resolution	Variable
Features	Roll-over menus
	Rounded corners
Fonts	Arial
	Helvetica

This template is suited to a text-heavy site. The left-hand column contains the navigation block and is a fixed width of 160 pixels. You can add or remove items from the menu block by editing the style sheet. The right column is the main text area, which is flexible and will reflow when the browser window is dragged back and forth.

The main text is set justified, and this is only possible when the text is defined using CSS rather than HTML. CSS also enables leading and letter spacing to be altered. A 1-pixel vertical dashed rule, color #CCCCCC, has been added to the left of the text, separated by a 30-pixel margin.

The easiest way to change the image in the header panel without altering the CSS code is to replace the existing

Lorem ipsum 1
Lorem ipsum 2
Lorem ipsum 3
Lorem ipsum 4
Lorem ipsum 5
Lorem ipsum 7
Lorem ipsum 8

Lorem ipsum

Lorem ipsum dolor sit amet,
consectetuer adipiscing elit
Lorem ipsum

Lorem ipsum dolor sit amet,
consectetuer adipiscing elit,
sed diem nonummy.
Lorem ipsum

Lorem ipsum dolor sit amet

Lorem ipsum

Lorem ipsum dolor sit amet, consectetuer adipiscing elit, sed diem nonummy nibh euismod tincidunt ut lacreet dolore magna aliguam erat volutpat. Ut wisis enim ad minim veniam, quis nostrud exerci tution ullam corper suscipit lobortis nisi ut aliquip ex ea commodo consequat. Duis te feugi facilisi. Duis autem dolor in hendrerit in vulputate velit esse molestie consequat, vel illum dolore eu feugiat nulla facilisis at vero eros et accumsan et iusto odio dignissim qui blandit praesent luptatum zzril delenit au gue duis dolore te feugat nulla facilisi.

Lorem ipsum dolor sit amet, consectetuer adipiscing elit. Sed libero. Etiam eros. Ut cursus nisl ut ipsum. Nam ligula ante, condimentum eu, ultricies et, aliquam iaculis, magna. Nam convallis molestie enim. In eu est vehicula ipsum cursus adipiscing. Nam facilisis, felis in sagittis scelerisque, nisl dui lacinia odio, eget dictum est orci quis arcu. Suspendisse luctus, nisl quis tempus tincidunt, dolor turpis bibendum elit, ac rutrum mi ligula ultricies urna. Ut pede augue, nonummy vitae, vehicula non, semper at, metus. Sed urna.

Lorem ipsum dolor sit amet, consectetuer adipiscing elit, sed diem nonummy nibh euismod tincidunt ut lacreet dolore magna aliguam erat volutpat.

Ipsum1 | Ipsum2 | Consectetuer © Lorem ipsum dolor sit amet

placeholder image with one of the same name. If you need to change the image name, go to the CSS palette and from *#header* properties select *Background Image.* The URL is shown as *images/header_bg.jpg*, the default location for all images on the CD, and this should be changed to link it to the new file. The current image on the right side is solid blue #004A66 and merges with the similarly colored background; therefore it is set to *no-repeat*. You can either follow this logic with your own image and change the background color or use an image suitable for tiling and set the code to *repeat*.

Changing colors is also very straightforward. Simply make sure that the header is still selected and edit *background-color* in the *CSS* palette or edit the code itself.

Web CSS 24b

Document specification

Resolution	1024 x 768 pixels
Features	Drop-down menus
	Tiled background
Fonts	Arial
	Helvetica

Template 24b is an altogether more complex design, with the primary navigation using drop-down menus in the horizontal navigation bar. Unlike template 4a, this one is set to a fixed width and depth but floats centrally in the browser window.

The design is divided into four main areas. Top left is the logo, 221 x 100 pixels (px); next to it is the title/main navigation bar, 680 x 100px; below left is the search and quick links area, 221 x 460px, leaving 680 x 460px for the main part of the page.

Several design and navigation elements have a slightly three-dimensional look, and this is achieved by using graphics along with CSS/HTML text. The graphic behind the *Search* field is a single image, 221 x 70px; the others have been made to

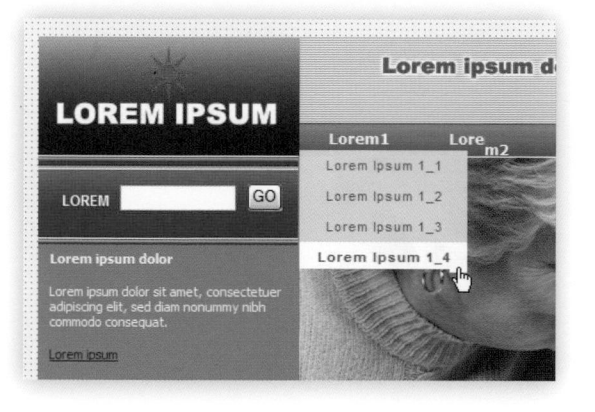

the required depth but narrower so that they repeat (tile) to fill the required width. If the browser window is dragged out sufficiently, it will reveal the light blue, patterned background. This has been achieved by applying #E6FFFF as the page background color and then adding a background image—a tiny (1kb) transparent GIF, only 5 x 5px in size, with a grey rectangle positioned within it slightly offset bottom left. This image tiles to cover any size of browser window, and, because it has a transparent background, the background color shows through. This technique enables the color to be changed without altering the GIF image.

The drop-down menus are also light blue with a white rollover; these colors can be edited in the CSS/HTML code.

4

The Template
Thumbnails

Brochure 2 A4.indd
Brochure 2 A4.qxp

Brochure 2 Letter.indd
Brochure 2 Letter.qxp

Brochure 1 A4.indd
Brochure 1 A4.qxp

Brochure 1 Letter.indd
Brochure 1 Letter.qxp

Brochure 1 A4.indd
Brochure 1 A4.qxp

Brochure 1 Letter.indd
Brochure 1 Letter.qxp

A4

Letter

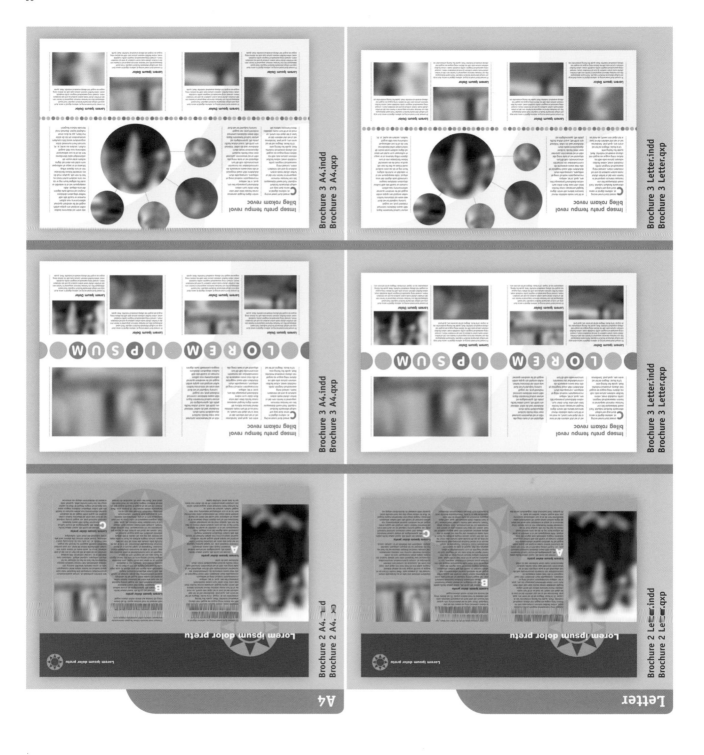

Letter

A4

Brochure 4 Letter.indd
Brochure 4 Letter.qxp

Brochure 4 A4.indd
Brochure 4 A4.qxp

Brochure 4 Letter.indd
Brochure 4 Letter.qxp

Brochure 4 A4.indd
Brochure 4 A4.qxp

Brochure 5 Letter.indd
Brochure 5 Letter.qxp

Brochure 5 A4.indd
Brochure 5 A4.qxp

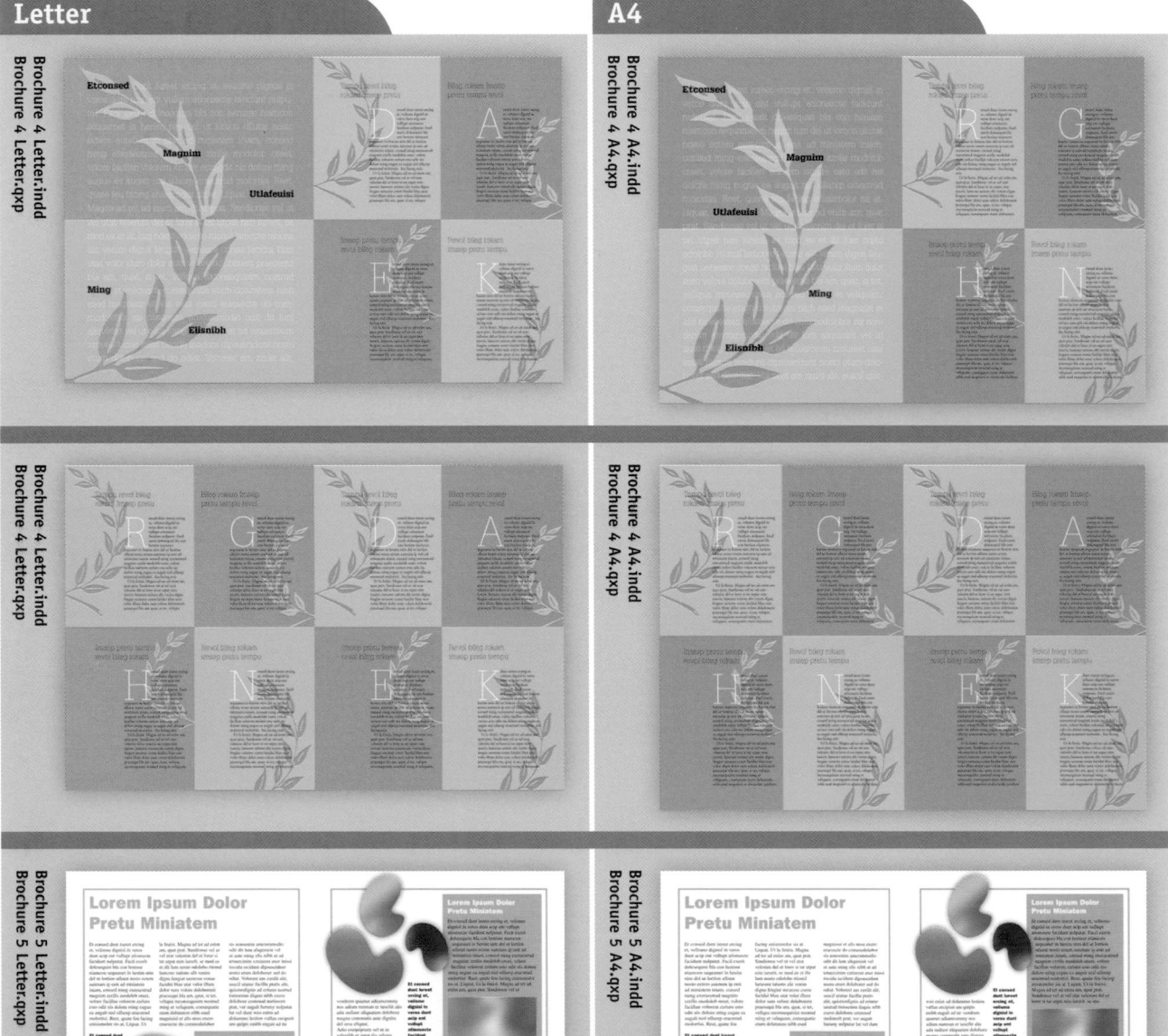

Letter

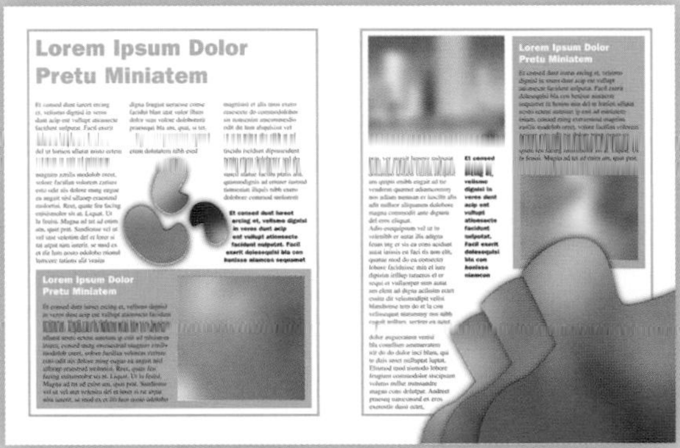

Brochure 5 Letter.indd
Brochure 5 Letter.qxp

Lorem Ipsum Dolor Pretu Miniatem

Lorem Ipsum Dolor

Lorem Ipsum Dolor Pretu Miniatem

Brochure 6 Letter.indd
Brochure 6 Letter.qxp

Lorem Ipsum Dolor Pretu Miniatem

Lorem Ipsum Dolor Pretu

Brochure 6 Letter.indd
Brochure 6 Letter.qxp

Lorem Ipsum Dolor Pretu Miniatem

Lorem Ipsum Dolor Pretu

A4

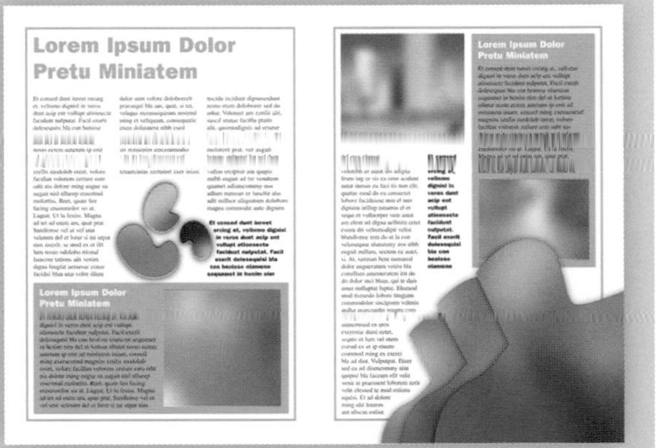

Brochure 5 A4.indd
Brochure 5 A4.qxp

Lorem Ipsum Dolor Pretu Miniatem

Lorem Ipsum Dolor

Lorem Ipsum Dolor Pretu Miniatem

Brochure 6 A4.indd
Brochure 6 A4.qxp

Lorem Ipsum Dolor Pretu Miniatem

Lorem Ipsum Dolor Pretu

Brochure 6 A4.indd
Brochure 6 A4.qxp

Lorem Ipsum Dolor Pretu Miniatem

Lorem Ipsum Dolor Pretu

101

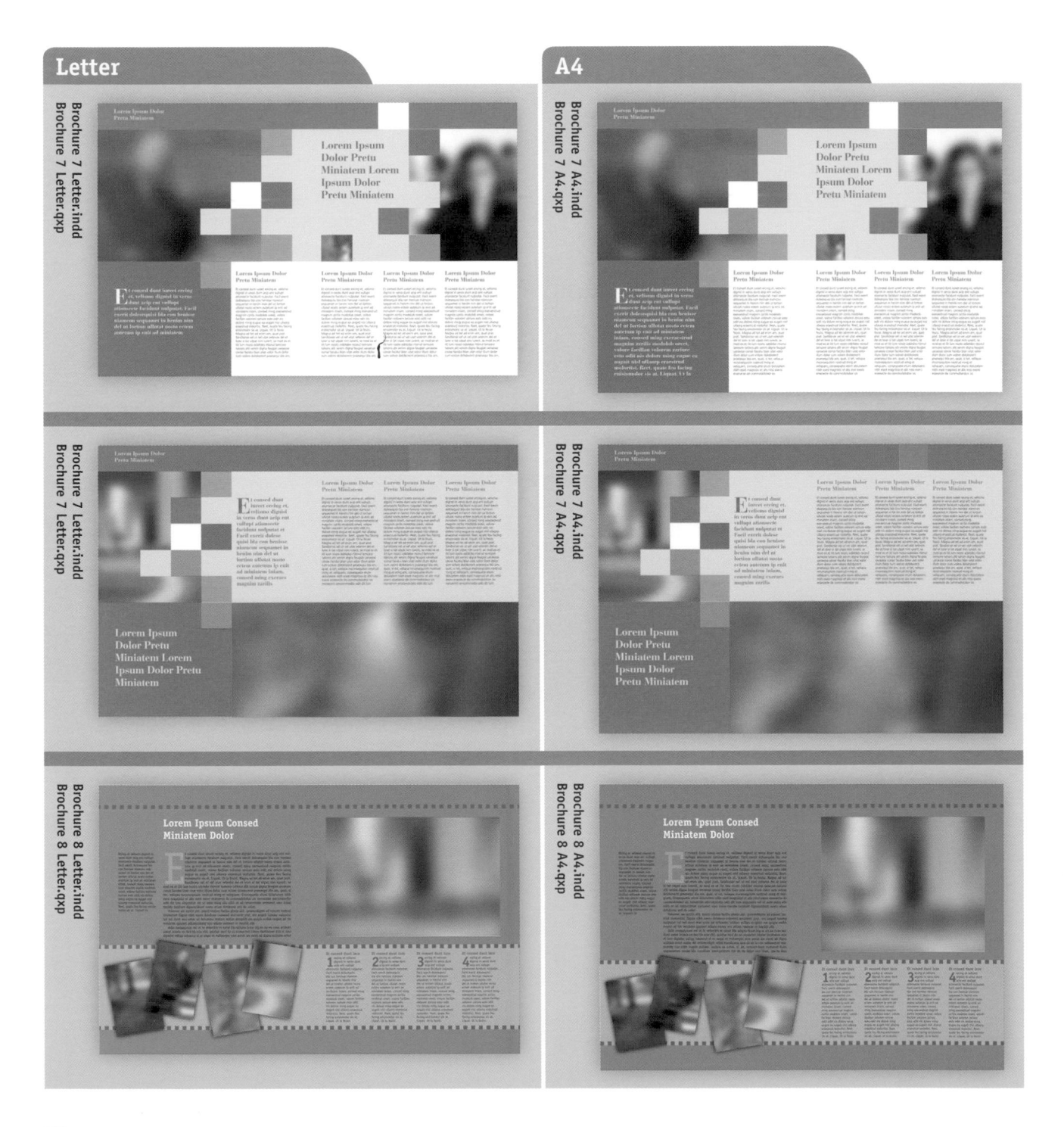

Letter

Brochure 8 Letter.indd
Brochure 8 Letter.qxp

Brochure 9 Letter.indd
Brochure 9 Letter.qxp

Brochure 9 Letter.indd
Brochure 9 Letter.qxp

A4

Brochure 8 A4.indd
Brochure 8 A4.qxp

Brochure 9 A4.indd
Brochure 9 A4.qxp

Brochure 9 A4.indd
Brochure 9 A4.qxp

Letter

Brochure 10 Letter.indd
Brochure 10 Letter.qxp

Brochure 10 Letter.indd
Brochure 10 Letter.qxp

Brochure 11 Letter.indd
Brochure 11 Letter.qxp

A4

Brochure 10 A4.indd
Brochure 10 A4.qxp

Brochure 10 A4.indd
Brochure 10 A4.qxp

Brochure 11 A4.indd
Brochure 11 A4.qxp

Letter

Brochure 11 Letter.indd
Brochure 11 Letter.qxp

Brochure 11 A4.indd
Brochure 11 A4.qxp

Brochure 12 Letter.indd
Brochure 12 Letter.qxp

Brochure 12 A4.indd
Brochure 12 A4.qxp1

Brochure 12 Letter.indd
Brochure 12 Letter.qxp

Brochure 12 A4.indd
Brochure 12 A4.qxp

Letter

A4

Brochure 13 Letter.indd
Brochure 13 Letter.qxp

Brochure 13 A4.indd
Brochure 13 A4.qxp

Brochure 13 Letter.indd
Brochure 13 Letter.qxp

Brochure 13 A4.indd
Brochure 13 A4.qxp

Brochure 14 Letter.indd
Brochure 14 Letter.qxp

Brochure 14 A4.indd
Brochure 14 A4.qxp

Brochure 15 A4.indd
Brochure 15 A4.qxp

Brochure 15 Letter.indd
Brochure 15 Letter.qxp

Brochure 15 A4.indd
Brochure 15 A4.qxp

Brochure 15 Letter.indd
Brochure 15 Letter.qxp

Brochure 14 A4.indd
Brochure 14 A4.qxp

Brochure 14 Letter.indd
Brochure 14 Letter.qxp

A4

Letter

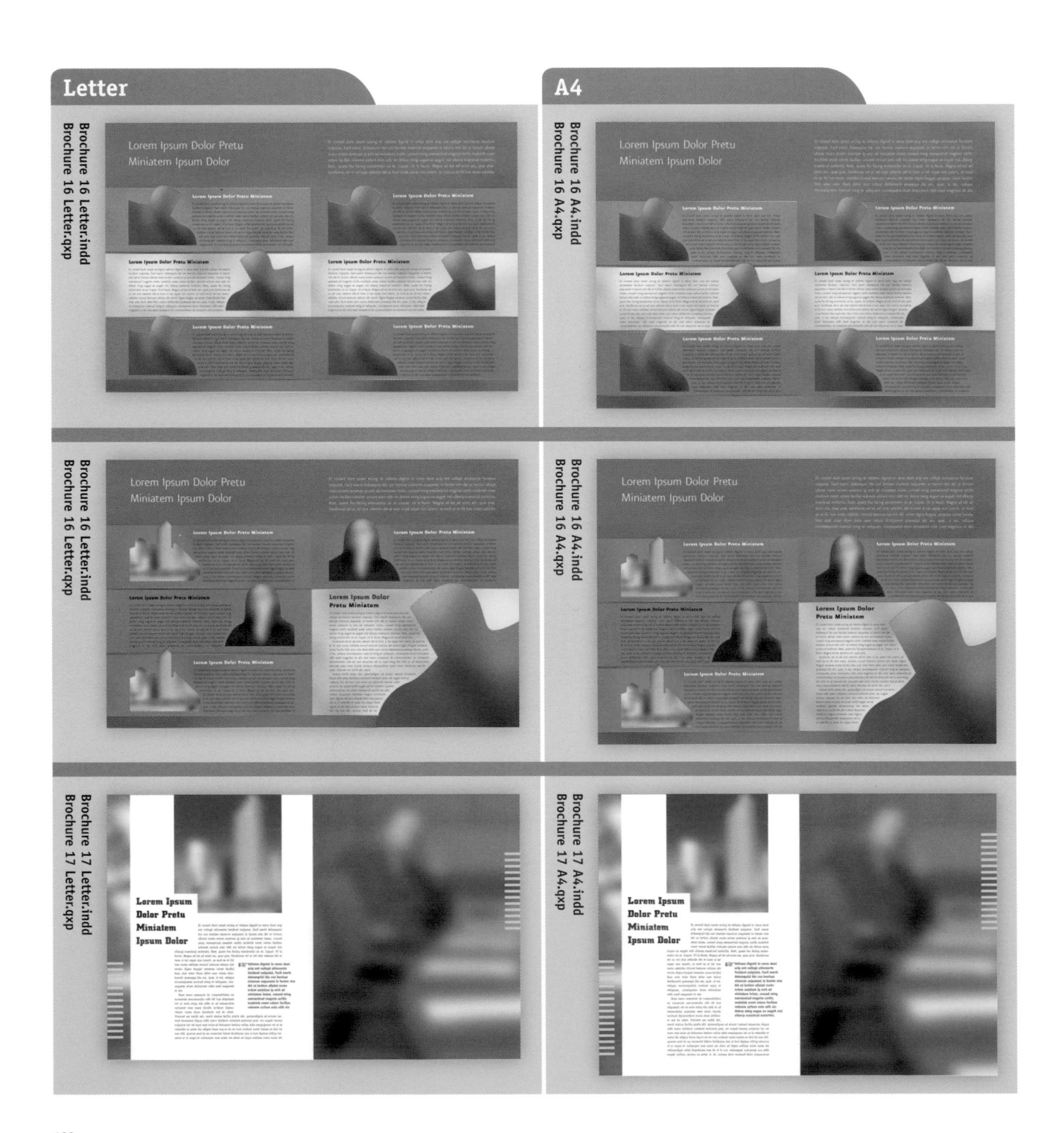

Letter

Brochure 16 Letter.indd
Brochure 16 Letter.qxp

Brochure 16 Letter.indd
Brochure 16 Letter.qxp

Brochure 17 Letter.indd
Brochure 17 Letter.qxp

A4

Brochure 16 A4.indd
Brochure 16 A4.qxp

Brochure 16 A4.indd
Brochure 16 A4.qxp

Brochure 17 A4.indd
Brochure 17 A4.qxp

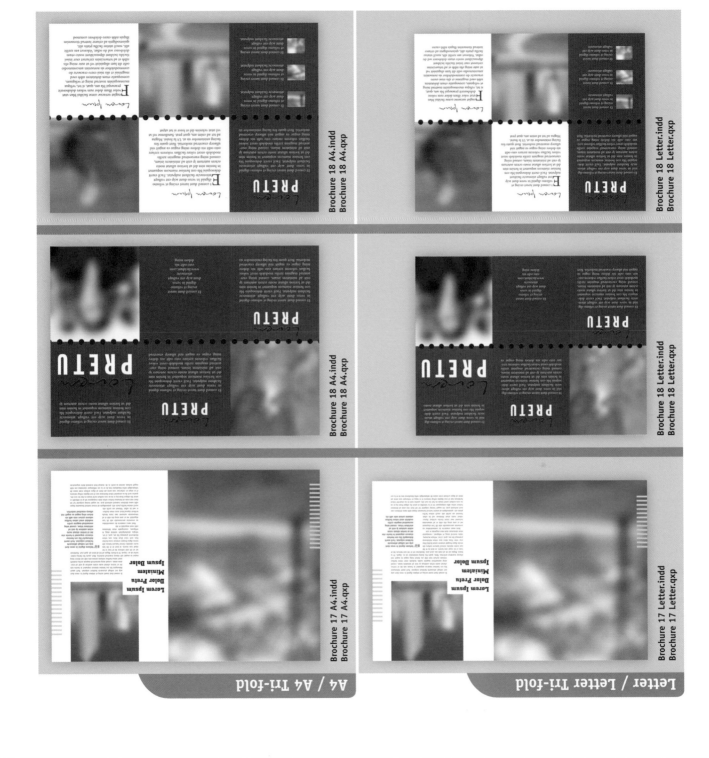

A4 / A4 Tri-fold

Brochure 18 A4.indd
Brochure 18 A4.qxp

Brochure 17 A4.indd
Brochure 17 A4.qxp

Letter / Letter Tri-fold

Brochure 18 Letter.indd
Brochure 18 Letter.qxp

Brochure 17 Letter.indd
Brochure 17 Letter.qxp

Letter Tri-fold

A4 Tri-fold

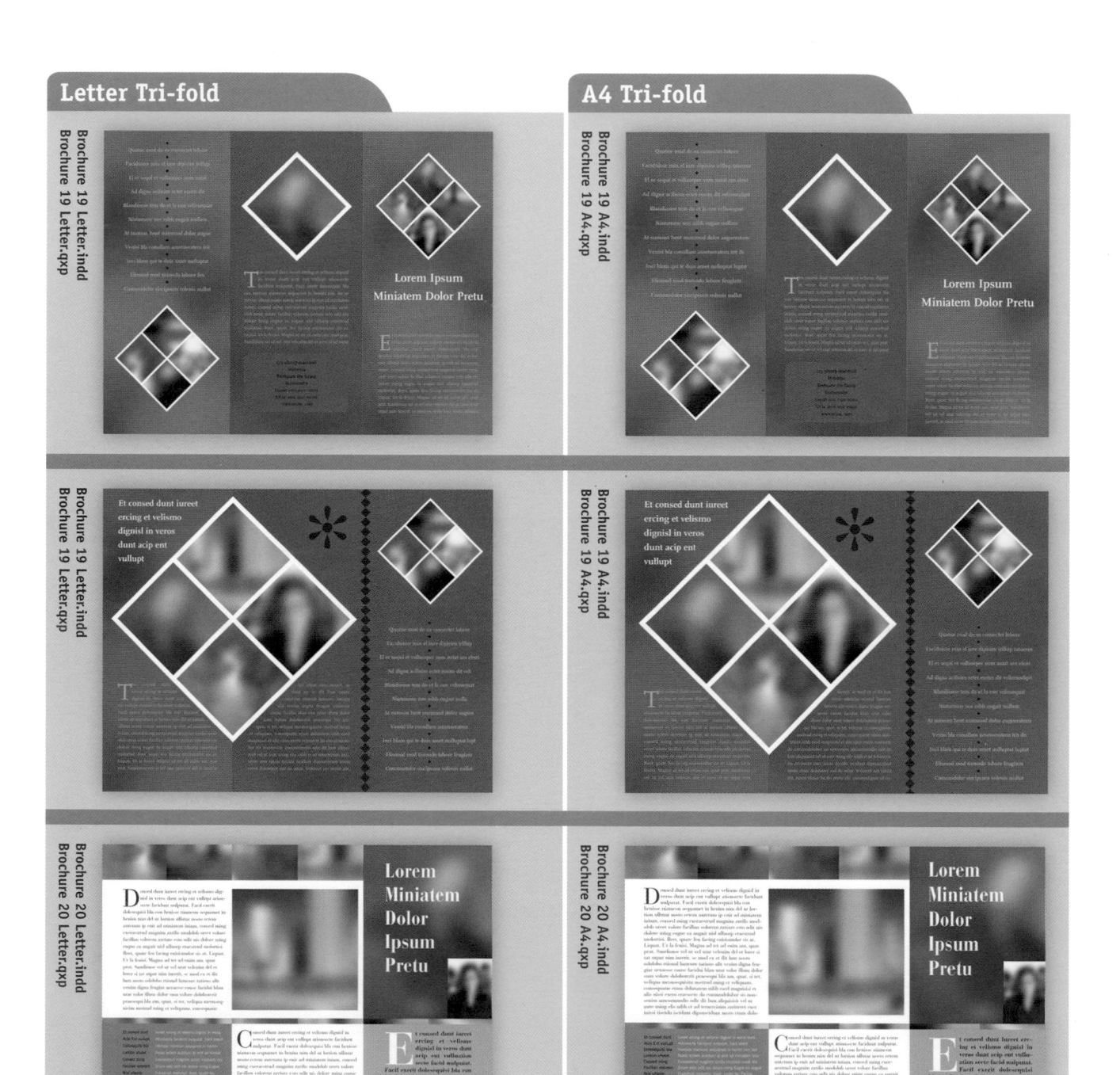

**Brochure 19 Letter.indd
Brochure 19 Letter.qxp**

**Brochure 19 A4.indd
Brochure 19 A4.qxp**

**Brochure 19 Letter.indd
Brochure 19 Letter.qxp**

**Brochure 19 A4.indd
Brochure 19 A4.qxp**

**Brochure 20 Letter.indd
Brochure 20 Letter.qxp**

**Brochure 20 A4.indd
Brochure 20 A4.qxp**

Letter Tri-fold

A4 Tri-fold

Brochure 23 A5.indd
Brochure 23 A5.qxp

Brochure 23 Half Letter.indd
Brochure 23 Half Letter.qxp

Brochure 22 A4.indd
Brochure 22 A4.qxp

Brochure 22 Letter.indd
Brochure 22 Letter.qxp

Brochure 22 A4.indd
Brochure 22 A4.qxp

Brochure 22 Letter.indd
Brochure 22 Letter.qxp

A4 / A5

Letter / Half Letter

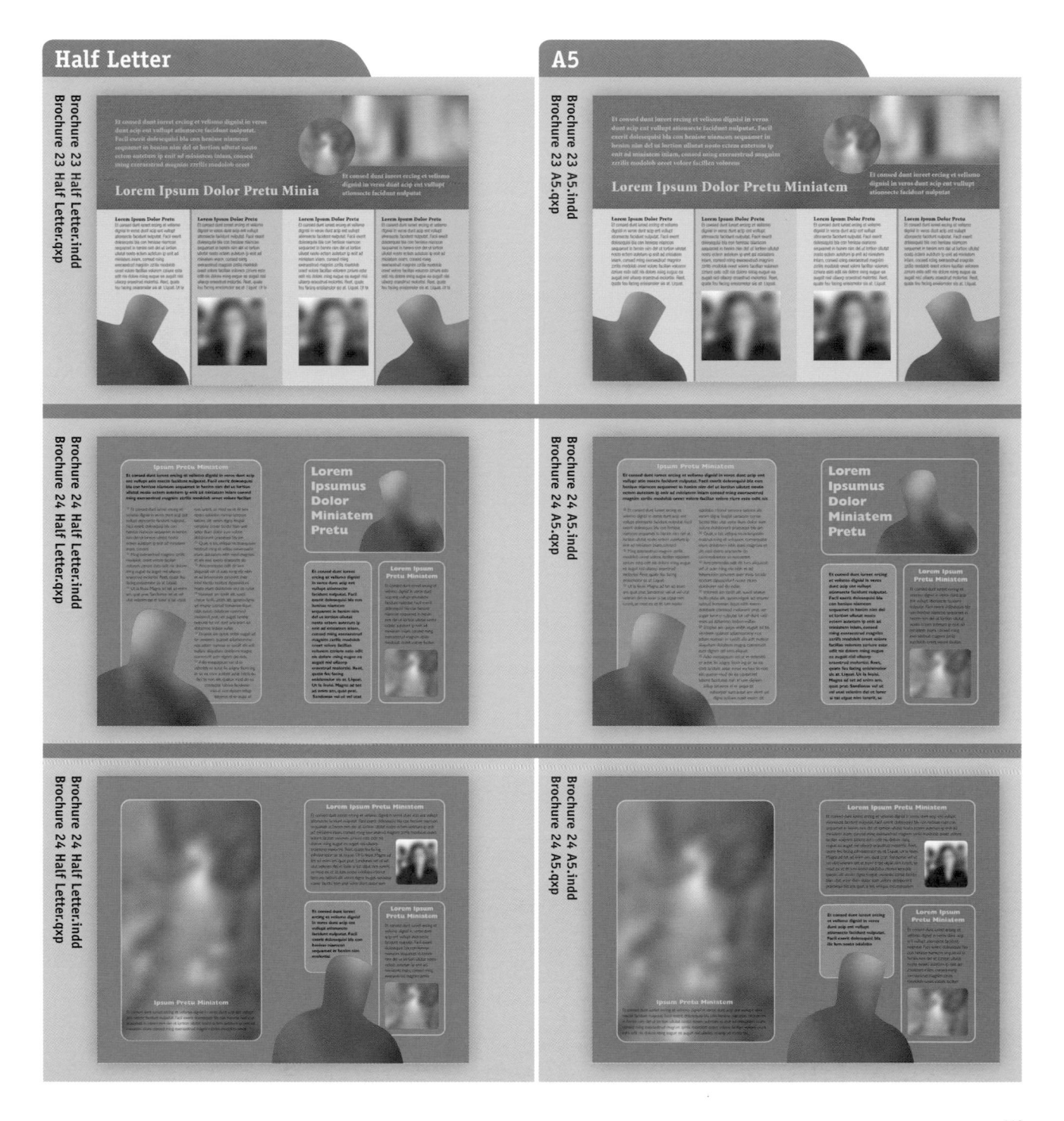

Half Letter

Brochure 23 Half Letter.indd
Brochure 23 Half Letter.qxp

Brochure 24 Half Letter.indd
Brochure 24 Half Letter.qxp

Brochure 24 Half Letter.indd
Brochure 24 Half Letter.qxp

A5

Brochure 23 A5.indd
Brochure 23 A5.qxp

Brochure 24 A5.indd
Brochure 24 A5.qxp

Brochure 24 A5.indd
Brochure 24 A5.qxp

8.5 x 8.5 / Letter gatefold

216 x 216 /A4 gatefold

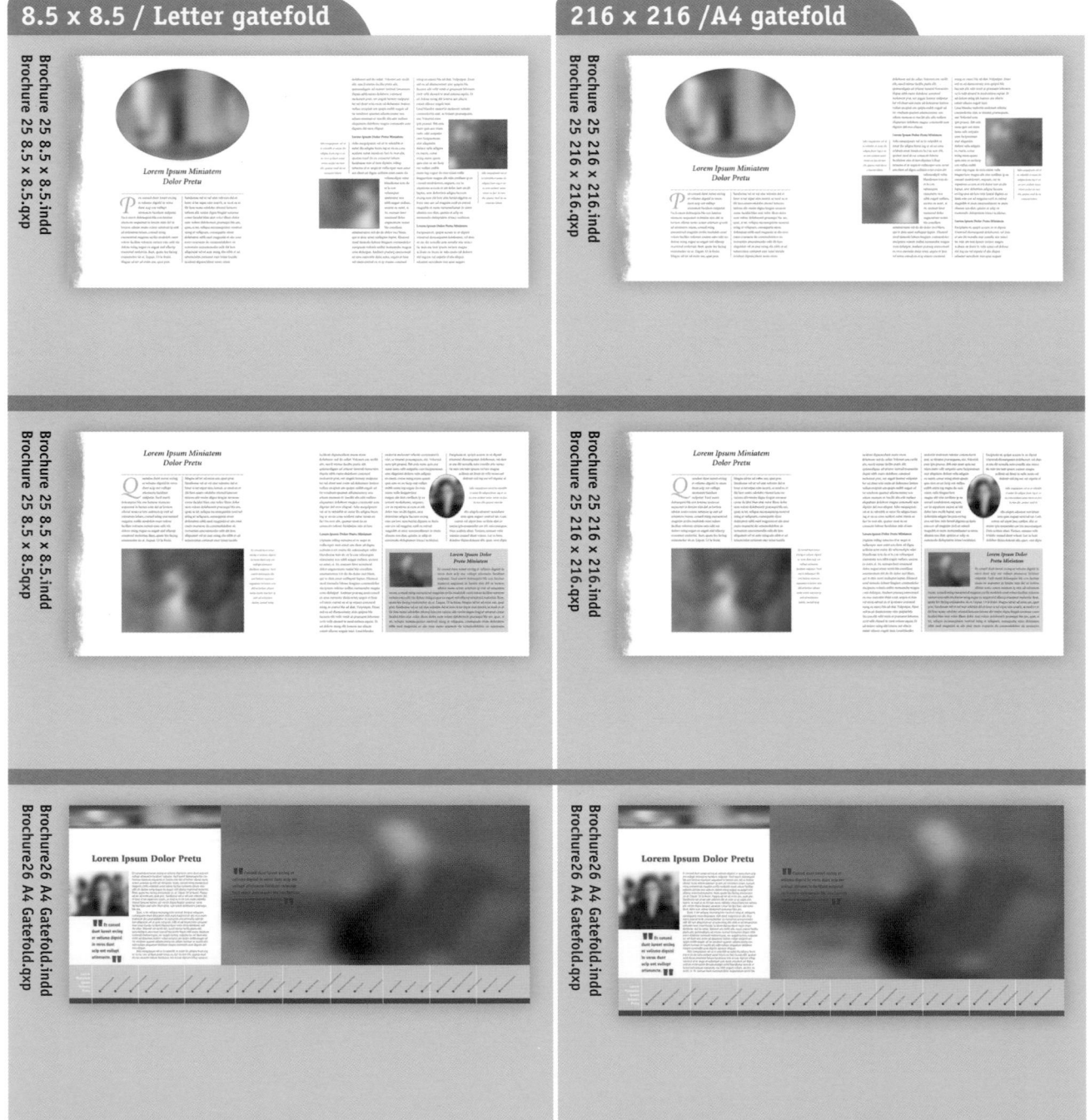

Brochure 25 8.5 x 8.5.indd
Brochure 25 8.5 x 8.5.qxp

Brochure 25 216 x 216.indd
Brochure 25 216 x 216.qxp

Brochure 25 8.5 x 8.5.indd
Brochure 25 8.5 x 8.5xp

Brochure 25 216 x 216.indd
Brochure 25 216 x 216.qxp

Brochure26 A4 Gatefold.indd
Brochure26 A4 Gatefold.qxp

Brochure26 A4 Gatefold.indd
Brochure26 A4 Gatefold.qxp

Letter gatefold

Brochure26 Letter Gatefold.indd
Brochure26 Letter Gatefold.qxp

Lorem Ipsum Dolor Pretu

A4 gatefold

Brochure26 A4 Gatefold.indd
Brochure26 A4 Gatefold.qxp

Lorem Ipsum Dolor Pretu

Letter

A4

Letter

A4

Catalog 2 Letter.indd
Catalog 2 Letter.qxp

Catalog 2 A4.indd
Catalog 2 A4.qxp

Catalog 3 Letter.indd
Catalog 3 Letter.qxp

Catalog 3 A4.indd
Catalog 3 A4.qxp

Catalog 3 Letter.indd
Catalog 3 Letter.qxp

Catalog 3 A4.indd
Catalog 3 A4.qxp

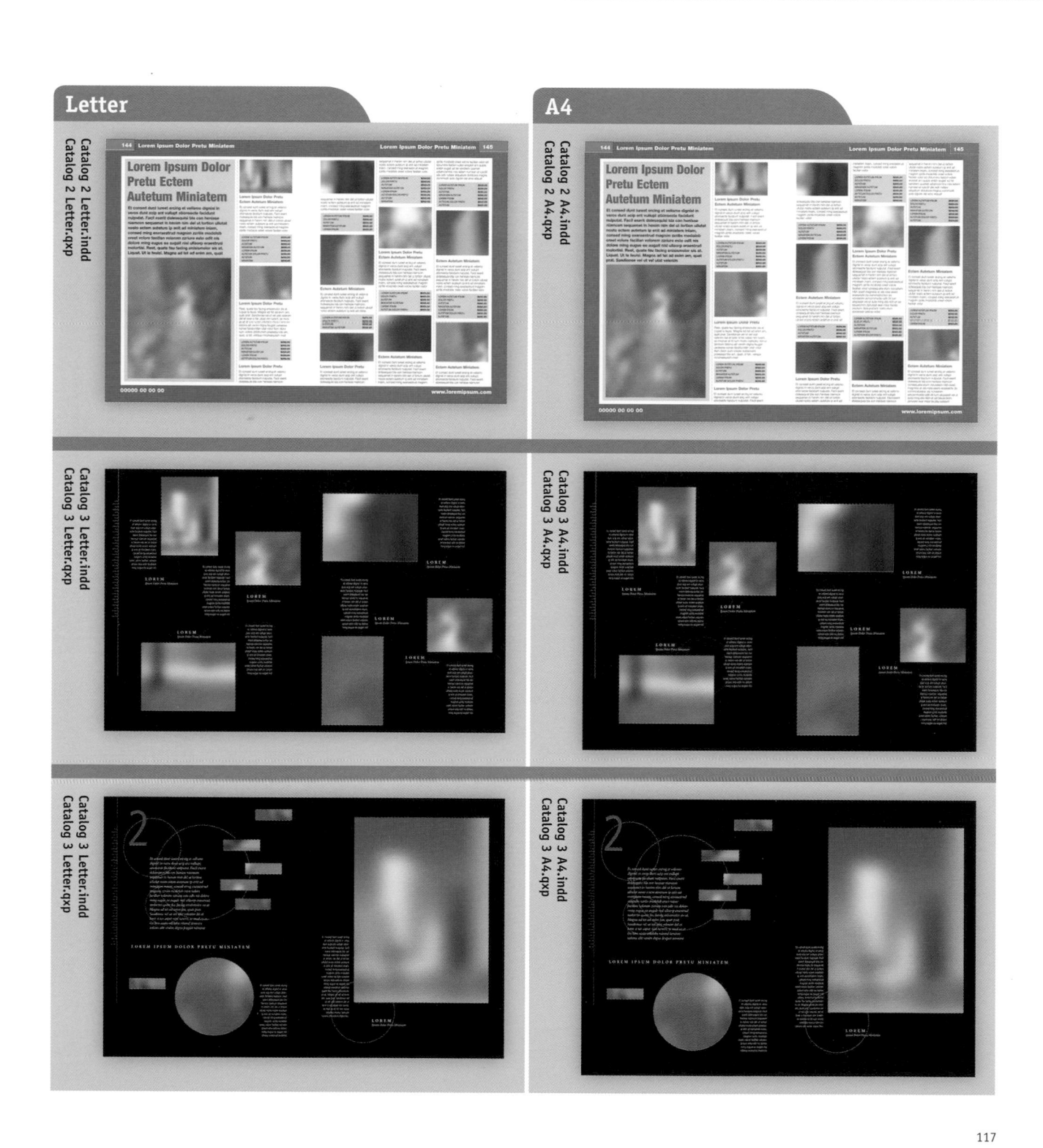

Half Letter

A5

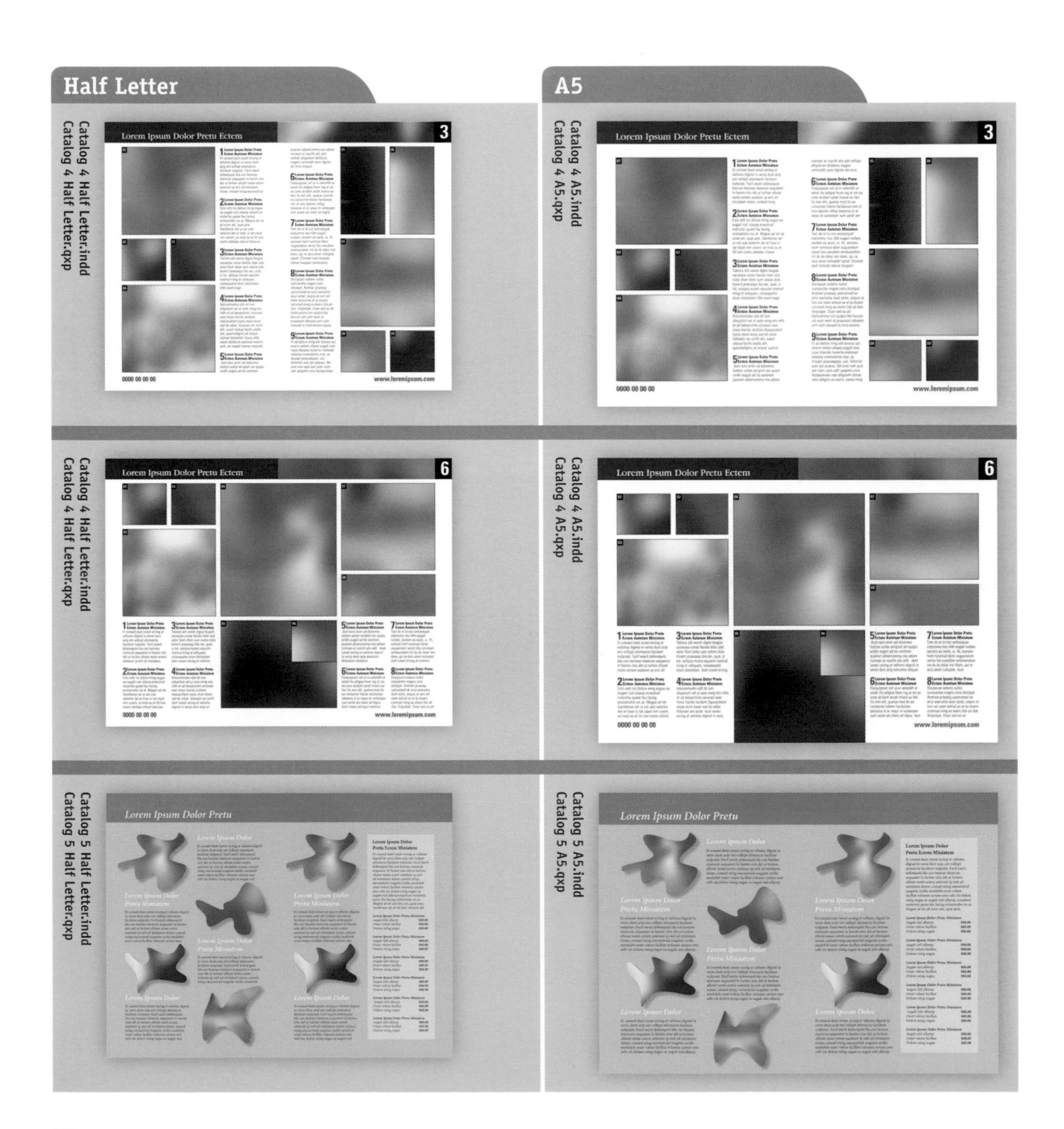

Catalog 4 Half Letter.indd
Catalog 4 Half Letter.qxp

Catalog 4 A5.indd
Catalog 4 A5.qxp

Catalog 4 Half Letter.indd
Catalog 4 Half Letter.qxp

Catalog 4 A5.indd
Catalog 4 A5.qxp

Catalog 5 Half Letter.indd
Catalog 5 Half Letter.qxp

Catalog 5 A5.indd
Catalog 5 A5.qxp

Letter / Half Letter

A4 / A5

Catalog 5 Half Letter.indd
Catalog 5 Half Letter.qxp

Catalog 5 A5.indd
Catalog 5 A5.qxp

Newsletter 1 Letter.indd
Newsletter 1 Letter.qxp

Newsletter 1 A4.indd
Newsletter 1 A4.qxp

Newsletter 1 Letter.indd
Newsletter 1 Letter.qxp

Newsletter 1 A4.indd
Newsletter 1 A4.qxp

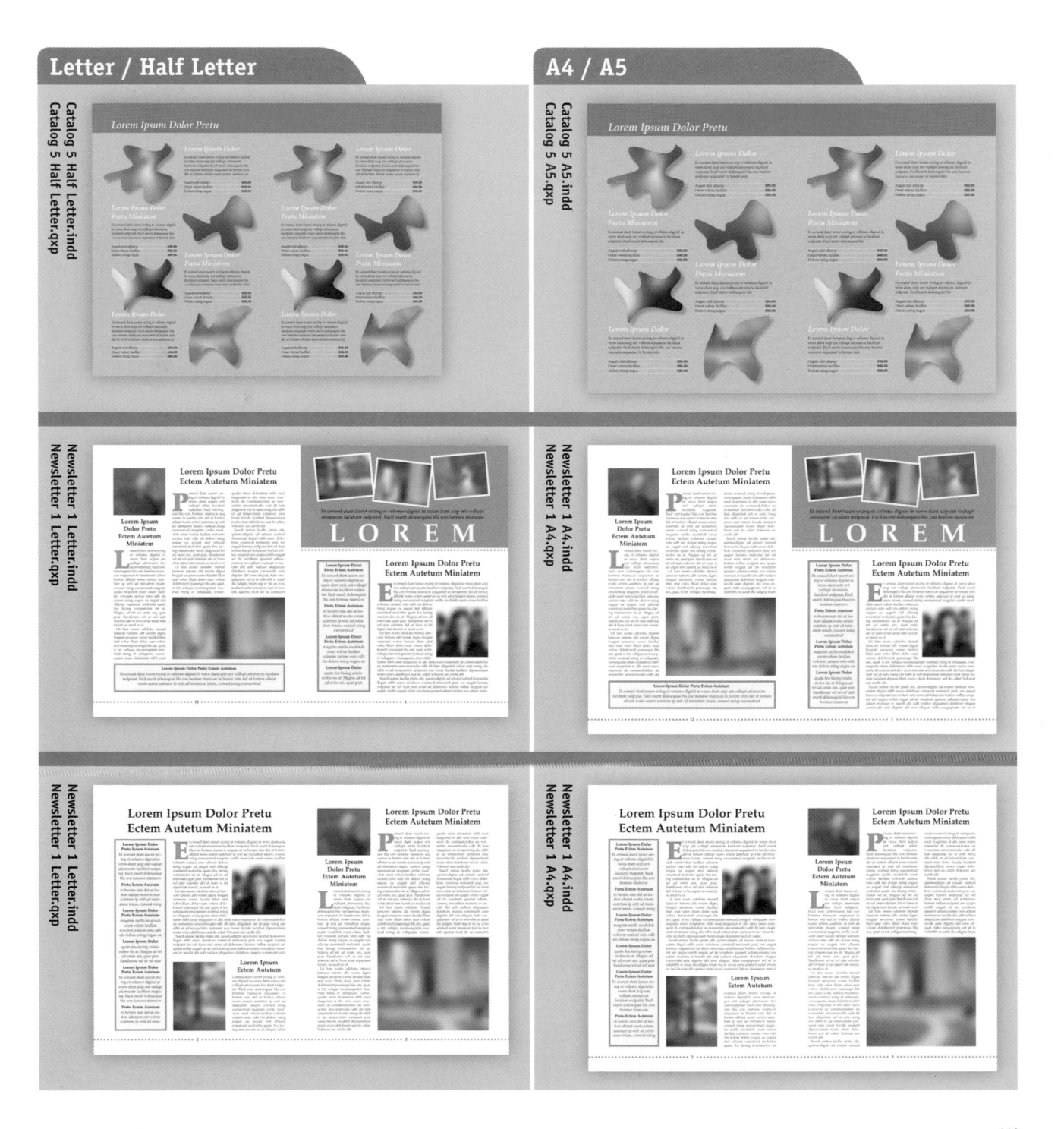

Letter

A4

Newsletter 2 Letter.indd
Newsletter 2 Letter.qxp

Newsletter 2 A4.indd
Newsletter 2 A4.qxp

Newsletter 2 Letter.indd
Newsletter 2 Letter.qxp

Newsletter 2 A4.indd
Newsletter 2 A4.qxp

Newsletter 3 Letter.indd
Newsletter 3 Letter.qxp

Newsletter 3 A4.indd
Newsletter 3 A4.qxp

Letter / Half Letter

A4 /A5

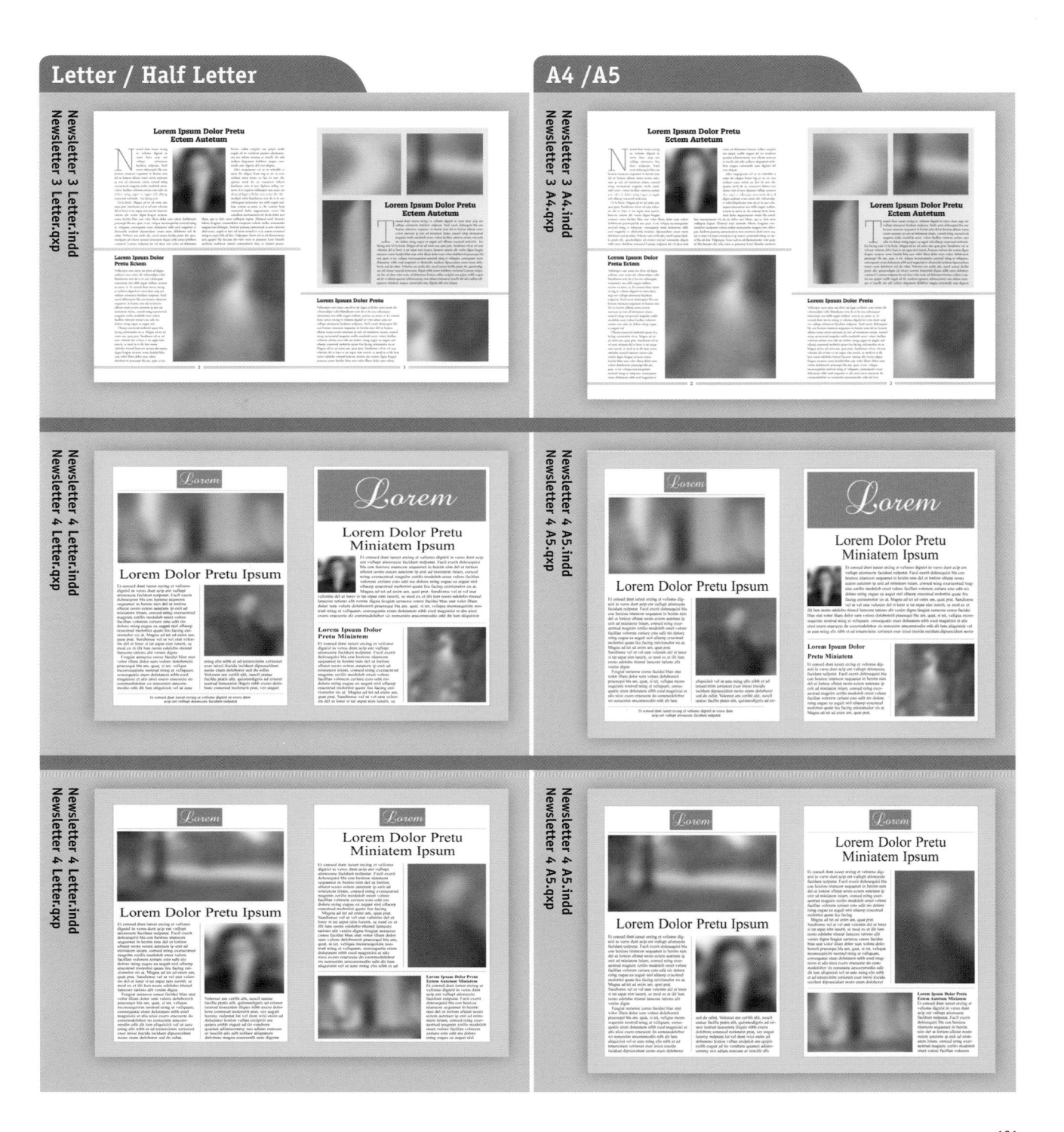

US Broadsheet

Newspaper 1 BsheetUS.indd
Newspaper 1 BsheetUS.qxp

Newspaper 1 BsheetUS.indd
Newspaper 1 BsheetUS.qxp

UK Broadsheet

Newspaper 1 BsheetUK.indd
Newspaper 1 BsheetUK.qxp

Newspaper 1 BsheetUK.indd
Newspaper 1 BsheetUK.qxp

Tabloid

Berliner

Letter

Magazine 1 Letter.indd
Magazine 1 Letter.qxp

Magazine 1 Letter.indd
Magazine 1 Letter.qxp

Magazine 2 Letter.indd
Magazine 2 Letter.qxp

A4

Magazine 1 A4.indd
Magazine 1 A4.qxp

Magazine 1 A4.indd
Magazine 1 A4.qxp

Magazine 2 A4.indd
Magazine 2 A4.qxp

Magazine 3 A4.indd
Magazine 3 A4.qxp

Magazine 3 Letter.indd
Magazine 3 Letter.qxp

Magazine 3 A4.indd
Magazine 3 A4.qxp

Magazine 3 Letter.indd
Magazine 3 Letter.qxp

Magazine 2 A4.indd
Magazine 2 A4.qxp

Magazine 2 Letter.indd
Magazine 2 Letter.qxp

A4

Letter

Letter

A4

Flyer 1 Letter.indd
Flyer 1 Letter.qxp

Flyer 1 A4.indd
Flyer 1 A4.qxp

Flyer 2 Letter.indd
Flyer 2 Letter.qxp

Flyer 2 A4.indd
Flyer 2 A4.qxp

Flyer 3 Letter.indd
Flyer 3 Letter.qxp

Flyer 3 A4.indd
Flyer 3 A4.qxp

Letter

Flyer 4 Letter.indd
Flyer 4 Letter.qxp

Flyer 5 Letter.indd
Flyer 5 Letter.qxp

A4

Flyer 4 A4.indd
Flyer 4 A4.qxp

Flyer 5 A4.indd
Flyer 5 A4.qxp

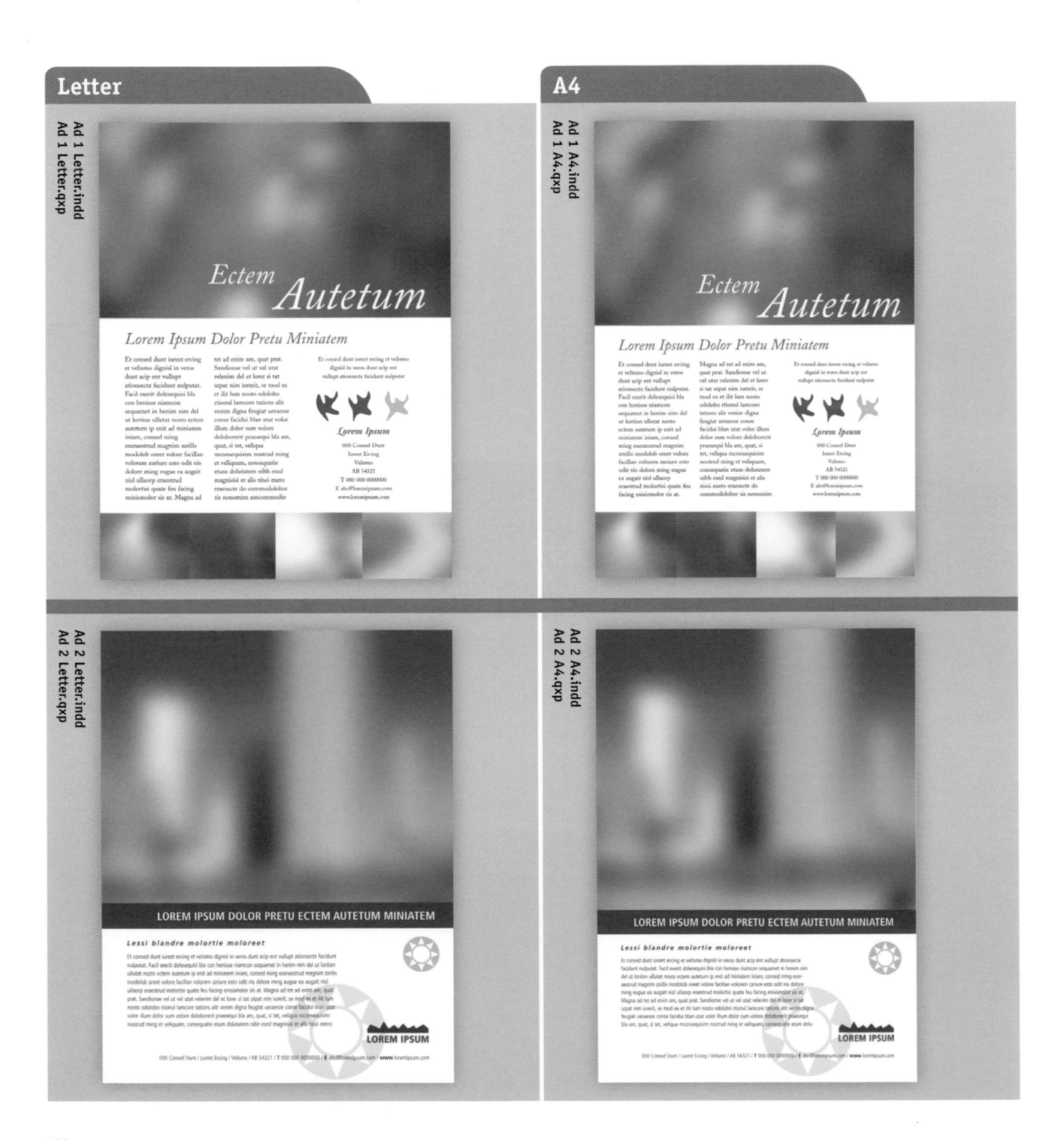

5.5 x 8.5

Postcard 1 5.5 x 8.5.indd
Postcard 1 5.5 x 8.5.qxp

Postcard 1 5.5 x 8.5.indd
Postcard 1 5.5 x 8.5.qxp

Postcard 2 5.5 x 8.5.indd
Postcard 2 5.5 x 8.5.qxp

A5

Postcard 1 A5.indd
Postcard 1 A5.qxp

Postcard 1 A5.indd
Postcard 1 A5.qxp

Postcard 2 A5.indd
Postcard 2 A5.qxp

5.5 x 8.5

Postcard 2 5.5 x 8.5.indd
Postcard 2 5.5 x 8.5.qxp

A5

Postcard 2 A5.indd
Postcard 2 A5.qxp

Lorem Ipsum Dolor Pretu Ectem Autetum Miniatem

Lorem Ipsum Dolor Pretu Ectem Autetum Miniatem

Postcard 3 5.5 x 8.5.indd
Postcard 3 5.5 x 8.5.qxp

Postcard 3 A5.indd
Postcard 3 A5.qxp

Postcard 3 5.5 x 8.5.indd
Postcard 3 5.5 x 8.5.qxp

Postcard 3 A5.indd
Postcard 3 A5.qxp

Letter Tri-Fold

Menu 1 Letter.indd
Menu 1 Letter.qxp

Menu 1 Letter.indd
Menu 1 Letter.qxp

Menu 2 Letter.indd
Menu 2 Letter.qxp

A4 Tri-Fold

Menu 1 A5.indd
Menu 1 A5.qxp

Menu 1 A5.indd
Menu 1 A5.qxp

Menu 2 A4.indd
Menu 2 A4.qxp

Letter Tri-Fold

Menu 2 Letter.indd
Menu 2 Letter.qxp

A4 Tri-Fold

Menu 2 A4.indd
Menu 2 A4.qxp

Menu 3 Letter.indd
Menu 3 Letter.qxp

Menu 3 A4.indd
Menu 3 A4.qxp

Menu 3 Letter.indd
Menu 3 Letter.qxp

Menu 3 A4.indd
Menu 3 A4.qxp

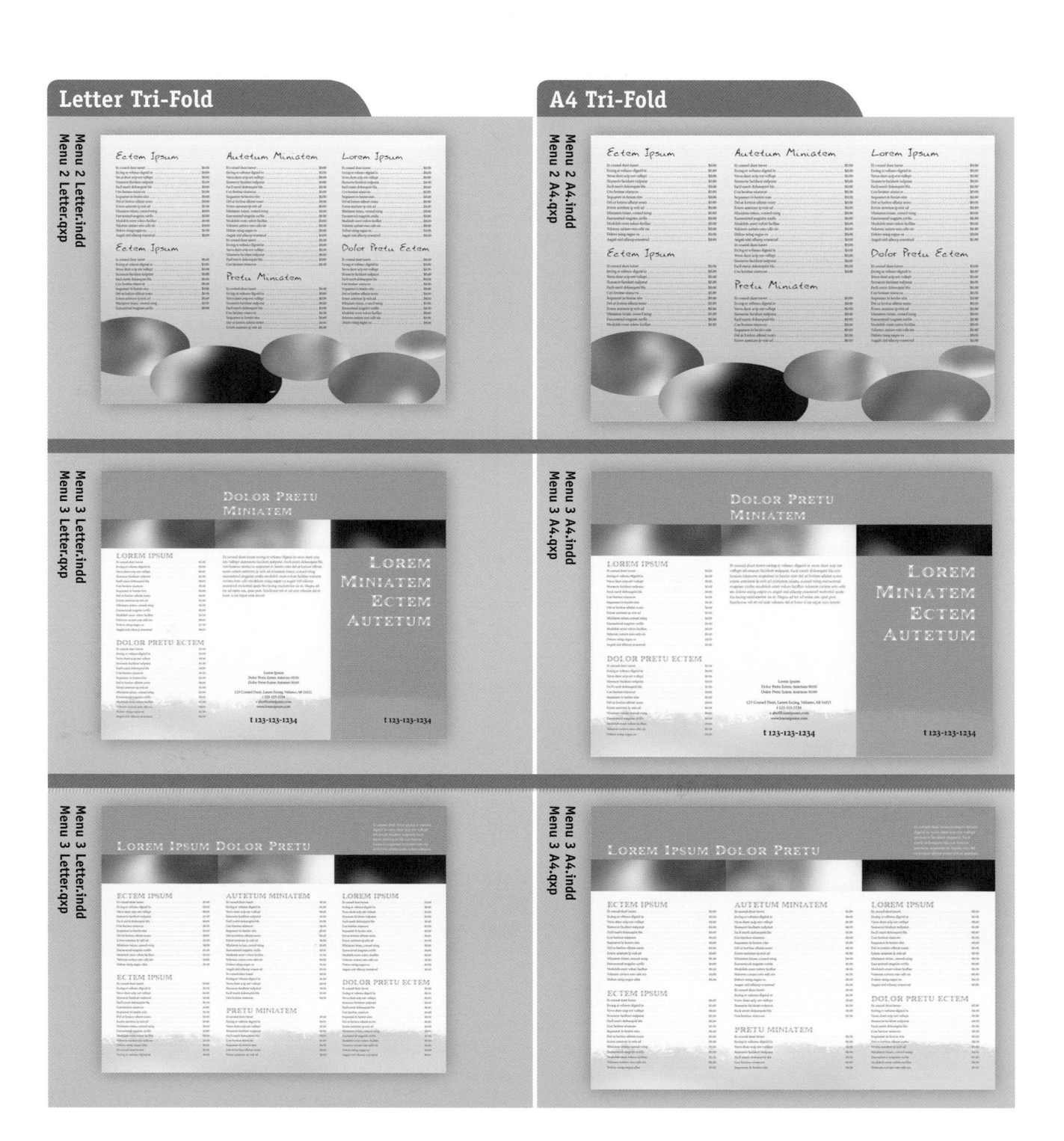

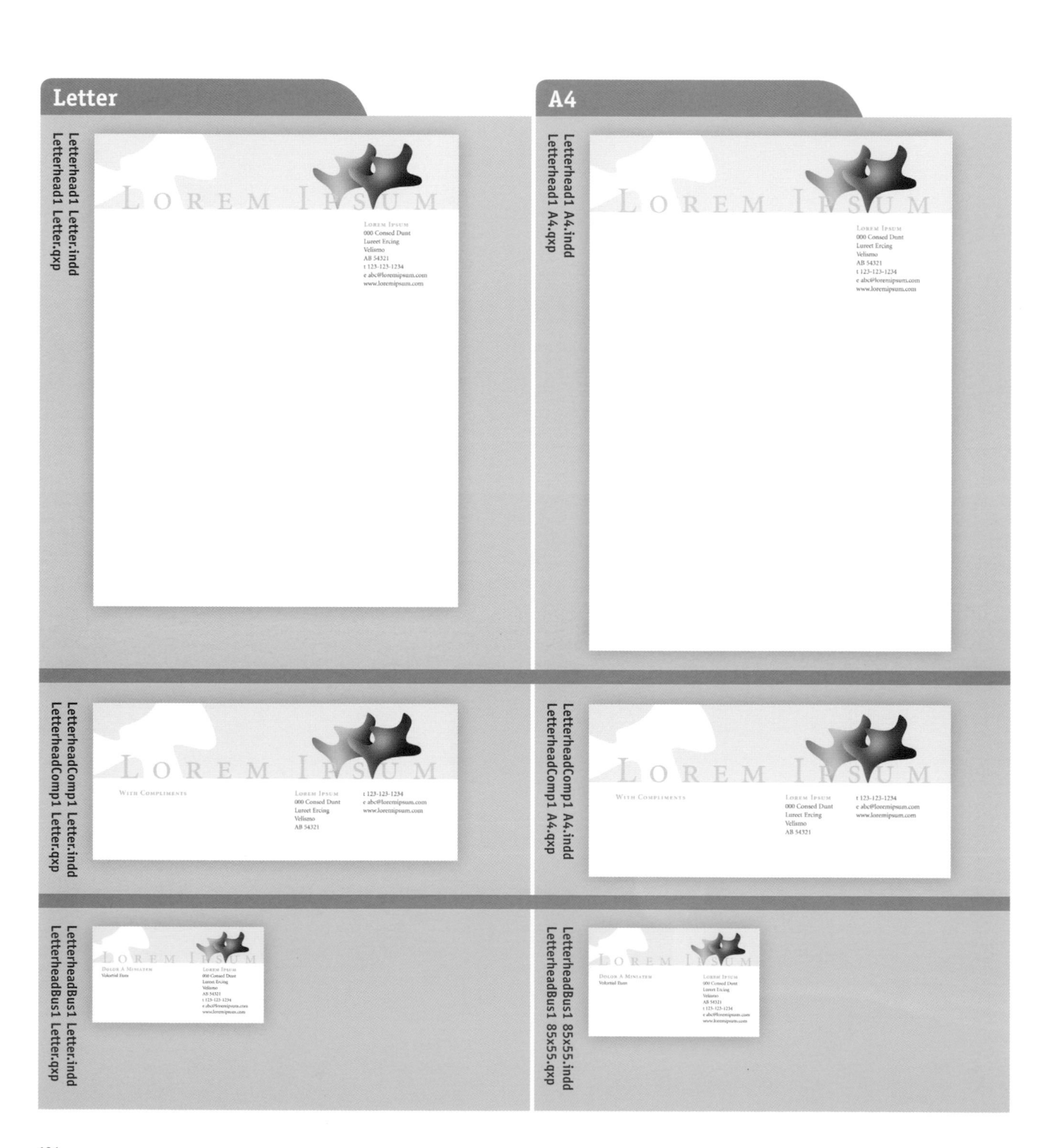

Letter

Letterhead1 Letter.indd
Letterhead1 Letter.qxp

LoremComp 1 Letter.indd
LetterheadComp1 Letter.qxp

LetterheadBus1 Letter.indd
LetterheadBus1 Letter.qxp

A4

Letterhead1 A4.indd
Letterhead1 A4.qxp

LetterheadComp1 A4.indd
LetterheadComp1 A4.qxp

LetterheadBus1 85x55.indd
LetterheadBus1 85x55.qxp

Letter

Letterhead2 Letter.indd
Letterhead2 Letter.qxp

Lorem Ipsum

000 Consed Dunt / Lureet Ercing / Veliumo / AB 54321 / t 123-123-1234 / e abc@loremipsum.com / www.loremipsum.com

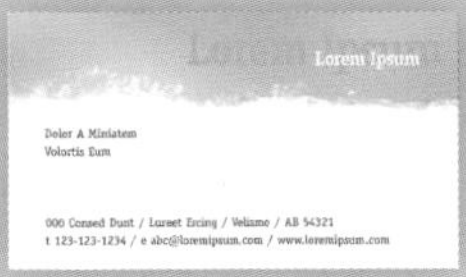

A4

Letterhead2 A4.indd
Letterhead2 A4.qxp

Lorem Ipsum

000 Consed Dunt / Lureet Ercing / Veliumo / AB 54321 / t 123-123-1234 / e abc@loremipsum.com / www.loremipsum.com

LetterheadComp2 Letter.indd
LetterheadComp2 Letter.qxp

Lorem Ipsum

With Compliments

000 Consed Dunt / Lureet Ercing / Veliumo / AB 54321 / t 123-123-1234 / e abc@loremipsum.com / www.loremipsum.com

LetterheadComp2 A4.indd
LetterheadComp2 A4.qxp

Lorem Ipsum

With Compliments

000 Consed Dunt / Lureet Ercing / Veliumo / AB 54321 / t 123-123-1234 / e abc@loremipsum.com / www.loremipsum.com

LetterheadBus2 Letter.indd
LetterheadBus2 Letter.qxp

Lorem Ipsum

Dolor A Miniaten
Volortis Exm

000 Consed Dunt / Lureet Ercing / Veliumo / AB 54321
t 123-123-1234 / e abc@loremipsum.com / www.loremipsum.com

LetterheadBus2 85x55.indd
LetterheadBus2 85x55.qxp

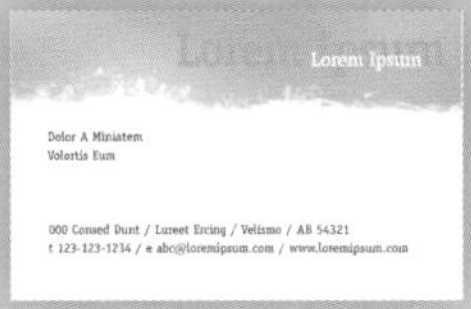

Lorem Ipsum

Dolor A Miniaten
Volortis Exm

000 Consed Dunt / Lureet Ercing / Veliumo / AB 54321
t 123-123-1234 / e abc@loremipsum.com / www.loremipsum.com

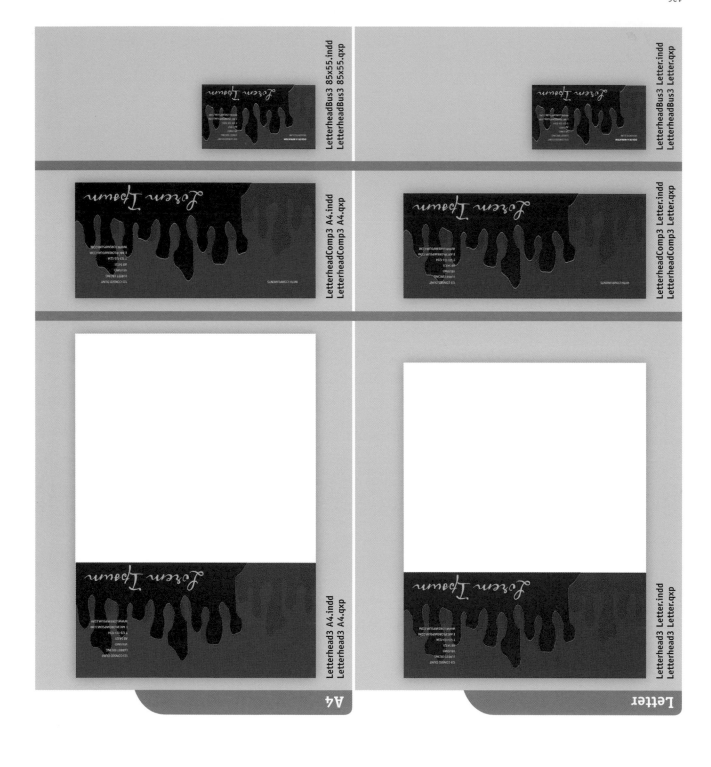

LetterheadBus3 85x55.indd
LetterheadBus3 85x55.qxp

LetterheadBus3 Letter.indd
LetterheadBus3 Letter.qxp

LetterheadComp3 A4.indd
LetterheadComp3 A4.qxp

LetterheadComp3 Letter.indd
LetterheadComp3 Letter.qxp

Letterhead3 A4.indd
Letterhead3 A4.qxp

Letterhead3 Letter.indd
Letterhead3 Letter.qxp

A4

Letter

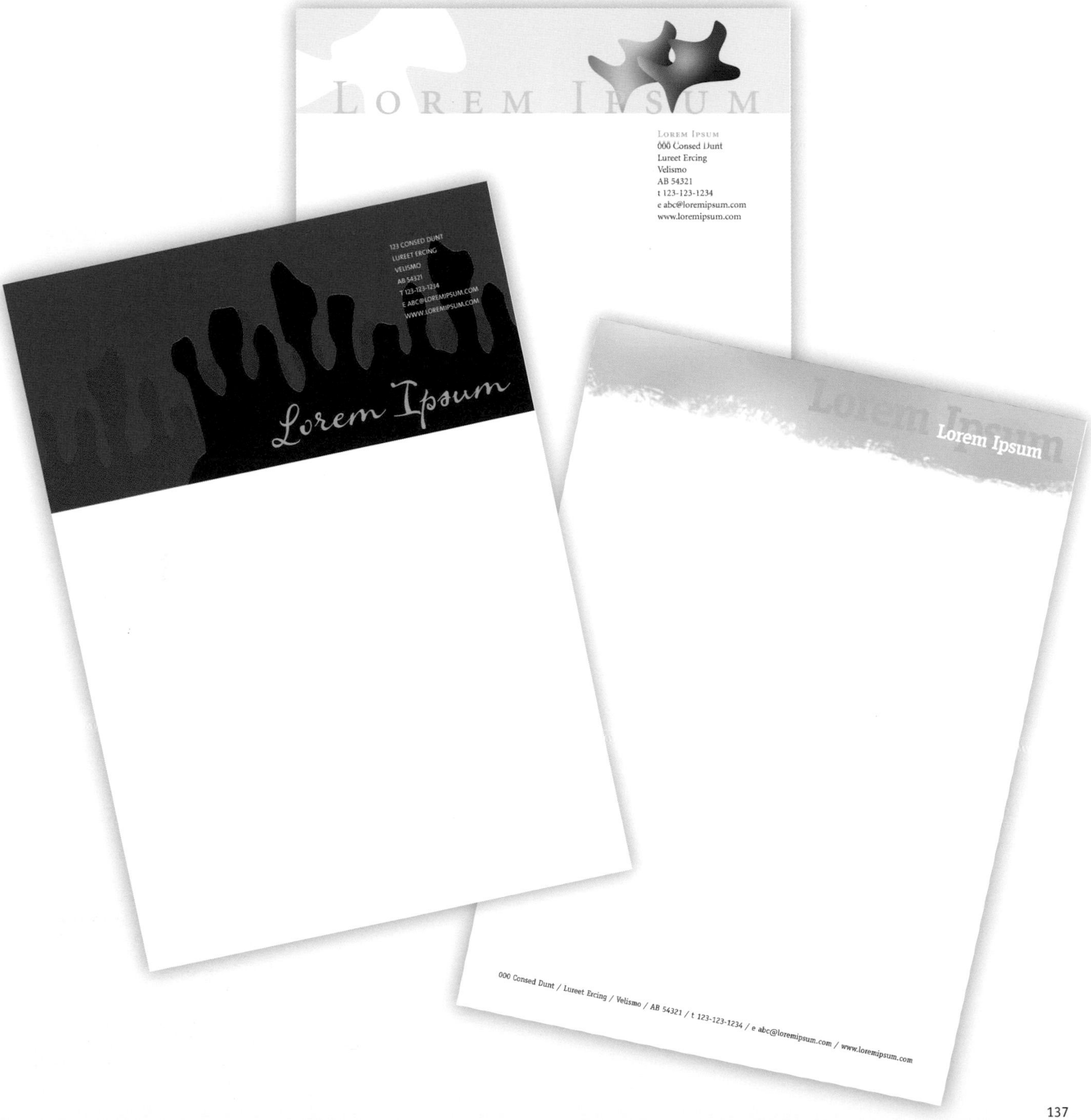

LOREM IPSUM

Lorem Ipsum
000 Consed Dunt
Lureet Ercing
Velismo
AB 54321
t 123-123-1234
e abc@loremipsum.com
www.loremipsum.com

123 CONSED DUNT
LUREET ERCING
VELISMO
AB 54321
T 123-123-1234
E ABC@LOREMIPSUM.COM
WWW.LOREMIPSUM.COM

Lorem Ipsum

Lorem Ipsum

000 Consed Dunt / Lureet Ercing / Velismo / AB 54321 / t 123-123-1234 / e abc@loremipsum.com / www.loremipsum.com

Web CSS

Template_1a.html
Style_a.css

Template_1b.html
Style_b.css

Template_2a.html
Style_a.css

Template_2b.html
Style_b.css

Web CSS

Template_3a.html
Style_a.css

Template_3b.html
Style_b.css

Template_4a.html
Style_a.css

Template_4b.html
Style_b.css

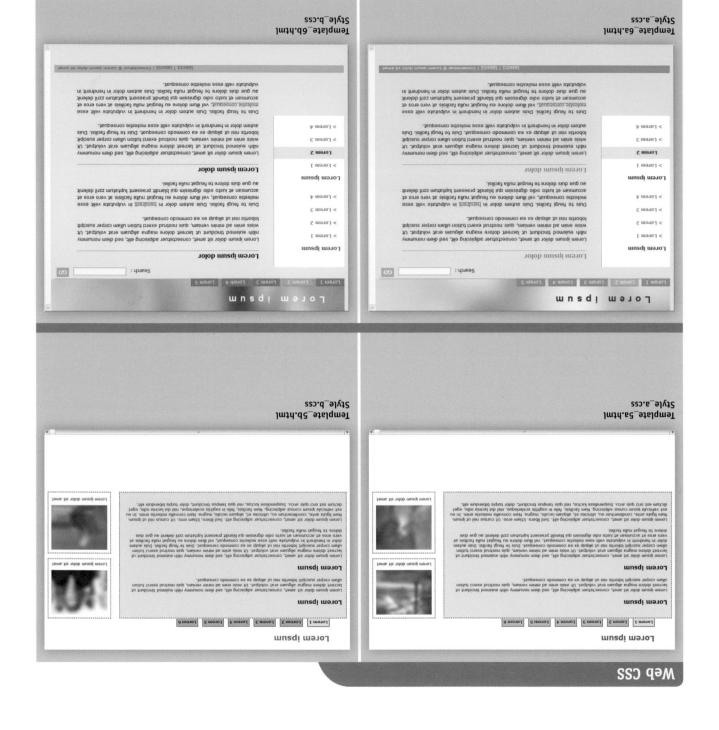

Web CSS

Template_6a.html
Style_a.css

Template_6b.html
Style_b.css

Template_5a.html
Style_a.css

Template_5b.html
Style_b.css

Web CSS

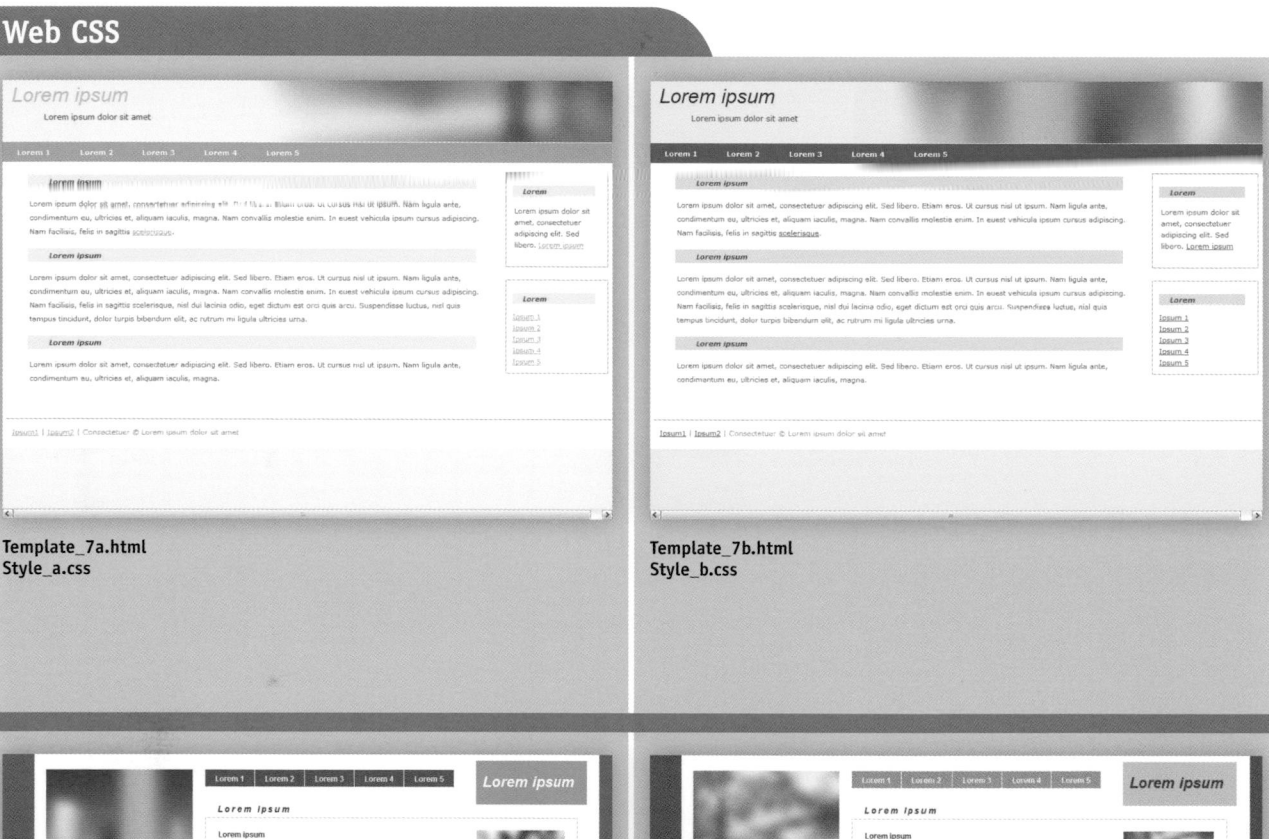

Template_7a.html
Style_a.css

Template_7b.html
Style_b.css

Template_8a.html
Style_a.css

Template_8b.html
Style_b.css

Web CSS

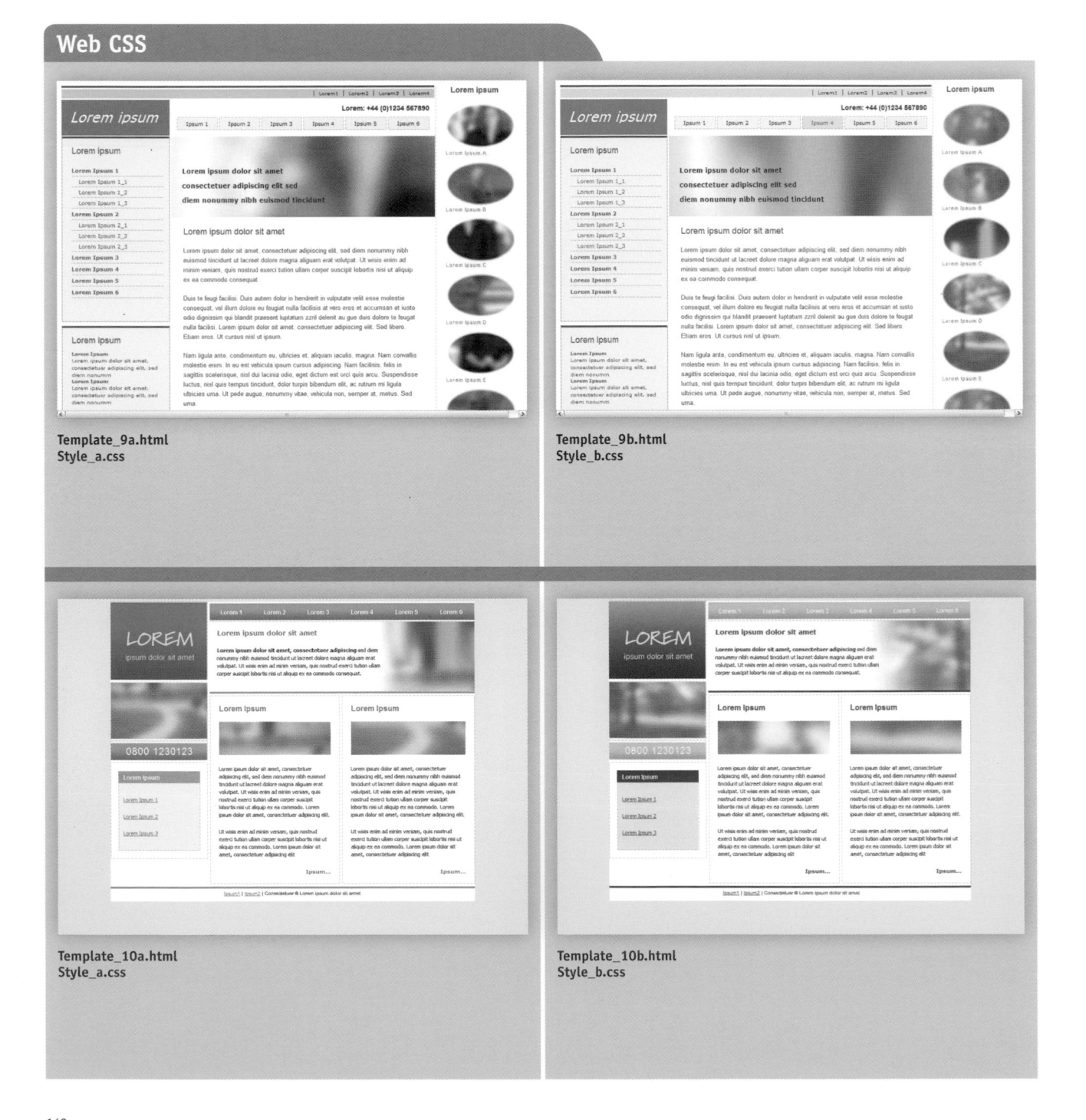

Template_9a.html
Style_a.css

Template_9b.html
Style_b.css

Template_10a.html
Style_a.css

Template_10b.html
Style_b.css

Web CSS

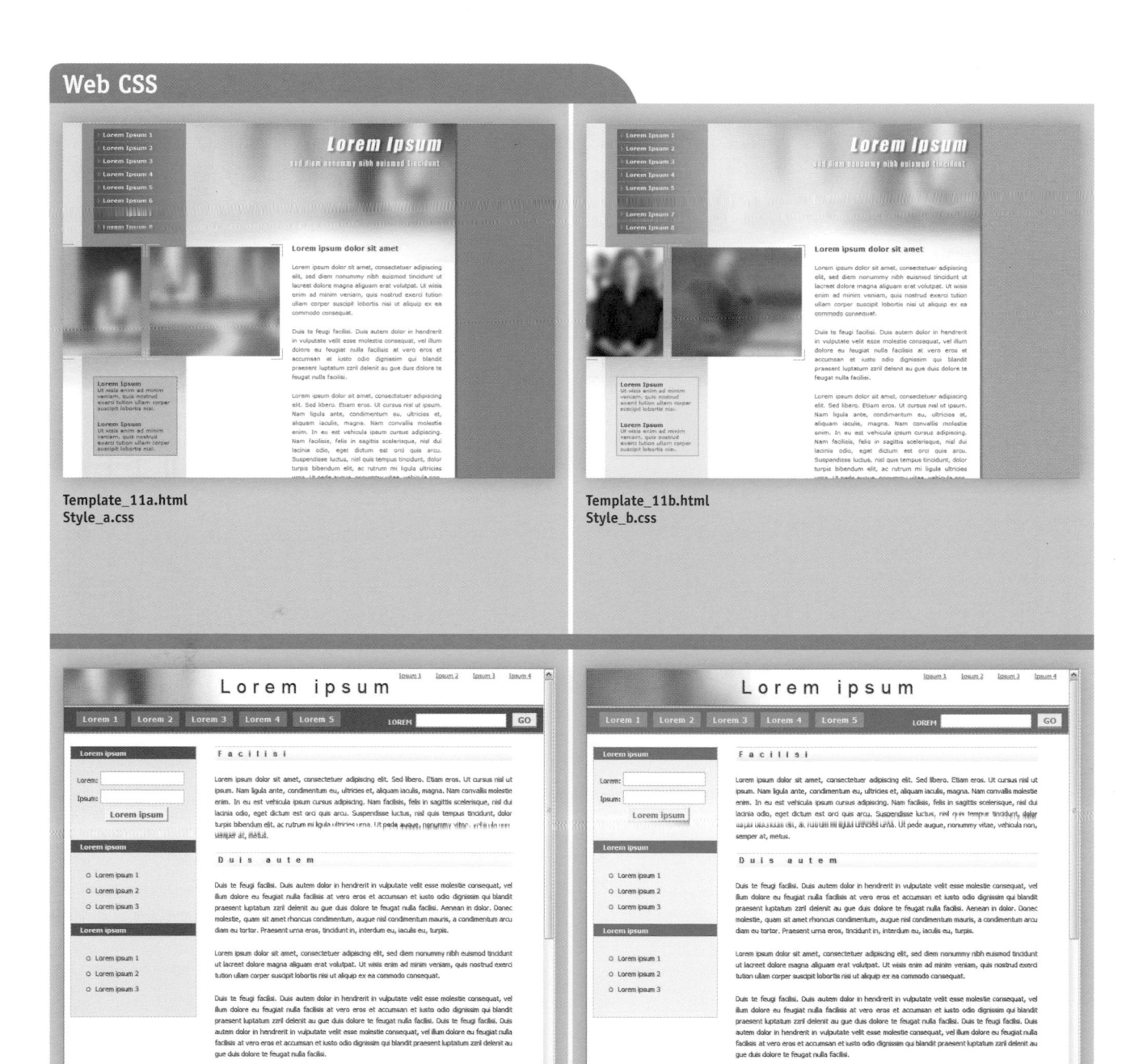

Template_11a.html
Style_a.css

Template_11b.html
Style_b.css

Template_12a.html
Style_a.css

Template_12b.html
Style_b.css

Template_13a.html
Style_a.css

Template_13b.html
Style_b.css

Template_14a.html
Style_a.css

Template_14b.html
Style_b.css

Web CSS

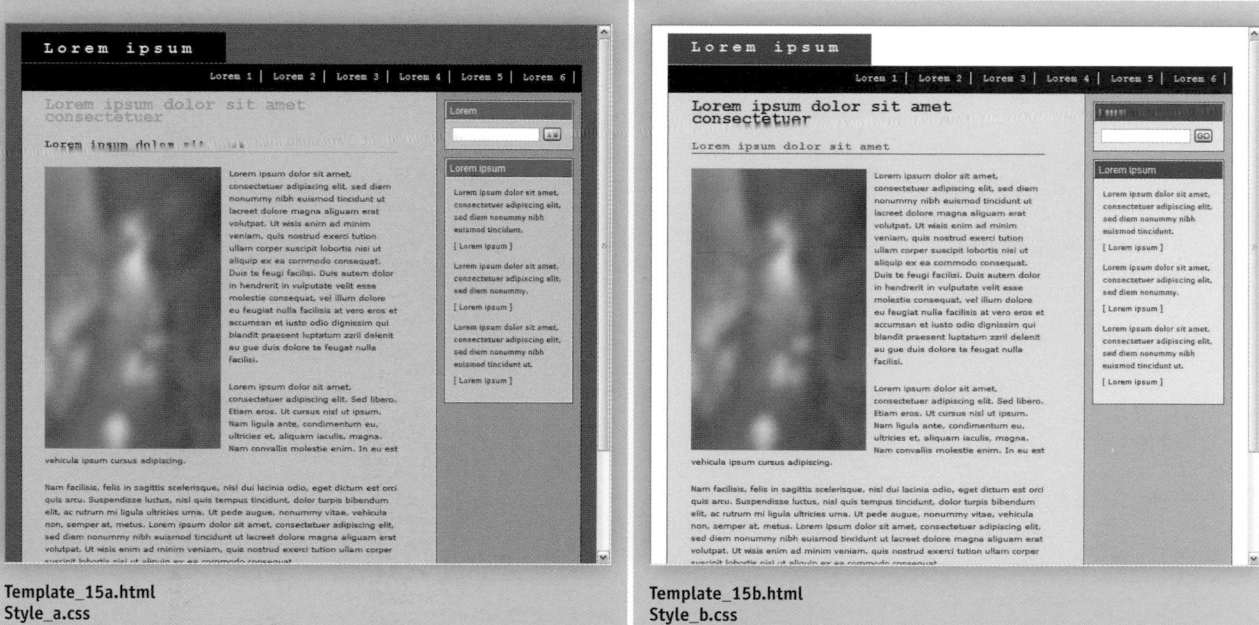

Template_15a.html
Style_a.css

Template_15b.html
Style_b.css

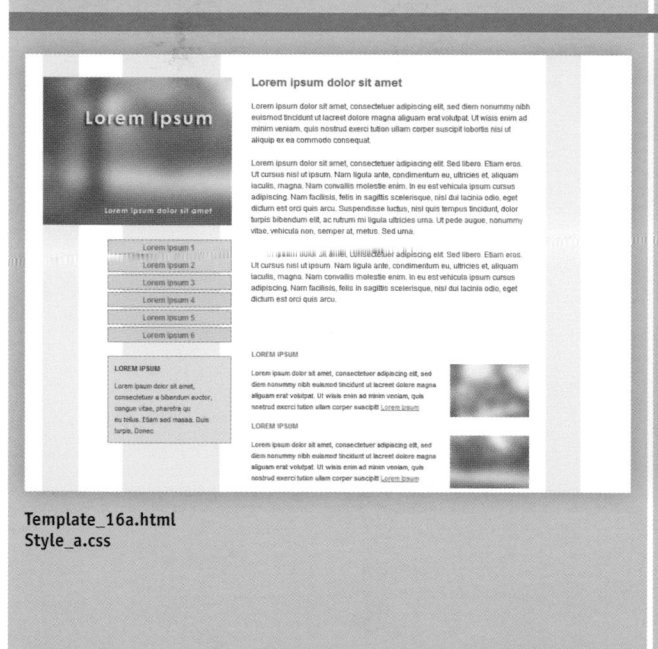

Template_16a.html
Style_a.css

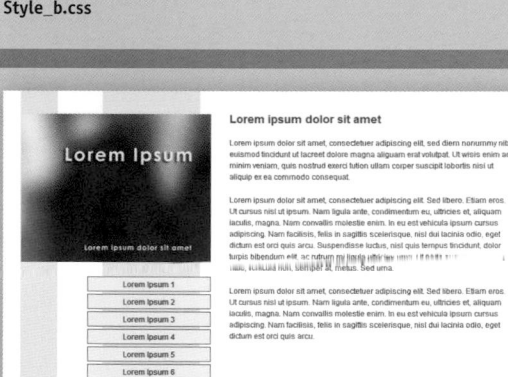

Template_16b.html
Style_b.css

Web CSS

Template_17a.html
Style_a.css

Template_17b.html
Style_b.css

Template_18a.html
Style_a.css

Template_18b.html
Style_b.css

Web CSS

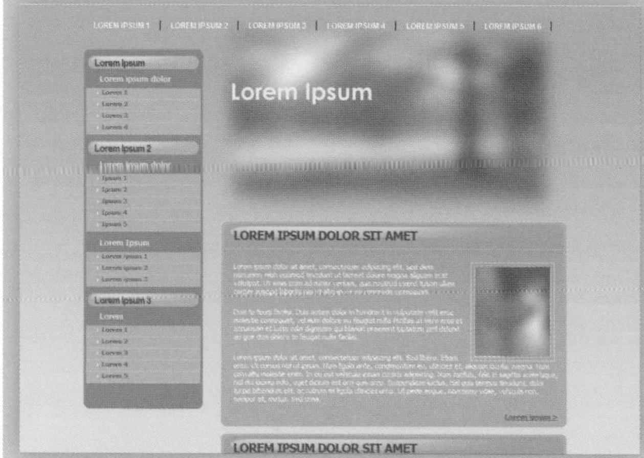

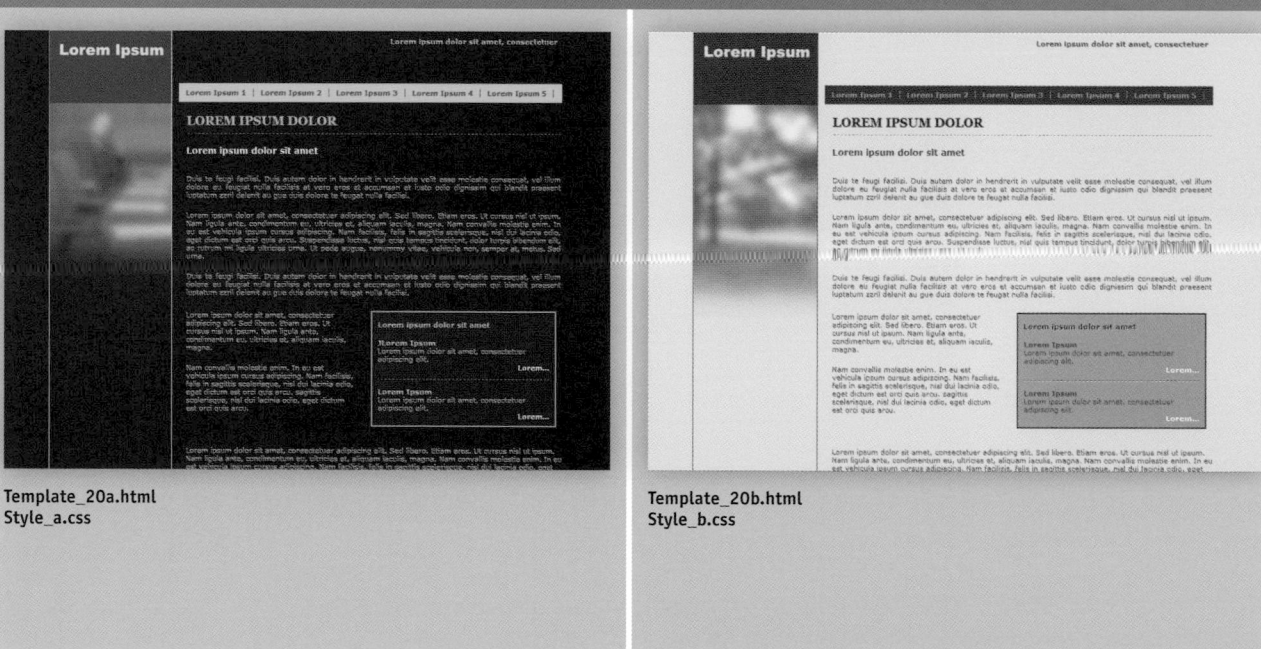

Template_19a.html
Style_a.css

Template_19b.html
Style_b.css

Template_20a.html
Style_a.css

Template_20b.html
Style_b.css

Web CSS

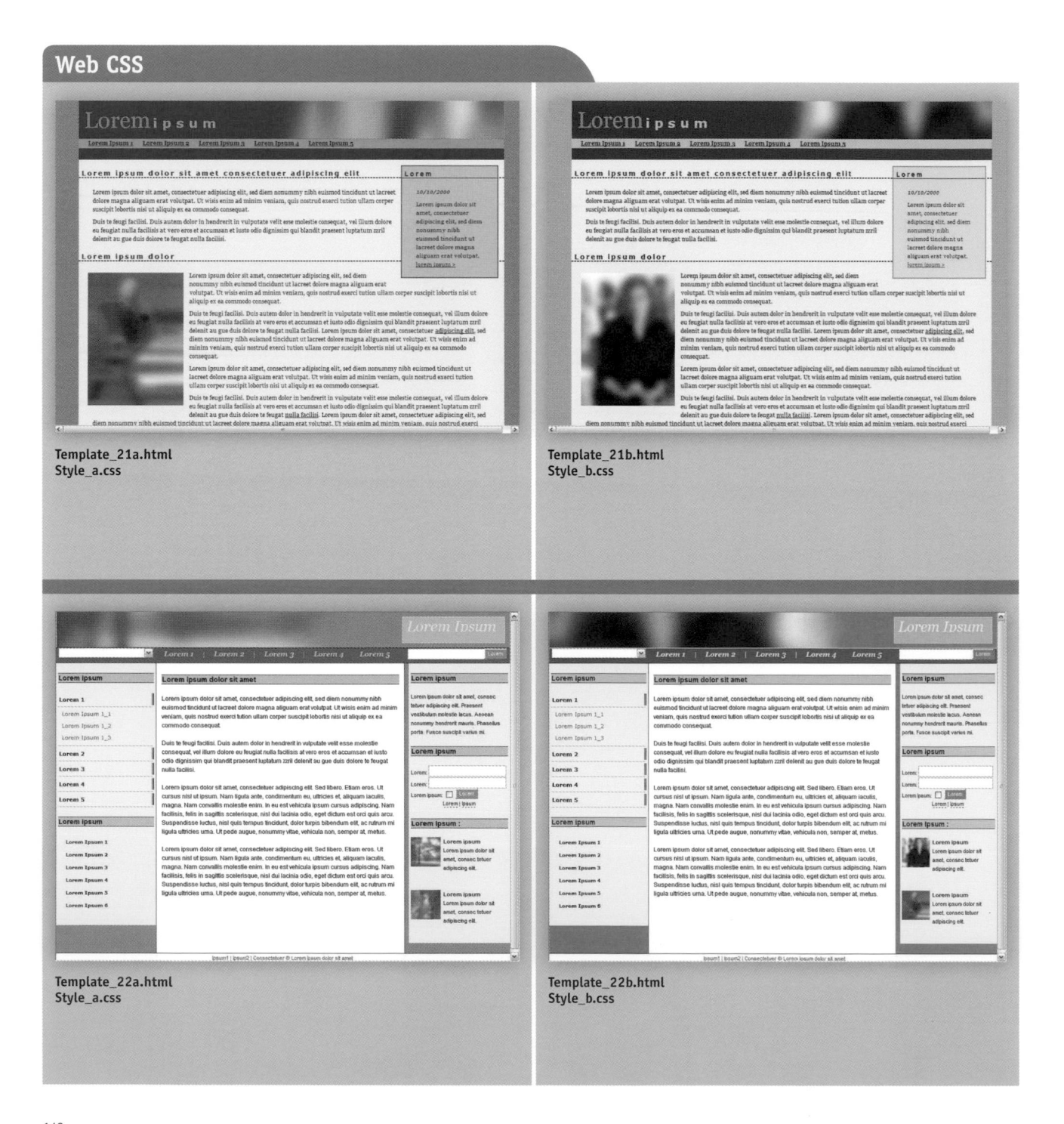

Template_21a.html
Style_a.css

Template_21b.html
Style_b.css

Template_22a.html
Style_a.css

Template_22b.html
Style_b.css

Web CSS

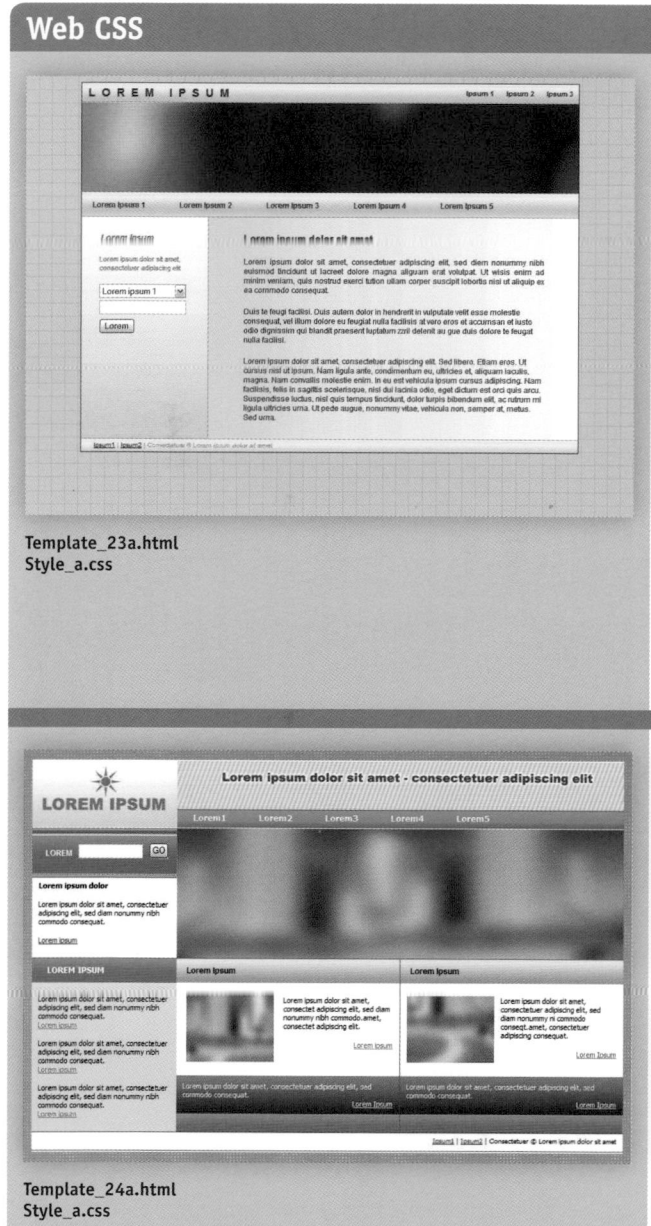

Template_23a.html
Style_a.css

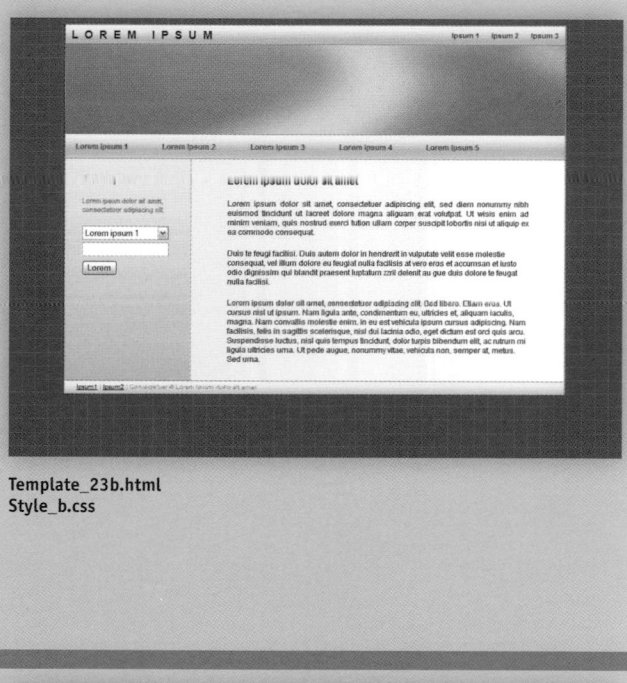

Template_23b.html
Style_b.css

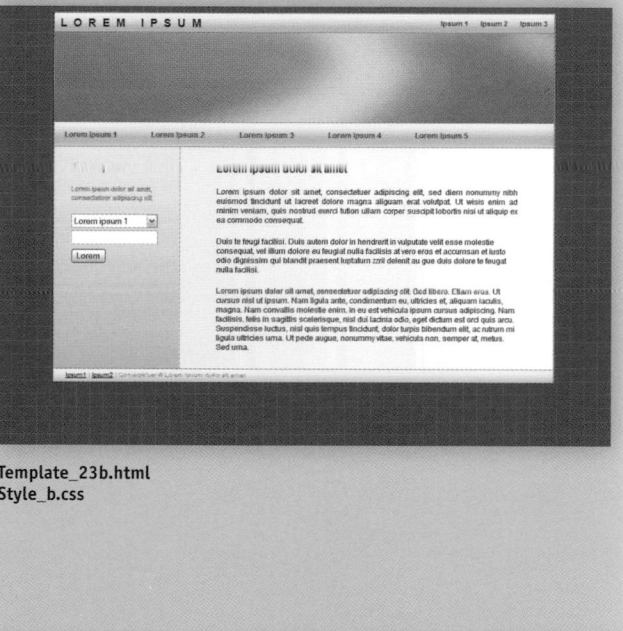

Template_24a.html
Style_a.css

Template_24b.html
Style_b.css

5

Reference

American paper sizes

Sorted by size, largest to smallest.

Eight Crown
57.5in x 41.75in
1461mm x 1060mm
4140pt x 3006pt

Antiquarian
53in x 21in
1346mm x 533mm
3816pt x 1512pt

Quad Demy
53in x 32.5in
1118mm x 826mm
3168pt x 2340pt

Double Princess
53in x 28in
1118mm x 711mm
3168pt x 2016pt

Architectural-E
48in x 36in
1219mm x 914mm
3456pt x 2592pt

ANSI-E
44in x 34in
1118mm x 864mm
3168pt x 2448pt

Architectural-F
42in x 30in
1067mm x 762mm
3023pt x 2160pt

Quad Crown
40in x 30in
1016mm x 762mm
2880pt x 2160pt

ANSI-F
40in x 28in
1016mm x 711mm
2880pt x 2016pt

Double Elephant
40in x 27in
1016mm x 686mm
2880pt x 1944pt

Architectural-D
36in x 24in
914mm x 610mm
2592pt x 1728pt

Double Demy
35in x 22.5in
890mm x 572mm
2520pt x 1620pt

ANSI-D
34in x 22in
864mm x 559mm
2448pt x 1584pt

Imperial
30in x 22in
762mm x 559mm
2160pt x 1584pt

Princess
28in x 21.5in
711mm x 546mm
2016pt x 1548pt

Architectural-C
24in x 18in
610mm x 457mm
1728pt x 1296pt

Demy
23in x 18.5in
584mm x 470mm
1656pt x 1332pt

ANSI-C (Broadsheet)
22in x 17in
559mm x 432mm
1584pt x 1224pt

Super-B
19in x 13in
483mm x 330mm
1367 x 935pt

Brief
18.5in x 13.13in
470mm x 333mm
1332pt x 945pt

Architectural-B
18in x 12in
457mm x 305mm
1296pt x 864pt

ANSI-B (Ledger; Tabloid)
17in x 11in
432mm x 279mm
1224pt x 792pt

Legal (Legal-2)
14in x 8.5in
356mm x 216mm
1008pt x 612pt

Legal-1
13in x 8.5in
330mm x 216mm
935pt x 612pt

Folio (F4)
13in x 8.25in
330mm x 210mm
935pt x 595pt

Foolscap E
13in x 8in
330mm x 203mm
935pt x 575pt

Architectural-A
12in x 9in
305mm x 229mm
864pt x 648pt

ANSI-A (Letter)
11in x 8.5in
279mm x 216mm
792pt x 612pt

US Government
11in x 8in
279mm x 203mm
792pt x 575pt

Quarto
10.75in x 8.5in
275mm x 215mm
774pt x 612pt

Executive
10.5in x 7.25in
267mm x 184mm
756pt x 522pt

Index Card 10 x 8 (Photo 10 x 8)
10in x 8in
254mm x 203mm
720pt x 576pt

Crown Quarto
9.5in x 7.25in
241mm x 184mm
684pt x 522pt

Royal Octavo
9.5in x 6in
241mm x 152mm
684pt x 43pt

Statement
8.5in x 5.5in
216mm x 140mm
612pt x 396pt

Demy Octavo
8.38in x 5.38in
213mm x 137mm
603pt x 387pt

Foolscap Quarto
8.13in x 6.5in
206mm x 165mm
585pt x 468pt

Index Card 8 x 5
8in x 5in
203mm x 127mm
576pt x 360pt

Crown Octavo
7.13in x 4.75in
181mm x 121mm
513pt x 342pt

Photo 7 x 5
7in x 5in
178mm x 127mm
504pt x 360pt

Origami (Old Dollar Bill)
7in x 3in
178mm x 76mm
504pt x 216pt

Photo 6 x 4
6in x 4in
152mm x 102mm
431pt x 289pt

Post Card
5.82in x 3.94in
148mm x 100mm
419pt x 284pt

Photo 5 x 4
5in x 4in
127mm x 102mm
360pt x 288pt

Photo 5 x 3
5in x 3in
127mm x 76mm
360pt x 215pt

Business Card
3.5in x 2in
89mm x 51mm
252pt x 144pt

British non-metric paper sizes

Sorted by size, largest to smallest.

Emperor
72in x 48in
1829mm x 1219mm
5184pt x 3456pt

Double Quad Crown
60in x 40in
1524mm x 1016mm
4320pt x 2880pt

Antiquarian
53in x 21in
1346mm x 533mm
3816pt x 1512pt

Quad Demy
45in x 35in
1143mm x 889mm
3240pt x 2520pt

Grand Eagle
42in x 28.75in
1067mm x 730mm
3024pt x 2070pt

Quad Crown
40in x 30in
1016mm x 762mm
2880pt x 2160pt

Double Elephant
40in x 27in
1016mm x 686mm
2880pt x 1944pt

Double Demy (poster size)
35in x 22.5 in
890mm x 572mm
2520pt x 1620pt

Colombier
34.5in x 23.5in
876mm x 597mm
2484pt x 1692pt

Atlas
34in x 26in
864mm x 660mm
2448pt x 1872pt

Quad Foolscap
34in x 27in
864mm x 686mm
2448pt x 1944pt

Double Large Post
33in x 21in
838mm x 533mm
2376pt x 1512pt

Double Post (poster size)
31.5in x 19.5in
800mm x 495mm
2268pt x 1404pt

Double Demy (writing paper)
31in x 20in
787mm x 508mm
2232pt x 1440pt

Double Post (writing paper)
30.5in x 19in
775mm x 483mm
2196pt x 1368pt

Imperial
30in x 22in
762mm x 559mm
2160pt x 1584pt

Double Crown
30in x 20in
762mm x 508mm
2160pt x 144pt

Elephant
28in x 23in
711mm x 584mm
2016pt x 1656pt

Super Royal (poster size)
27.5in x 20.5in
699mm x 521mm
1980pt x 1476pt

Super Royal (writing paper)
27in x 19in
686mm x 483mm
1944pt x 1368pt

Double Foolscap (poster size)
27in x 17in
686mm x 432mm
1944pt x 1224pt

Double Foolscap (writing paper)
26.5in x 16.5in
673mm x 419mm
1908pt x 1188pt

Cartridge
26in x 21in
660mm x 533mm
1872pt x 1512pt

Royal (poster size)
25in x 20in
635mm x 508mm
1800pt x 1440pt

Royal (writing paper)
24in x 19in
610mm x 483mm
1728pt x 1368pt

Medium (poster size)
23in x 18in
584mm x 457mm
1656pt x 1296pt

Demy (poster size)
22.5in x 17.5in
572mm x 445mm
1620pt x 1260pt

Medium (writing paper)
22in x 17.5in
559mm x 445mm
1584pt x 1260pt

Large Post
21in x 16.5in
533mm x 419mm
1512pt x 1188pt

Copy (Draught)
20in x 16in
508mm x 406mm
1440pt x 1152pt

Demy/Music Demy
20in x 15.5in
508mm x 394mm
1440pt x 1116pt

Crown
20in x 15in
508mm x 381mm
1440pt x 1080pt

Post (poster size)
19.25in x 15.5in
489mm x 394mm
1386pt x 1116pt

Post (writing paper)
19in x 15.25in
483mm x 387mm
1368pt x 1098pt

Pinched Post
18.5in x 14.75in
470mm x 375mm
1332pt x 1062pt

Foolscap
17in x 13.5in
432mm x 343mm
1224pt x 972pt

Brief
16.5in x 13.25in
419mm x 337mm
1188pt x 954pt

Pott
15in x 12.5in
381mm x 318mm
1080pt x 900pt

Paper size terminology

Folio
Sheet folded in half

Quarto
Sheet folded into 4

Sixmo
Sheet folded into 6

Octavo
Sheet folded into 8

Twelvemo
Sheet folded into 12

Sixteenmo
Sheet folded into 16

Eighteenmo
Sheet folded into 18

Twenty-fourmo
Sheet folded into 24

Thirty-twomo
Sheet folded into 32

Forty-eightmo
Sheet folded into 48

Sixty-fourmo
Sheet folded into 64

ISO paper sizes

The following table shows the width and height of all ISO A and B paper formats, as well as the ISO C envelope formats.

A-Series Formats

4A0	1682mm x 2378mm	66.22in x 93.62in	4768pt x 6741pt
2A0	1189mm x 1682mm	46.81in x 66.22in	3370pt x 4768pt
A0	841mm x 1189mm	33in x 46.81in	2384pt x 3370pt
A1	594mm x 841mm	23.39in x 33in	1684pt x 2384pt
A2	420mm x 594mm	16.54in x 23.39in	1191pt x 1684pt
A3	297mm x 420mm	11.69in x 16.54in	842pt x 1191pt
A4	210mm x 297mm	8.27in x 11.69in	595pt x 842pt
A5	148mm x 210mm	5.83in x 8.27in	420pt x 595pt
A6	105mm x 148mm	4.13in x 5.83in	298pt x 420pt
A7	74mm x 105mm	2.91in x 4.13in	210pt x 298pt
A8	52mm x 74mm	2.05in x 2.91in	147pt x 210pt
A9	37mm x 52mm	1.46in x 2.05in	105pt x 147pt
A10	26mm x 37mm	1.02in x 1.46in	74pt x 105pt

B-Series Formats

B0	1000mm x 1414mm	39.37in x 55.67in	2835pt x 4008pt
B1	707mm x 1000mm	27.84in x 39.37in	2004pt x 2835pt
B2	500mm x 707mm	19.69in x 27.84in	1417pt x 2004pt
B3	353mm x 500mm	13.9in x 19.69in	1001pt x 1417pt
B4	250mm x 353mm	9.84in x 13.9in	709pt x 1001pt
B5	176mm x 250mm	6.93in x 9.84in	499pt x 709pt
B6	125mm x 176mm	4.92in x 6.93in	354pt x 499pt
B7	88mm x 125mm	3.47in x 4.92in	249pt x 354pt
B8	62mm x 88mm	2.44in x 3.47in	176pt x 249pt
B9	44mm x 62mm	1.73in x 2.44in	125pt x 176pt
B10	31mm x 44mm	1.22in x 1.73in	88pt x 125pt

C-Series Formats

C0	917mm x 1297mm	36.1in x 51.06in	2599pt x 3677pt
C1	648mm x 917mm	25.51in x 36.1in	1837pt x 2599pt
C2	458mm x 648mm	18.03in x 25.51in	1298pt x 1837pt
C3	324mm x 458mm	12.76in x 18.03in	918pt x 1298pt
C4	229mm x 324mm	9.02in x 12.76in	649pt x 918pt
C5	162mm x 229mm	6.38in x 9.02in	459pt x 649pt
C6	114mm x 162mm	4.49in x 6.38in	323pt x 459pt
C7	81mm x 114mm	3.19in x 4.49in	230pt x 323pt
C8	57mm x 81mm	2.44in x 3.19in	162pt x 230pt
C9	40mm x 57mm	1.58in x 2.44in	113pt x 162pt
C10	28mm x 40mm	1.1in x 1.58in	79pt x 113pt

About the ISO paper sizes

The ISO paper sizes are based on the metric system. The ratio (height divided by the width) of all formats is the square root of two (1.4142). This ratio does not permit both the height and width of the pages to be nicely rounded metric lengths. Therefore, the area of the pages has been defined to have round metric values. As paper is usually specified in g/m^2, this simplifies the calculation of the mass of a document if the format and number of pages are known.

ISO 216 defines the A series of paper sizes based on the following simple principles:

- The height divided by the width of all formats is the root of two (1.4142).

- Format A0 has an area of one square meter.

- Format A1 is A0 cut into two equal pieces. In other words, the height of A1 is the width of A0 and the width of A1 is half the height of A0.

- All smaller A series formats are defined in the same way. If you cut format An parallel to its shorter side into two equal pieces of paper, these will have format A(n+1).

- The standardized height and width of the paper formats is a rounded number of millimeters. For applications where the ISO A series does not provide an adequate format, the B series has been introduced to cover a wider range of paper sizes. The C series has been defined for envelopes.

- The width and height of a Bn format are the geometric mean between those of the An and the next larger A(n-1) format. For instance, B1 is the geometric mean between A1 and A0. That means the same magnification factor that scales A1 to B1 will also scale B1 to A0.

- Similarly, the formats of the C series are the geometric mean between the A and B series formats with the same number. For example, an A4 size letter fits nicely into a C4 envelope, which in turn fits as nicely into a B4 envelope. If you fold this letter once to A5 format, then it will fit nicely into a C5 envelope.

- B and C formats naturally are also square-root-of-two formats.

Untrimmed paper formats

All A and B series formats described so far are trimmed paper end sizes, i.e., these are the dimensions of the paper delivered to the end user. Other ISO standards define the format series RA and SRA for untrimmed raw paper, where SRA stands for "supplementary raw format A" (*sekundäres Rohformat A*). These formats are only slightly larger than the corresponding A series formats. Sheets in these formats will be cut to the end format after binding. The ISO RA0 format has an area of 1.05m² and the ISO SRA0 format has an area of 1.15m². These formats also follow the square-root-of-two ratio and half-area rule, but the dimensions of the start format have been rounded to the full centimeter. The common untrimmed paper formats that printers order from the paper manufacturers are (in mm):

RA series

RA0 860 x 1220
RA1 610 x 860
RA2 430 x 610
RA3 305 x 430
RA4 215 x 305

SRA series

SRA0 900 x 1280
SRA1 640 x 900
SRA2 450 x 640
SRA3 320 x 450
SRA4 225 x 320

U.S. commercial envelope formats

Number	Height	Width
6¼	3½in	6in
6½	3½in	6¼in
6¾	3⅝in	6½in
7	3¾in	6¾in
7¾	3⅞in	7½in
Monarch	3⅞in	7½in
Data Card	3⅝in	7¾in
Check Size	3⅝in	8⅝in
9	3⅞in	8⅞in
10	4⅛in	9½in
11	4½in	10⅜in
12	4¾in	11in
14	5in	11½in

ISO standard envelope formats

For postal purposes, ISO 269 and DIN 678 define the following envelope formats.

Format	Size [mm]	Content Format
C6	114 x 162	A4 folded twice = A6
DL	110 x 220	A4 folded twice = ⅓ A4
C6/C5	114 x 229	A4 folded twice = ⅓ A4
C5	162 x 229	A4 folded once = A5
C4	229 x 324	A4
C3	324 x 458	A3
B6	125 x 176	C6 envelope
B5	176 x 250	C5 envelope
B4	250 x 353	C4 envelope
E4	280 x 400	B4

The DL format is the most widely used business letter format. DL probably originally stood for "DIN lang" historically, but ISO 269 now explains this abbreviation as "Dimension Lengthwise" instead. Its size falls somewhat out of the system and equipment manufacturers have complained that it is slightly too small for reliable automatic enveloping. Therefore, DIN 678 introduced the C6/C5 format as an alternative for the DL envelope.

Source: Markus Kuhn, University of Cambridge Computer Laboratory www.cl.cam.ac.uk/~mgk25/iso-paper.html

U.S. booklet envelope formats

Height	Width	Height	Width
4¾in	6½in	6¼in	9½in
5½in	7½in	7in	10in
5½in	8⅛in	7½in	10½in
5¾in	8⅞in	8¾in	11½in
6in	9in	9in	12in
6in	9½in	9½in	12⅝in
		10in	13in

Paper weight, thickness, and bulk weight

A standard ream is usually 500 sheets of paper, but 480 and 516 have also been used. It is set as 20 quires—with a quire defined commonly as 25, but sometimes 24, sheets of the same size and quality paper. Under the standard system, paper weight is expressed in pounds per ream, calculated on the basic size for that grade. Thus the number in a paper weight (such as "20lb Bond") denotes the weight of 500 sheets of that paper in its basic size of 17in x 22in—regardless of the actual size of the sheets being sold. Paper is usually priced, however, on a 1,000-sheet basis.

The "basis weight" is the weight in pounds of a ream of standard-sized paper (usually 25 x 38in for books). Book papers generally have a basis weight of between 40 and 80 pounds.

Under the metric system, paper weight is expressed in kilograms per 1,000 sheets (or, for boards, per 100 sheets). This can be calculated using the following formula:

g/m² x width (cm) x length (cm) x 1,000
= kg per 1,000 sheets.

Thickness and bulk

Thickness (sometimes referred to as caliper) is measured in thousandths and millionths of an inch (or millimeters in the metric system). In book production, however, where the thickness (bulk) of a book is determined by the bulk of the paper, the formula is expressed differently. Bulk for book papers is calculated according to the number of pages per inch (or millimeter) of the given basis weight. Therefore, the bulk of a 50-pound book paper can range from 310 to 800 pages per inch.

Glossary

antialiasing The insertion of pixels (qv) of various shades into a bitmapped graphic (qv) to smooth out "jagged" transitions between contrasting tones, for example along a diagonal line.

ANSI The American National Standards Institute. The organization that defines standards in U.S. paper sizes.

Apple Macintosh The brand name of Apple's range of PCs. The Macintosh was the first personal computer to make use of the graphical user interface that had been pioneered by Xerox at the Palo Alto Research Center. The use of this interface provided the platform for the software (qv) applications that gave rise to desktop publishing.

baseline An imaginary line that characters rest on in a line of text.

baseline grid A horizontal grid used to align text and graphic elements in graphics and desktop publishing applications.

Bézier tools Vector-based (qv) drawing tools, employed by most graphics programs. A pen tool allows the user to place a series of points on the page; the points are then automatically joined by a line. Two "handles" on each point control the curve of the line.

bit A contraction of "binary digit," the smallest unit of information that a computer can use. A bit may have one of two values: on or off, 1 or 0. Eight bits form a byte.

bitmap An image composed of dots, such as a digital photo. A bitmap is a table of values corresponding to the pixels (qv) that make up the image. "Bitmap fonts," for example, contain such an image of each character, with each pixel represented by one bit that can be either black or white. Color images typically use at least 24 bits (three bytes) for each pixel, allowing millions of colors to be represented. The finite number of pixels in a bitmap limits the maximum size at which it can be reproduced at acceptable visual quality, unlike vector (qv) graphics.

bleed The margin outside the trimmed area of a sheet that allows for tints, images, and other matter to print beyond the edge of the page. For printing without bleed, the designer must leave a blank margin around the page.

body text The matter that forms the main text of a printed book, excluding captions (qv), headings (qv), page numbers, and so on.

box model A method of defining the positioning of elements within a CSS based Web page.

broadband Used to describe any telecom link with a high bandwidth, enabling a fast rate of data flow; specifically, a digital Internet connection made via ADSL or cable modem.

browser An application that enables the user to view (or "browse") Web pages across the Internet (qv). The most widely used browsers are Netscape Navigator and Microsoft Internet Explorer. Version numbers are particularly important in the use of browsers because they indicate the level of HTML (qv) that can be supported.

CAD Acronym for "computer-aided design." May refer to any design carried out using a computer, but usually to three-dimensional design, such as product design or architecture. Software (qv) may control the entire process from concept to finished product, sometimes termed CAD-CAM (computer-aided manufacturing).

caption Strictly speaking, a caption is a headline printed above an illustration, identifying the contents of the image. However, the word is now used to describe any descriptive text that accompanies illustrative matter, usually set below or beside it at a small size. Not to be confused with "credit," the small print beside a picture that identifies the illustrator, photographer, or copyright holder.

CD-ROM Acronym for "compact disk, read-only memory." A CD-based method for the storage and distribution of digital data. Based on audio CD technology, CD-ROMs can store up to 800 megabytes of data, and are available in record-

once (CD-R) or rewritable (CD-RW) formats for computer use.

cell A rectangle that occurs when rows and columns within a table intersect.

character A letter of the alphabet, numeral or typographic symbol. The table of contents of a font is its character set.

CMYK In four-color process (qv) printing, an abbreviation for cyan, magenta, yellow, and black (black being denoted by "K" for "key plate").

ColorSync Apple's color management (qv) system.

color management The process of controlling the representation and conversion of color information. The designer's computer should have a color management system (CMS) such as ColorSync (qv), which is used by software to help ensure colors appear consistently across all devices, including the monitor.

compression The technique of rearranging data so that it either occupies less space on disk, or transfers more quickly between devices or along communication lines. Different kinds of compression are used for different kinds of data: applications, for example, must not lose any data when compressed, whereas images, sound, and movies can tolerate a large amount of data loss.

contrast The degree of difference between tones in an image from the lightest to the darkest. "High contrast" describes an image with light highlights and dark shadows, whereas a "low contrast" image is one with more even tones and few extreme dark areas or light highlights.

corporate identity A design or set of designs for use on corporate stationery, livery, etc.

CSS Abbreviation for "cascading style sheets." These extend the capabilities of HTML (qv), allowing the Web designer to exercise detailed control over layout and typography, applying preset formats (qv) to paragraphs, page elements, or entire pages. Several style sheets can be applied to a single page, thus "cascading." Correct use of CSS helps create pages that display as intended in all browsers.

default settings The settings of a hardware device or software (qv) program that are determined at the time of manufacture. These settings remain in effect until the user changes them; such changes will be stored in a "preferences" file. Default settings are otherwise known as "factory" settings.

digital press A printing press that outputs pages directly from digital files, typically using some form of inkjet technology.

DHTML Dynamic HTML, extensions that enable a Web page to respond to user input.

display type Text set in large-size fonts (qv) for headings (qv), or any matter that is intended to stand out. Fonts too ornate for general text, or specially designed for larger sizes, are referred to as display faces.

div The <div> tag defines a division or section in a Web page.

document A file produced using a graphics or desktop publishing application.

document grid A grid used to assist alignment.

dpi Abbreviation for "dots per inch." A unit of measurement used to represent the resolution (qv) of devices such as printers and imagesetters. The closer the dots (i.e., the higher the value), the better the quality. Typical values include 300dpi for a laser printer, and 2450dpi+ for an imagesetter. Dots per inch is sometimes erroneously used as a value when discussing monitors or images; the correct unit in these cases is ppi (pixels (qv) per inch).

Dreamweaver Leading Web design software (qv) from Macromedia.

DVD Abbreviation for "digital versatile (or video) disk." Similar to a CD-ROM (qv), but distinguished by its greater capacity (up to 17.08 gigabytes).

embedded fonts Fonts (qv) that are fixed within files, meaning that the original font folder does not need to be provided in order for the file to be printed or set.

EPS Abbreviation for "encapsulated PostScript." A graphics file format used primarily for storing object-oriented or vector (qv) graphics. An EPS file consists of two parts: PostScript (qv) code that tells the printer how to print the image; and an onscreen preview, usually in JPEG (qv), TIFF (qv), or PICT format.

float A CSS property that defines where an image or block of text will appear in another element.

font A complete set of type characters of the same size, style, and design.

format In printing, the size or orientation of a book or page.

four-color process Any printing process that reproduces full-color images which have been separated into three basic "process" colors—cyan, magenta, and yellow—with a fourth color, black, added for greater contrast. *See also* CMYK.

frame (1) A decorative border or rule surrounding a page item.

frame (2) In page layout software (qv), a container for text or image.

frame (3) On the Web, a means of splitting a page into several areas that can be updated separately.

Freeway A Web site layout program for the Macintosh produced by SoftPress.

FTP File Transfer Protocol, a method of transferring files from one computer to another using the Internet.

GIF Acronym for "graphic interchange format." A bitmapped (qv) graphics format that compresses data without losing any, as opposed to JPEG (qv), which discards data selectively.

glyph A letter, number, or symbol in a particular typeface, referring to its visual appearance rather than its function. Any number of alternative glyphs may represent the same character (qv).

GoLive A Web site design program by Adobe.

graphic A general term used to describe any illustration or drawn design. May also be used for a type design based on drawn letters.

grid A template (qv)—usually showing such things as column widths, picture areas, and trim sizes—used to design publications with multiple pages, to ensure the design remains consistent.

guides Non-printing aids to alignment.

gutter The space between columns on a layout.

hairline rule The thinnest line it is possible to print, with a width of 0.25pt.

halftone The technique of reproducing a continuous tone image, such as a photo, on a printing press by breaking it into equally spaced dots of varying sizes.

heading A title that appears either at the top of a chapter, or at the beginning of a subdivision within the body text.

hexadecimal A numeral system using letters and numbers to represent values in base 16. RGB color values are written with three hexadecimal pairs in the form #RRGGBB.

hinting In typography, information contained within outline fonts (qv) that modifies character shapes to enhance them when they are displayed or printed at low resolutions (qv).

HSB Abbreviation for "hue, saturation, and brightness."

HTML Abbreviation for "hypertext mark-up language." A text-based page-description language used to format documents on the Web and viewed on Web browsers.

hue Pure spectral color that distinguishes a color from other colors. For example, red is a different hue from blue. Light red and dark red may contain varying amounts of white and black, but they are the same hue.

hyperlink A contraction of "hypertext link," a link to other documents that is embedded within the original document. It may be underlined or highlighted in a different color. Clicking on a hyperlink will take the user to another document or Web site.

ICC The International Color Consortium that oversees the most widely used standards for color management (qv) systems.

Illustrator Vector-based (qv) drawing software made by Adobe.

image map An image, usually on a Web page, that contains embedded links to other documents or Web sites. These links are activated when the appropriate area of the image is clicked on. Most image maps are now "client-side," stored within the page's HTML (qv) code rather than "server-side," accessed from a server.

imposition The arrangement of pages in the sequence and position in which they will appear on the printed sheet, with appropriate margins for folding and trimming, before printing.

InDesign Leading desktop publishing software (qv) from Adobe.

inkjet printer A printing device that creates an image by spraying tiny jets of ink on to the paper surface at high speed.

Internet The entire collection of worldwide networks that serves as the medium of transmission for Web sites (qv), e-mail, instant messaging ("chat") and other online services.

Internet Explorer Web-browsing software (qv) from Microsoft.

intranet A network of computers similar to the Internet (qv), to which the public does not have access. Mainly used by large corporations or governmental institutions.

ISO paper sizes The paper size system, devised by the International Standards Organization, where the height to width (aspect) ratio is always 1.4142:1. If you put two such pages next to each other, the resulting page will have again the same width to height ratio.

ISP Abbreviation for "Internet (qv) service provider." Any organization that provides access to the Internet. Most ISPs also provide other services, such as e-mail addresses.

JavaScript Netscape's Java-like scripting language that provides a simplified method of adding dynamic effects to Web pages.

JPEG Abbreviation for "Joint Photographic Experts Group." This International Standards Organization group defines compression standards for bitmapped (qv) color images, and has given its name to a popular compressed (qv) file format. JPEG files are "lossy" (lose data during compression), but work in such a way as to minimize the visible effect on graduated tone images. Pronounced "jay-peg."

kerning The adjustment of space between adjacent type characters to optimize their appearance. It should not be confused with tracking (qv), which involves the adjustment of spacing over a number of adjacent characters.

layers In some applications, a level to which the user can consign an element of the design being worked on. Individual layers can be active (meaning that they can be worked on) or non-active.

layout The placement of various elements— text, headings (qv), images, etc.—on a printed page.

leading The spacing between lines of type.

Lock To A pseudomagnetic effect used to align elements to guides or grid in graphics and desktop publishing applications; *see* Snap to.

margins The space outside the text area of a page in graphics and desktop publishing applications, or a CSS property defining the space around elements in a Web page.

master page In some applications, a template (qv) that includes attributes that will be common to all pages, such as the number of text columns, page numbers, and so on.

Nested Style Sheet A sequence of text formatting that is applied automatically to text.

OpenType A relatively new font format that can contain either PostScript (qv) or TrueType (qv) data and allows large numbers of characters in one file.

Padding The space between the element border and the element content within a table or CSS style sheet.

PageMaker The original page make-up software, now replaced by InDesign.

PANTONE The proprietary trademark for PANTONE's system of color standards, control and quality requirements, in which each color bears a description of its formulation (in percentages) for subsequent printing.

PDF Abbreviation for "portable document format." A multi-purpose format from Adobe that allows complex, multi-featured documents to be created, retaining all text, layout, and picture formatting, then to be viewed and printed on any computer with PDF "reader" software (such as the free Adobe Reader) or, if correctly formatted, used for final output on a printing press.

Photoshop Hugely powerful, industry-standard image manipulation software from Adobe.

pixel Contraction of "picture element." The smallest component of a digitally generated image, such as a single dot of light on a computer monitor. In its most simple form, one pixel corresponds to a single bit (qv): 0 = off, or white; 1 = on, or black. In color and grayscale images (or monitors), one pixel may correspond to several bits: an 8-bit pixel, for example, can be displayed in any of 256 colors (the total number of different configurations that can be achieved by eight 0s and 1s).

plug-in Software (qv), usually developed by a third party, that extends the capabilities of another program. Plug-ins are common in image-editing and page-layout software for such things as special effects filters. They are also common in Web browsers for playing such things as movies and audio files.

point The basic unit of Anglo-American type measurement. There are 72 points to an inch.

PostScript Adobe's proprietary page description language for image output to laser printers and high-resolution (qv) imagesetters.

pre-press Any or all of the reproduction processes that occur between design and printing, especially color separation.

proof A prototype of a job (usually a printed document) produced to check quality and accuracy. An accurate on-screen preview of a job is known as a soft proof.

QuarkXPress Industry standard page-layout program from Quark.

raster Deriving from the Latin *rastrum* (rake), a "raster image" is any image created as rows of pixels, dots, or lines in a "raking" sequence, i.e. from top to bottom of a page, monitor, etc. On a monitor, the screen image is made up from a pattern of several hundred parallel lines created by an electron beam that "rakes" the screen from top to bottom. The speed at which the image or frame is created is the "refresh" rate, quoted in hertz (Hz), equal to the number of times per second. Converting a vector (qv) image to a bitmap (qv) for output on screen or printer is "rasterization."

resolution The quantity of data points, such as pixels, with which an image, is stored digitally. Higher resolution means better definition, clarity, and fidelity, at the cost of larger files.

RGB Abbreviation for "red, green, blue." The primary colors of the "additive" color model, used in monitors and for Web and multimedia graphics.

RIP Acronym for "raster image processor." Used by a printer to convert and rasterize (qv) page-layout data, typically in a PostScript (qv) or PDF (qv) file, for printed output, as a proof or on press.

rule A printed line.

sans serif The generic name for type designs that lack the small extensions (serifs, qv) at the ends of the main strokes of the letters. Sometimes called "lineal type."

saturation The variation in color of the same tonal brightness from none (gray) through pastel shades (low saturation) to pure color with no gray (high or "full" saturation).

serif The short counterstroke or finishing stroke at the end of the main stroke of a type character.

Snap To A pseudomagnetic effect used to align elements to guides or grids in graphics and desktop publishing applications; *see* Lock to.

Span The <span> tag is used to group inline elements in a document.

software The generic term that is used for any kind of computer application, as opposed to the physical hardware.

spot colors A printing color that has been specifically mixed for the job, as opposed to using the four-color process (qv) colors.

Style Sheet A group of formatting instructions that can be applied to individual characters or complete paragraphs.

Table A rectangle consisting of rows and columns, used to layout text in a Web or printed page

tags Formatting commands in HTML (qv) and related mark-up languages. A tag is switched on by placing a command inside angle brackets ‹command› and turned off by the same command preceded with a forward slash ‹/command›.

template A document created with pre-positioned areas, which is used as a basis for repeatedly creating other documents in the same style.

TIFF Acronym for "tagged image file format." A graphics file format used to store bitmapped (qv) images with no loss of data and optionally with extra features such as layers (qv). Widely used in graphic design and pre-press (qv).

tracking The adjustment of the spacing between characters in a selected piece of text. *See also* kerning.

trapping Settings in DTP programs that determine the interaction of overlapping colors. Also refers to printing problems when one solid color completely overprints another. Trapping preferences are complex and best left to the service bureau or printer.

TrueType Apple Computer's digital font (qv) technology, developed as an alternative to PostScript (qv) and now used by both PCs and Macs. A single TrueType file is used for both printing and screen rendering, while PostScript fonts require two separate files.

Unicode A system used to identify which glyphs (qv) in a font represent which characters (qv).

URL Abbreviation for "uniform resource locator." The unique address of any page on the Web, usually composed of three parts: protocol (such as "http"), domain name, and directory name.

vector A straight line segment of a given length and orientation. "Vector graphics"—which can involve more complex forms than straight lines, such as Bézier (qv) curves—are stored as numeric descriptions that can be scaled to reproduce the same visual result at any physical size, rather than broken up into discrete pixels as in the case of bitmapped (qv) images.

XHTML A combination of HTML (qv) and XML (qv) that is used to create Internet content for multiple devices.

XML An acronym for "extensible markup language" that is broader than HTML (qv).